'Unputdownably delicious . . . the [ . . . ]
[but] better'

'Terrific . . . shows the emptiness be[ . . . ]
Nick Cohen, *The Observer*, Book of the Week

'A meticulously researched and enjoyably lively account'
*The Daily Telegraph*

'Forensic and riveting'
*The New Statesman*

'An incredible book, transforming a complex financial scandal into a rich character drama'
Bradley Hope, co-author of *New York Times* bestseller *Billion Dollar Whale*

'Quite simply, one of the best books of investigative journalism I have ever read. Duncan Mavin is a natural storyteller and a brilliant sleuth'
Matthew d'Ancona, author of *Post-Truth*

'Leaves little doubt that much is indeed wrong in the excessively close relationship between some financiers and politicians . . . [who] stood to gain millions of pounds'     Simon Clark, author of *The Key Man*

'A keen eye for the colourful and at times absurd human drama'
*Reuters*

'Powerful'
*Money Week*

'Mavin knows how to keep you hooked . . . gripping'
*Financial World*

'Mavin expertly demystifies the rise and fall of Greensill Capital and weaves an intriguing tale at the cross section of sleaze, power and greed at the heart of UK politics and global finance. A fascinating – and prescient – read'
Karl Holbrook, Executive Editor, *Daily Express*

'The definitive account of the Greensill Capital's rise and spectacular meltdown . . . and a searing inquisition into the political connections that make it all possible'

Mary Childs, co-host of NPR's *Planet Money*
and author of *The Bond King*

'A classic cautionary tale, as fun to read as it is disturbing. Meticulously reported and brilliantly narrated'

Katherine Bell, formerly Editor in Chief,
*Quartz* and *Barron's*

'The extraordinary story of Greensill's rise and collapse is a microcosm of global finance in the last decade . . . a keen eye for the colourful – and at times absurd – human drama'

Peter Thal Larsen, EMEA Editor *Reuters Breakingviews*

'Mavin expertly unfolds a searing, unflinching, incisive, and definitively reported narrative on one of the great financial scandals of our time and the wreckage left in its wake . . . a must-read cautionary tale'

Sean Silcoff, co-author, *Losing the Signal:
The Extraordinary Rise and Spectacular Fall of BlackBerry*

# PYRAMID
# OF LIES

# About the Author

Duncan Mavin is a seasoned international financial journalist, and started his career as a chartered accountant in the City and in Toronto. He has been a reporter and editor for Dow Jones publications including *The Wall Street Journal* and was the *Journal*'s Financial Editor for Europe, the Middle East and Africa. He has also been Managing Editor for Barron's Group and a reporter for Canada's *National Post*. Currently, he is a senior assignment editor at *The Washington Post*. He lives with his family in the UK.

# PYRAMID OF LIES

## THE PRIME MINISTER, THE BANKER AND THE BILLION-POUND SCANDAL

### DUNCAN MAVIN

PAN BOOKS

Hardback edition *The Pyramid of Lies* first published 2022 by Macmillan

This paperback edition *Pyramid of Lies* published 2023 by Pan Books
an imprint of Pan Macmillan
The Smithson, 6 Briset Street, London EC1M 5NR
*EU representative*: Macmillan Publishers Ireland Ltd, 1st Floor,
The Liffey Trust Centre, 117–126 Sheriff Street Upper,
Dublin 1, D01 YC43
Associated companies throughout the world
www.panmacmillan.com

ISBN 978-1-5290-8892-2

1 3 5 7 9 8 6 4 2

A CIP catalogue record for this book is available from the British Library.

Typeset in Minion Pro by Jouve (UK), Milton Keynes
Printed and bound by CPI Group (UK) Ltd, Croydon, CR0 4YY

Visit **www.panmacmillan.com** to read more about all our books
and to buy them. You will also find features, author interviews and
news of any author events, and you can sign up for e-newsletters
so that you're always first to hear about our new releases.

# Contents

# Author's Note

When Greensill Capital began its rapid meltdown in March 2021, the effects were felt around the world, from the UK to Japan, from Australia to the coal fields of West Virginia.

Billions of dollars of investors' money was missing, billions more simply written off. Top politicians and financiers began desperately trying to distance themselves from their entanglement with a start-up firm that had promised to make them rich and then imploded in spectacular fashion. Lex Greensill, the firm's charismatic, super-salesman CEO, was supposed to be the next-big-thing in global finance. Suddenly, he was an arch-villain, his grinning photo appearing on nightly news and on front pages everywhere.

Greensill Capital's rise had been swift, but its demise was even speedier. Most of the 1,000 or so employees had had no idea of the failings at the company they worked for, or the allegations of fraud. And then it was over.

By then, Greensill had gone mainstream. A photo I had been given by a source showed ex-UK Prime Minister David Cameron and Lex Greensill sitting cross-legged, in twin blue suits, at the desert retreat of the controversial leader of Saudi Arabia. When we published it at *The Wall Street Journal*, the photo instantly went viral. Within a couple of hours, it popped up on the main BBC News bulletin. Then it started to appear on news websites. The next day, it was republished on just about every front page in the UK press. That didn't surprise me – the photo of the Australian banker and the former Prime Minister lounging at the luxurious desert campsite of the Saudi Prince seemed to underscore everything the public felt was wrong about the revolving door of politics and business. For me, it also illustrated Lex's rapid and unlikely ascent to global power player.

As a reporter, I'd first written about Lex Greensill in 2019. Greensill Capital was a difficult firm to cover, not least because accurate information was always hard to get your hands on. Greensill's corporate public relations strategy was aggressive and erratic. On several occasions, they would tell me one thing was true and then tell me the opposite days later. The firm's lawyers were quick to pull the trigger threatening legal action – they frequently denied things that later turned out to be accurate. I've never before worked on a story where so many potential sources would ask for financial reward before they would agree to talk (naturally, I always refused).

Greensill Capital also suffered from an incredibly gossipy culture, perhaps because so much centred on Lex himself. Even seasoned, senior executives were often left relying on second-hand bits of information to ascertain what was going on at the company they worked for. Sometimes, very plugged-in sources would tell me something they believed to be true because it came from Lex himself or someone very close to him, but they were later proved wrong.

Lex's rapid downfall was a surreal moment. For most of the time I'd been covering Greensill, it felt as if I was shouting into an abyss. I would bore friends and colleagues, harping on about a fast-growing supply chain finance (SCF) business that was either going to change banking for ever or would be the next major financial scandal. But I couldn't tell if anyone else cared. Then suddenly Greensill blew up, and everyone cared.

I wasn't the only journalist covering Greensill's rise and fall. Far from it. Reporters at Bloomberg, the *Financial Times*, *The Sunday Times* and Reuters all did sterling work uncovering the reality about Lex's business – as did several of my Dow Jones colleagues at *Financial News* and *The Wall Street Journal*. Many of these reporters had their own brushes with Greensill's aggressive public relations and legal strategies. At one point, Greensill even took Reuters to court – and lost.

When a big business collapses, the reasons are complex. Greensill was no different. Covid-19 helped trigger Greensill's collapse – it shocked the markets and rattled through Greensill's business. But Greensill Capital also just wasn't very profitable. It aimed to hit overly ambitious revenue targets to sustain its sky-high valuation. It grew too fast and was far too reliant on just a handful of key relationships, despite Lex's claims that it had a diverse pool of clients, funders and other critical partners.

Above all, Lex Greensill was telling investors they were buying into a super-safe form of financing when he was actually making billions of dollars in loans to risky enterprises that could not pay them back. The whole scheme had echoes of the worst elements of the financial crisis, when risky US home mortgages were dressed up as something much safer and sold off to unwitting investors.

All of that made for a fascinating story to cover. But what most interested me about Greensill was Lex and the incredible network of supporters he had gathered along the way. Lex was smart and hardworking. He was a compelling salesman. He was certainly driven. But he was otherwise unremarkable. He didn't party hard. He dressed conservatively. He often seemed bland, robotic.

Somehow, he had won over big banks, giant asset managers, the world's biggest investors, top politicians, long-tenured financial executives. They were all on board. They were all believers. For anyone reporting on the company, it was a constant challenge to reconcile the presence of this extraordinary group of powerful supporters with the numerous red flags about Lex and his business.

This book is an attempt to build on years of reporting to explain what happened at Greensill, and to figure out why so many top bankers, investors and politicians went along for the ride, why they got behind Lex even when it was clear he was taking aggressive risks with other people's money.

My reporting draws on interviews with hundreds of individuals who graciously shared their time and knowledge to help reveal the truth. These include former Greensill executives, staff, shareholders and investors in the assets that Greensill sold; staff at Greensill's business partners, including the giant Wall Street banks and the asset managers, the insurance companies and the tech platforms that Greensill's business relied upon; friends and old colleagues; lawyers; regulators; politicians and other government officials. I've also drawn on emails, letters, internal reports, financial presentations, spreadsheets, legal contracts, photos, audio and video recordings, and other documentary evidence.

In almost all cases, my sources agreed to help me on the condition that I did not reveal their identities. Some of them cited nondisclosure agreements. Others feared retribution from parties involved in the Greensill scandal.

In some cases, I have reconstructed scenes and dialogue based on information gleaned from these sources. Readers should not assume that a person named in the book or quoted here has spoken to me. Where there have been conflicting accounts, I have relied on the most plausible description and the most credible sources. Sometimes I have included notes to reflect alternative views.

Lex Greensill declined several requests to be interviewed for this book. He was presented with the key facts I intended to include about him. I also talked with Lex Greensill and his senior staff several times over the years of reporting on the firm. Some of these meetings were on the record. At other times, they requested that we talk off the record – where it later turned out that what they had told me during such meetings was not accurate, I consider that our agreement of confidentiality does not apply.

The book also follows a key rule to which all *Wall Street Journal* reporters adhere. Key people mentioned in this book have been made aware, and they've been given the opportunity to comment too.

# Prologue

By January 2020, Greensill Capital had hit the big time. In the previous few months, the start-up finance firm had received a jackpot injection of $1.5 billion in funding from Vision Fund 1, an investment fund run by Japan's SoftBank Group Corp. That influx of cash had dwarfed an earlier investment of around $250 million from a well-regarded US private equity shop called General Atlantic (GA).

The firm's founder, Lex Greensill, and a handful of early investors collectively took hundreds of millions of dollars in cash out of the business. They were rich, and Lex made sure everyone knew it.

He bought a fleet of private jets, a wardrobe full of expensive, custom-made suits and a glass-fronted beachside property in his native Queensland, Australia. He picked up awards, became a regular guest on business television, and lavished a £2.5 million donation on the University of Manchester, where he had attended business school. Lex even planned to buy hundreds of acres of land around his Cheshire home to 're-wild' – it was the kind of thing, he told his senior staff, that billionaires like him did with their money.

While the trappings of wealth were hugely rewarding, Lex was just as desperate for the status he got from hanging around politicians and top bankers. It was exhilarating to zip around the world in your own Gulfstream 650 – an elite plane even among global private aircraft owners. But showing off your star power over dinner with the great and good of international finance and politics at the World Economic Forum in Davos or at a Buckingham Palace garden party or as a trustee of the famed Monteverdi Choir and Orchestra was just as big a thrill.

On a cold, sunny day in January 2020, Greensill's top management meeting took place in London. The programme started with an 8 a.m. breakfast meeting in a grand boardroom on the lower floor of the Savoy. The storied hotel is a 130-year-old art deco masterpiece, dubbed London's 'most famous hotel' and renowned as a favourite haunt of kings and presidents, Hollywood stars and fashionistas. Its restaurants have been run by celebrity chefs like Gordon Ramsay and Marcus Wareing. The hotel sits on the Strand, right across the street from Greensill's own headquarters. The finance company, despite being relatively unknown and still in its infancy, was a major client of the hotel, often reserving a fifth or more of the rooms at exorbitant rates for clients and the firm's own executives from around the world, many of whom flew into London on a Greensill plane. Lex himself kept a suite there, and the hotel's staff dealt with the dry cleaning of his tailor-made suits.

The morning was taken up by a big meeting, recapping the past month's work and mulling the next stage of Greensill's rapid global expansion. A tighter group met in the afternoon, an inner circle of senior executives and board members who had been taken into King Lex's confidence.

Everything at Greensill flowed through Lex. All the major deals. All the discussions with regulators and major investors. He didn't exactly hide the true perilous state of Greensill's business from the board and senior managers. Its corporate governance processes – the checks and balances that prevent wrongdoing and mishaps – had not kept up with the pace of the company's expansion. German regulators were circling a bank the company owned there. One of the firm's biggest clients was in a perilous state itself – if it defaulted on loans from Greensill, both firms would be in deep trouble. Lex was open about all of this. It was all disclosed to the management team. But he'd also wave away any concerns. Everything was in hand.

Finally, in the evening, there was a lavish dinner. About fifty guests attended on this occasion; sometimes it was as many as seventy. Lex ruled the room like a mandarin, surrounded by his courtiers.

The guest list was filled with powerful figures from politics and finance who were all backing Lex. Invites went out to top Greensill executives such as Bill Crothers, who was previously the UK government's chief commercial officer; to board members like Julie Bishop, formerly Australia's foreign minister, and Maurice Thompson, who was once the head of US bank Citigroup in the UK. Top executives from SoftBank and GA were also invited.

At Greensill's board dinners or management meetings or Christmas parties, Lex would show who was in favour by carefully selecting who got to sit next to whom. New hires he wanted to celebrate or those whose bits of the Greensill business were excelling would get to sit next to Lex. Anyone who had clashed with Lex would sit further away. He personally drew up the table plan, with the studious attention to detail of a general strategically deploying his army.

This time, Lex's top table was heavily weighted in favour of executives with experience in so-called 'fintechs' – financial technology companies that had proliferated across London since the financial crisis. Many of those were Silicon Valley clones, based in cool former warehouses or hot, new, wired office spaces in London's trendy Shoreditch, where the office culture was relaxed and informal, with baristas preparing flat white coffees and music playing in the background.

These new technology firms were attracting heady valuations

among investors. The stock prices of tech firms had soared around the world. For founders of fast-growing tech businesses, as well as investors that bought into them early, the potential pay-off could be huge. It was like winning the lottery a hundred times over.

Lex had taken to calling Greensill a fintech too. In reality, it was nothing like that, culturally or in a business sense. In contrast to the uber-casual tech scene, Greensill's senior executives were buttoned-up and formally dressed. And while the company shared much of the 'move fast and break things' ethos of big tech companies, it had little in the way of actual new or proprietary technology. But that didn't really matter. If Lex said the business was a fintech enough times, others would repeat it, and the money flowed in.

There was another term frequently applied to Greensill: 'shadow bank'. In the aftermath of the financial crisis, tougher regulations had forced traditional banks to set aside large amounts of capital to cover for another calamity. That had driven the banks from newly burdensome businesses, and money that previously ran through big global finance houses instead washed up in companies that were much less tightly regulated, and which thrived by skirting rules designed to prevent a financial scandal. Greensill was one of them.

That January dinner was a conservative affair – a reflection of Lex's personality. Greensill Capital was no hedonistic hedge fund or investment bank. Lex could be charming, but he was not gregarious. He was usually serious, rarely talked about anything but business. He didn't even talk much about his family. He sometimes said he didn't have any friends.

His biggest quirk was an odd obsession with wanting to fit into the upper echelons of British society and high finance. He seemed to have a strange preoccupation with the British royal family. He spoke in a staged manner that masked his upbringing on a dusty farm in one of the most rural regions of Australia. Employees mocked his verbal tics like the pompous, 'Indeed, sir.'

He always dressed the part too – even as a junior banker, fifteen or so years earlier, he wore handmade suits from one of his tailors, on Jermyn Street or near his home in Cheshire, and an expensive watch. Lex would regularly remind senior Greensill executives of the need to dress well. He'd inspect their suits, lifting the collars as if to check out the stitching, mocking them if they'd got a lesser cut or poorer cloth.

Though there was none of the wackiness of the tech scene or the wild partying of the seedier corners of the City, Greensill Capital was anything but cheap. The Savoy meal was expensive. Lex personally didn't drink much – rarely more than a single glass of wine – but he always ordered expensive vintages, impressing guests and business partners.

As the guests finished their desserts, up stepped David Cameron, the former UK prime minister. Greensill had worked for Cameron's government as an unpaid adviser on trade finance. He'd walked the corridors of Whitehall and around Number 10 Downing Street as if he owned the place. He'd pitched his supply chain finance ideas, some of which even saved the government some money, he said. And in return Lex received a CBE – Commander of the Order of the British Empire. The honour played to Lex's ego. The certificate hung in the lobby of the Greensill office. A video of the ceremony, Prince Charles bestowing the honour on a beaming Lex, ran on the company website landing page. Many partners and clients of Greensill felt that it all seemed a bit gauche. But the CBE got Lex noticed and bought him some credibility. Over the years, he'd often presented two business cards – one for Greensill Capital and the other noting his role at Number 10.

By 2019, he had repaid Cameron's support, hiring the former PM as an adviser to Greensill Capital. Cameron flew around the world helping Lex work deals and conduct business in the US, Japan, Saudi Arabia and Australia. He sent hundreds of emails to company executives recommending that they use Greensill's services. Cameron also lobbied his former UK government colleagues to open their doors for Lex. For his part, the ex-PM was well remunerated for his work, raking in millions of pounds in salary, bonus and stocks in the company.

When Cameron stood up to make the after-dinner speech at the Savoy, he heaped praise on Lex – as he did frequently at events inside and outside Greensill, and in texts and meetings with his former government colleagues. Greensill, according to the former PM, was a saviour of small business, democratizing access to sophisticated forms of finance that had hitherto been the reserve of only the world's most powerful corporations.

And then, in a gear switch, Cameron launched into an analysis of the UK's landmark Brexit referendum, the vote on European Union membership that had unseated Cameron, precipitating the end of his premiership. As the former prime minister sketched out his thoughts on a whiteboard, some Greensill executives were taken aback by his brazenness in explaining a referendum that had been a major black eye and an embarrassing, terminal defeat for Cameron's government. Some executives were unsure what skills or attributes Cameron really brought to the company at all.

For Lex, though, the moment was another triumph. This was exactly where he always thought he belonged: in a fancy, historic hotel, at the top of the head table, with seasoned bankers coveting his attention and a major political power player dancing to his tune. It was the perfect evening.

Yet, less than eighteen months later, the whole business was insolvent. By spring of 2021, Greensill was in tatters and a bunch of establishment banks and investors were picking through the pieces, like vultures, or trying to cover up for losses that Greensill's business had brought their way. His major backers wrote down their multibillion-dollar investments to zero. Authorities in Germany, the UK and Switzerland came looking for evidence of criminal wrongdoing. Parliamentarians levelled allegations of corruption and accused Lex of fraud. Months after Greensill's collapse, billions of dollars belonging to investors were still missing.

Shortly after Greensill's collapse, I was given an Excel spreadsheet prepared by the company's top executives and titled 'High Risk Franchise Names'. The document listed about $14 billion in loans to more than thirty companies. In each case, the existence of the loan was a cause for major concern. Alongside the loan amount, Greensill insiders had typed brief descriptions like 'Defaulted, fraud' and 'Exposure to a company with no revenue', indicating that recovering the loan was highly unlikely. The spreadsheet showed that several companies were either owned by or associated with a single businessman, steel magnate Sanjeev Gupta. In five more cases, the description simply said 'SoftBank', meaning the loans were to other companies where Greensill's biggest shareholder also had a significant stake. Others showed that the borrowers had ties to Greensill's board or senior management.

This is the story of Greensill's rise and spectacular fall. Of the farmer from Bundaberg, Australia, whose ambition and smarts grew a multibillion-dollar empire, before it was exposed as a house of cards. It is a story about an aggressively risk-taking entrepreneur who didn't like to hear 'no' for an answer, supported by a group of experienced politicians and businessmen who each stood to gain millions of pounds from backing him. It's a story about weak governance and lax oversight. It's a story about the revolving door between government and business, and the inability of regulators to act on a scandal even when it is staring them in the face. It's a story about the skewed incentives that lead to poor outcomes in the world of high finance. And it's also a tale of the stock market, where heady valuations are fuelled by massive global investors who never seem to lose, even when a company they bet on turns out to be a failure.

This is a story that echoes many of the biggest financial and business scandals of all time. Politicians have accused Lex of running a Ponzi scheme, named for a 1920s Italian-born US financier. Like Lex,

Charles Ponzi was a natty dresser, and an outsider who slipped into high society. Ponzi convinced investors to part with their money and offered them huge profits. But his investments were an illusion, using money from new investors to pay off older investors. The whole scam kept running only so long as he could get his hands on more cash. Eventually, the scam was exposed, in part by Dow Jones, my own employer, and Charles Ponzi ended up in jail.

Like Greensill, the disgraced American financier Bernie Madoff ran an eponymous investment business and lived the high life for years, attracting the support of wealthy backers and smart investors. Madoff's establishment connections ran deep and sceptics were dismissed out of hand, told they didn't understand how clever Madoff was. His fund grew to $65 billion and promised steady returns year after year. But Madoff's funds collapsed, revealed as a mirage. The sceptics were proved right. Madoff went to prison, and died there in April 2021.

The surge in new, disruptive technology companies after the financial crisis is not without its villains too. Elizabeth Holmes, the disgraced US founder of Theranos, is chief among them. Like Lex, Holmes made fanciful claims and promises. Like Lex, she was backed by big names from business and politics. Holmes's health technology firm raised hundreds of millions of dollars in funding from supporters in Silicon Valley and got the backing of a roster of supposedly smart businesspeople and politicians. She was hailed as a visionary, a game-changer. Until *The Wall Street Journal* revealed that Theranos's claims of breakthrough technology were false. The company collapsed and Holmes was brought to trial, accused of fraud.

But Greensill's story is different to all of these. In some ways, it's even more outlandish. There is a political chapter that has taken on a life of its own. In the UK, the collapse of Greensill has spurred a broad public outcry over ethics in Westminster. And it has sparked a renewed furore over allegations of sleaze at the heart of the ruling Conservative (Tory) Party. With echoes of the 1990s, when more than a decade of Tory rule descended into farce and almost daily revelations about misconduct of one sort or another, the current Conservative government also finds itself hit by a seemingly endless stream of allegations. And though Cameron is long since out of office, the exposure of his role in the Greensill affair fuelled a resumption of concerns about sleaze in the current era.

Cameron, who had shown up whenever Lex needed his support, immediately distanced himself from the firm once it collapsed – a spokesperson said that as he 'was neither a director of the company, nor involved in any lending decisions, he has no special insight into what ultimately happened.' But the revelations about Cameron's lobbying of his former government colleagues will not go away. He has been hauled in front of Parliament, his reputation sullied.

ALONG THE WAY, there were plenty of opportunities to stop the Greensill crisis before it snowballed. I began writing about Greensill in the spring of 2019. My stories were sceptical. Lex hated them and as a result he hated me too. His staff told me. His business partners told me too. His pugilistic public relations chief told me, and demanded that I stop asking awkward questions. It was personal, at least for Lex.

The story had long taken over my professional life. Shortly after that Greensill board meeting at the Savoy in January 2020, the story began to spill over into my personal life too. The nineteenth of February 2020 was a dark, wintry London day, when the wind is too strong for you to use an umbrella, and the Tube platforms are slippery with rainwater. I took a taxi from our office at the News Building near Tower Bridge to meet a contact at Brown's Hotel in Mayfair across town. The contact understood a lot about Greensill, and I was hoping they would help with my reporting. We met in the lobby cafe of the swanky hotel and ordered coffee. It was mid-afternoon. As usual, I looked around to make sure our conversation wouldn't be overheard.

Most of the other people in the hotel cafe were wealthy tourists, and there was a useful buzz of noise that meant we could chat freely without being overheard. We talked. The source had useful insights. After a while, the source passed me a package in a Jiffy bag. It was a gift, a book they thought I'd find interesting. To anyone watching, the package could have looked like something much more significant. I got up, said goodbye and left.

It was also my kids' birthday that day and I'd arranged to meet them and my wife for dinner just off Oxford Street. I wandered up through London's busy streets, my coat wrapped tightly against the rain. I was thinking about some of the great material I'd just heard that could prove useful for stories. My family was waiting in the car, parked just off the busy main road, and I opened the boot and threw my bag in. It went to the front of the boot, nearest the seats, beyond some birthday presents in shopping bags that the kids had picked up. Near the car, a man in a trench coat was talking loudly on his mobile phone. My wife remarked that there was something odd about him, but we didn't think too much about it. As we left the car to head for dinner, I double-checked that the doors were locked.

Ninety minutes later, after burgers and ice cream, we returned to the car. Something didn't feel right. The doors were still locked and there was no damage, but the parcel shelf above the boot was ruffled. I opened the boot. All the brand-new birthday presents were still there in shopping bags, but my own bag was gone. Someone had managed to break in without damaging the car and while leaving the locks undisturbed. They'd reached across a half-dozen bags filled with shopping, and they'd taken my battered old gym bag. I immediately thought about the odd man who was hanging about earlier. If he had stolen my bag, all he'd find inside it was a sweaty gym kit, my house keys and a book in a jiffy bag that the source had given me. Nevertheless, the theft was a shock that felt like a violation of our personal space.

Later, as I called to have the locks changed at home, I thought about the odd break-in. It didn't feel random. Why had they not taken the brand-new gifts? How had the thief entered the locked car without damaging it? Could it have been related to the meeting I'd had with the source earlier in the day? I called the Dow Jones security chief, a tense, serious man with a militaristic disposition. I described what had happened, what story I was working on, and what companies were involved. Before I got to the end, he stopped me and said, 'I know who did it. They're not very sophisticated, mostly just thugs.' It wasn't reassuring, though the security chief made it clear I should change locks and passwords, and be wary when meeting contacts on the Greensill story from then on.

It was very unsettling. Was I safe? Was I being paranoid? It's certainly not unheard of for big companies to hire private investigators. Credit Suisse, whose clients had invested billions in Greensill's funds, had recently become embroiled in its own 'spygate' affair after it emerged that one of the bank's leaders had hired spooks to follow a former executive. Executives at SoftBank, Greensill's biggest investor, had spied on their own people and even set up a honey-trap plot for one senior partner of the firm, according to a report by my colleagues at *The Wall Street Journal*. Reporters at the *Financial Times* had also come face to face with dirty tricks of exactly this kind during their intrepid reporting on Wirecard, a German payments business that turned out to be a fraud.

I became deeply concerned that Greensill was connected to the break-in. The thief had stolen my bag containing something a source had handed to me earlier that afternoon. Someone must have followed me, I reasoned. They must have been looking to intimidate me or to uncover my sources, I thought. Maybe I was paranoid. Maybe I was wrong. But dealing with Greensill left me thinking anything was possible.

# ONE

# Betting the Farm

In the years following the Second World War, thousands of Australians took to the land and began a new life in farming. One of these was Roy Greensill, who planted and harvested sugar cane, watermelons and peanuts on a small plot outside Qunaba, Queensland. The township lies a few miles to the east of the nearest large urban centre, Bundaberg. It was named for the only local landmark, the Qunaba Mill, which was previously known as the Mon Repos Mill until it was taken over, in 1900, by the Queensland National Bank. Qunaba is a kind of portmanteau of the bank's own name.

Farming was tough. This part of Queensland is subtropical and prone to extreme weather conditions. It was remote, especially back then – Bundaberg itself is about 230 miles from the state capital, Brisbane. The township, which is named after the Bunda kinship group of the local indigenous Taribelang people, was entirely flooded in the 1960s, an event that caused widespread economic pain and lived long in the memories of the region's farmers.

Success in Bundaberg demanded sheer hard work and bloody-mindedness – a resolute refusal to accept that ongoing hardship or the occasional outright calamity would finish you off. It required relentless optimism even in the face of a terrible storm or catastrophic harvest. It was the sort of place where you had to ignore the dire reality of your circumstances from time to time, because if you acknowledged just how bad things were, you'd be finished.

Despite everything, it was possible to dig out a decent living. From Roy Greensill's original sixty-six acres of sugar cane, the farm tripled in size within twenty years. By the time Roy's grandson, Alexander 'Lex' David Greensill, was born on 29 December 1976, the family owned hundreds of acres of farmland. Bundaberg itself had grown too. The population was still just about thirty thousand, but they were increasingly wired into the Queensland and Australian economy.

Still, when Lex and his two brothers were growing up, the family often struggled for money. The farm did all right, but they sometimes had to wait months for the supermarkets that bought their produce to pay up. Young Lex thought it was grossly unfair the way big business could use its massive buying power to bully farmers into accepting payment on their terms.

Years later, Lex's apocryphal backstory always started this way when he retold it time and time again. The point of the retelling was always clear: the financial system is rigged against the little guy, and fixing it was a mission. It was certainly a convenient and compelling creation myth.

In fact, the Greensill farm had mostly run well enough under the stewardship of Lex's parents, Judy and Lloyd. At school, Lex was smart and studious. He was small and not especially athletic – as an adult, he became an avid long-distance runner and cycled too, and he tried his hand at golf, squash, surfing and water-skiing. But not being on the sports teams was a knock against him in the sports-oriented environment. Combined with his bookishness, this meant he was the occasional target of jockish bullies.

But he was hard-working, becoming school captain and a leading member of the school debating team. In the tough farming landscape of Bundaberg, Lex was learning there was another way to rise to the top. If he couldn't rely on brawn, then he could certainly win with his brains, his words, his perseverance, his sheer, indefatigable willpower. To make it big, he'd have to work incredibly hard and project remarkable self-confidence.

In Lex's later retelling, his parents couldn't afford to send him to college, so he studied for a law degree by correspondence. I could never substantiate this claim that attending university in person was out of his financial reach. There are plenty of people who are not very well off and still attend university, and the Greensills weren't so poor. Certainly, however, the story embellished his credentials as extremely hard-working and driven and supported his 'helping-out-the-little-guy' mission statements.

Either way, Lex worked as a clerk for a local law firm and earned his degree from the Queensland University of Technology by listening to cassette tapes mailed to the farm. 'I can tell you that is a tough way to earn your degree,' he told me later. 'Work full-time, discover girls, and do a law degree all at the same time.'

He also worked voluntarily with an industry group for farmers where he tried to get a better deal out of the supermarkets and wholesale fruit and vegetable buyers. He'd work on the terms in their sales contracts, including how and when they were paid. He claimed that his pro bono work for the farmers' association had a far-reaching impact. 'Basically, the little guys get screwed by the big guys,' he told me. 'The market in Australia has completely reformed, in no small part, because basically from the point I started my legal career I spent a chunk of my time working gratis on that to help farmers get a better deal.'

BY 1999, LEX had completed his legal studies and articles at Payne Butler Lang, a prominent Bundaberg law firm. He briefly spent some time at Deacons Graham & James, another law firm, with connections across Asia and a focus on intellectual property and new technologies.

He'd also expanded his CV, collecting a list of impressive accolades: world champion of the 1998 Junior Chamber International Public Speaking Competition; finalist in the 1999 Young Australian of the Year Awards (he was beaten by Bryan Gaensler, an astronomer and expert in magnetic fields and supernova remnants); two-term appointee to the Asia Pacific Development Council on bilateral trade and education ties; 1998 Young Citizen of the Year for Shire of Burnett in Queensland. He could speak a little Japanese and he'd become a Justice of the Peace. He was the director of five separate companies, including Greensill Corporation Pty.

Lex was, he said, skilled in law, wireless applications, international trade, insurance, capital raising, sales and marketing, public speaking, written communications, corporate governance, training, organization and management, the etiquette of shareholder and board meetings, and in navigating Asian markets. He'd worked with teams in Australia, New Zealand, Japan, China, Hong Kong, Macau, Thailand, Pakistan, Philippines and Austria.

He said he was 'tenacious, disciplined and committed . . . my personal drive, fiercely competitive nature, and the ability to perform under pressure for extended periods make me an ideal business associate.'

The CV ran to ten pages in total. For a twenty-four-year-old embarking on his first career steps, the résumé was filled with bold claims and exactly the kind of eye-catching statements that carried Lex through the next two decades. It was also over the top, brash, boastful, and rather less impressive if you parsed the details. You could poke fun at it. But you had to admire the audacity. In my view, the document was in many ways a very fair reflection of Lex Greensill.

*

IT WAS THE era of the dotcom boom – even farmers in remote Bundaberg had taken notice. Tech or internet businesses were all the rage. If you wanted to earn a fortune, the tech scene was where you needed to be. Lex wanted in on it and moved to Sydney's richer pastures.

He went to the office of Robert Cleland, a wealthy Australian businessman who'd run some of Australia's biggest construction and architectural firms. He was a smart, eloquent speaker with movie-star looks. Lex strode into his office as though he owned the place, brimming with confidence.

'I want to come work for you,' he told Cleland. 'And here are my terms.' Greensill laid out a package that would make seasoned executives blush. He had hardly any experience to speak of, but wanted a bigger salary than Cleland would have paid an experienced company director. Cleland declined Lex's proposal. But he was impressed by Lex's chutzpah. Cleland had some space at Australia Square, an office and shopping complex on George Street, in Sydney's Central Business District. He let hungry young executives who were interested in e-commerce work there. It was a kind of skunkworks for wannabe Australian tech entrepreneurs. Lex took a desk. He quickly made a name for himself, though it wasn't always a good one. Sure, he was bright and ambitious. But he also came across as rude and arrogant, as though he thought he was better than everyone else. Still, Lex had a foot in the door.

CLELAND WAS AN architect by training. He had studied at Melbourne University and Harvard, and then become chairman at Stephenson and Turner, one of Australia's top architectural firms, responsible for the design of some of the country's most prominent buildings. By the 1990s, S&T was an international business, with offices in New Zealand, Singapore and Hong Kong.

And then it all went wrong.

The business was too closely concentrated on relationships with just six key clients. When a shift in the Australian economy sent interest rates spiralling, five of S&T's clients were unable to pay for work they'd commissioned. Cleland took the advice of his accountants and closed shop.

Then in his fifties, Cleland was not going to retire to the golf course or the beach. He enjoyed work and a new venture was never too far from the front of his mind. He had been fascinated by the potential of computers since the 1980s, when he'd picked up Apple Mac parts from a street-side reseller in Taiwan and put it together himself in his hotel room. A couple of decades later, the internet promised to revolutionize business. Cleland saw an opportunity.

At S&T, one problem the company had faced on large projects was how to make cash flow efficiently from property owners to contractors, subcontractors and suppliers. It was in everyone's interest to make cash move fast and have supplies turn up on time. But things didn't always work that way. Cleland and a couple of close associates dabbled in electronic invoice settlement – paying invoices over the internet. That would get funds moving through the supply chain more quickly and prevent costly hiccups and delays in construction projects.

After S&T collapsed, Cleland and a couple of his former colleagues began to put together a business plan for a kind of prototype 'supply chain finance' firm. An electronic platform would process invoices instantly, with funding from a bank that would take a small fee. Suppliers would be paid early. Buyers could make their payments later. The whole system would mean that the payments and invoices shuttling between companies would work more smoothly than in the past, and Cleland and his team would make a very tidy profit along the way. They talked to potential clients, including some of Australia's largest companies. The feedback was positive. A new business named OzEcom was born. Almost.

By September 1999, Lex was working full-time on OzEcom. He

was a kind of roving salesman, research consultant and fundraiser rolled into one. Lex worked on the business plan, developed a sales strategy, marketed OzEcom to clients, and sought out new investment. They began rolling out OzEcom to a handful of businesses on a trial basis. Cleland had already attracted a few hundred thousand dollars in venture capital, from a few dozen investors, including friends and family of staff. But they were constantly looking for more sources of investment. Lex tapped up his mother and brother and other Bundaberg connections too.

In November, the start-up was looking at a potential $5 million equity fundraising. Cleland hired investment bankers. They had accountants Arthur Andersen providing advice. French bank Société Générale was to fund the SCF deals. But the deal never got off the ground. Within months, the dotcom bubble had well and truly burst, leaving OzEcom thoroughly deflated. There was suddenly far less appetite for floating shares in internet-based businesses.

Cleland believed that part of the problem was the Australian market. It was too small. He decided to restart the business in London. He flew to the UK, leaving OzEcom in the hands of the – mostly – young guns in the Sydney office. Cleland's idea was that he'd relaunch the business, and then reverse-engineer a takeover of OzEcom from the UK. After all, he was still the biggest shareholder in what was left of the company. Instead, while he was away, the team in Sydney tried to kick Cleland out altogether. A legal battle ensued, with each side accusing the other of dirty tricks. Cleland, who firmly believed that the future of the business lay in London, cut his losses. OzEcom folded soon after.

Lex later told me that he had put A$250,000 into OzEcom and lost it all. He said OzEcom collapsed because 'the big people at the top of the company were not able to keep up with my ability to sell.' The experience, he said, left him 'like a dog with a bone,' determined never to lose his grip on success again.

*

ON 11 SEPTEMBER 2001, while the world watched in horror as terrorists flew planes into the World Trade Center in New York, Lex Greensill was at the British Potato Conference. Lex had moved to the UK and taken a consulting role with Robert Cleland's new, UK-based SCF business, Transaction Risk Mitigation, or TRM. It was a kind of supercharged version of OzEcom, based in Golden Square, in Soho, London. Lex was researching potential clients, especially agricultural business. He was talking with QV Foods, one of the UK's largest potato-packing businesses, which counted Tesco, Sainsbury's and Marks & Spencer as key customers. Lex reported back that QV's leadership would 'support, endorse and would immediately participate in a TRM Programme that paid both growers and themselves for potatoes as they are packed.'

This was mundane stuff. The grubby work of a junior staffer at a start-up business trying to make a go of it at the unglamorous end of trade and finance. Lex's notes were detailed and thorough. He also met with a pea-producing cooperative that sold most of its peas to a giant frozen food company. Lex was not constrained by the humdrum nature of the TRM business. Despite being a very junior member of the team, he was ambitious and cast the net far and wide for new opportunities. He flew round the world and stayed at luxurious hotels and spoke to senior executives at grocery chains, food wholesalers and agribusiness groups in Australia and Asia and Europe.

Cleland had very particular views on the UK's business culture. The rules were different from the laid-back scene in Australia. It was critically important to wear the right suit, the right tie, the right shirt. These were class markers that would open doors and get deals done.

'In business, you have to be ready for combat,' he'd tell his associates. 'You have to play the game. Dressing down is a game for juniors, because the seniors are dressing up.'

It was a message that Lex took on board and held dear for decades. He and Cleland were close. Greensill started wearing a single-breasted cashmere banker's coat, identical to the one the veteran Cleland always wore. When Greensill decided to go to business school in Manchester and study for an MBA (Master of Business Administration) in 2004, Cleland wrote a letter supporting his admission and his visa application. 'We have found Lex's entrepreneurial skills equally at home with senior management of established leading City firms and regional small businesses.' Cleland had made a habit of supporting young staff if they needed funding or support for study programmes. He had given Lex a full-time role at TRM to help pay him through the studies. When Lex got married, to a British doctor named Victoria, in a traditional ceremony close to her home in northwest England, Cleland was asked to make a speech. He talked about starting the greatest adventure life can give you; that it was important not to take things too seriously, but always give it your best shot; to take the bad days and the good days with the same spirit.

Lex could also be a difficult employee and colleague. At one meeting of TRM's directors Lex attended, though he was a junior member of the team, he slammed the board for not following up on leads and he complained that targets were always changing. It was a step out of line for the young Greensill. Cleland pushed back, vigorously defending his track record. The older man held firm, but Lex was clearly bristling with ambition.

Ultimately, though Lex sometimes upset his colleagues, there was a view that his frustration was born out of commitment, competitiveness and a sense of urgency, none of which were particularly bad traits at an entrepreneurial firm like TRM, so long as there were others who could keep him in line.

Cleland was also a stickler for documentation. Everything was conducted in meticulous fashion. He was putting together a kind of blueprint for a new type of supply chain financing. If it was successful, it could be rolled out around the world. The roadmap was all laid out for Cleland, Lex and others involved to use over and over.

TRM was gaining traction. Cleland had attracted an experienced board and heavyweight supporters. Merrill Lynch and Deutsche Bank and HSBC were interested in his work. Barclays agreed to a potential funding deal – the bank discussed providing about $200 million of funding for an SCF-type programme. German software company SAP, Hong Kong-based conglomerate Jardine Matheson, UK water company United Utilities and many others were interested in becoming clients. Cleland had an agreement with French insurance company CoFace to provide trade credit insurance to the TRM programme too.

And then, almost at the last minute, the rug was pulled out from under the firm. CoFace found that its own backers no longer had an appetite for the SCF programme. Without the insurance, Barclays also withdrew. The proposal collapsed. TRM struggled on for a while. It morphed into another similar electronic trade finance business. But the momentum was gone. Cleland eventually returned to Australia.

Lex meanwhile had enjoyed some better luck. For a short time, towards the end of OzEcom, he'd done some work for another tech start-up called 5th Finger. It was a kind of SMS marketing venture that used mobile phones to deliver content and advertising. Lex had helped the company's founders develop a business plan and pitch it to telecoms companies. When he moved to the UK, he'd tried to set up a 5th Finger office there and develop an international strategy. It was hard to gain a foothold though, and the start-up cut him loose in early 2001 as it focused on Australia. Years later, when 5th Finger was sold to a unit of Microsoft, the early stakeholders, including Lex, each made a small fortune.

By the time TRM ended, Lex had already moved on. He was studying at Manchester, and he was making inroads elsewhere. He lost touch with Cleland, though he'd taken a lot from being around the seasoned businessman. He'd seen Cleland's blueprint for a technology-driven supply chain finance solution up close and personal. He'd also seen how good business ideas could suffer from fickle business partners. And he'd learned that, if you want to get on, dressing the part is important too.

# TWO

# Lex and the City

Getting into Morgan Stanley's MBA internship programme is one of the toughest tickets in banking. Tens of thousands of eager wannabes apply for the coveted positions. A tiny handful make it through. In 2005, the giant Wall Street bank only accepted applications from a select group of elite international universities – the likes of Oxford or Cambridge, INSEAD (Institut Européen d'Administration des Affaires) and NYU (New York University). The University of Manchester's Alliance Manchester Business School, where Lex Greensill was studying for his MBA, was not on the Morgan Stanley approved list.

For Lex, that was a challenge, not a firmly shut door.

In the mid 2000s, the big global banks were booming, riding a wave of deregulation, new technology and cheap funding to greater and greater profit. Ambitious, aspiring executives on the make knew that the most direct path to extraordinary riches began at the doors of the biggest banks in the world.

Lex had two of the most fabled institutions in his sights – both appealed to his desire for high status and his unwavering belief that he would one day sit at the top of the global financial establishment. One was Rothschild, the centuries-old, blue-blooded London investment bank whose hushed halls are decked with Old Masters. The other was Morgan Stanley, Wall Street's so-called 'white shoe' bank (white buck suede Oxfords were once the hallmark of upper-class American bankers). Both institutions were known for a traditional, slightly stuffy culture. In the introspective hierarchy of the banking industry, they were also at the very peak.

In Lex's later version of events, he could have chosen to work at either firm, but he rejected Rothschild in favour of the American bank. It was more exciting, more forward-looking, better suited to his sense of enterprise and drive. He had also found an inside track that would help him secure a place there.

David Brierwood was a veteran of Morgan Stanley's UK business since the 1980s. A guitar-loving British banker, Brierwood had risen through the ranks for two decades, becoming the chief operating officer of the securities division – a highly prominent role in Morgan Stanley's London office. He had a profile and network that spanned the bank's global reach.

Brierwood was also an alumnus of Manchester Business School. For many senior bankers, like Brierwood, it was a part of the role to scout your alma mater for talent at campus drinks and social events. That's where Lex came in. The young Australian was impressive, relentless, convincing and full of self-belief. He was an arch-networker, focused and determined, a standout even among the MBA types eyeing their next high-paying gig. Lex was also evangelical about a unique-sounding idea for a new business based around providing short-term loans to clients who were backed by invoices from their own suppliers. It was a form of factoring, or supply chain finance, that involved funding short-term loans to clients backed by the invoices they owed their suppliers. What Lex was pitching was a version of the blueprint put together by Robert Cleland and his team at OzEcom and Transaction Risk Mitigation (TRM).

Lex's potential was not hard to spot – even if he hadn't gone to the right school. His enthusiasm was infectious, and his supply chain finance idea was potentially a money-spinner, even if it wasn't quite the winning lottery ticket Lex claimed it would be. His career track was interesting – growing up on the farm, his turbulent time in the Australian start-up scene, the law degree, and his work with the Australian farm producers. His background was not typical, and Lex had to jump through hoops. He met with literally dozens of Morgan Stanley executives and answered hour after hour of questions. He had to impress them all. And he did.

Not only was Lex admitted to the programme, but the super-salesman also secured a few special footnotes to his contract. The high achievers who'd made the cut were put on a strict rotation, spending a few weeks in one department of the bank before being rolled onto another and then another. Lex instead managed to persuade his new bosses to let him work exclusively in a single business unit – the fixed income division, which consisted of a couple of hundred people on the lower floors of Morgan Stanley's Canary Wharf headquarters. He also got the Morgan Stanley chiefs to agree to let him focus entirely on building up the firm's trade finance programme. Most of Lex's new colleagues in fixed income had never heard of supply chain finance. It sounded interesting and small enough to be a very low risk. Senior executives saw it as a kind of low-risk research and development experiment and decided to let the young Australian upstart run with his own project, beavering away with minimal supervision.

Even among the alpha types at the bank, Lex was abnormally hard-working and confident about his own success. Other bankers approvingly talked about Lex the 'demon', Lex the 'psychopath', possessed by his own ambition, uber-focused and working extraordinarily long hours.

He would make outlandish claims about his SCF experiment, too. 'We're going to make billions and billions of pounds,' Lex told his bosses and colleagues. 'We're going to be rich.'

Nobody took the boldest of Lex's statements too seriously, but the Morgan Stanley chiefs figured that even if he earned the bank a fraction of what he boasted he could deliver, it would be worth it. And given Lex's drive and self-belief, who would bet against him?

Lex was racing ahead of the other MBA interns. He still had to take part in the same team-building events – trips to cookery schools or to greyhound tracks. When he joined them for social drinks or dinners, he'd never truly let loose like the others. And when the internship programme ended, and the rest of his cohort went back to school to finish their MBAs, Lex stayed on at Morgan Stanley, completing his studies part-time. Soon, Lex was running the trade finance team, known as TReFS, short for Trade Receivable electronic Financing System.

(Several of his Morgan Stanley colleagues later became key members of the Greensill team too. Among them were Roland Hartley-Urquhart and Dave Skirzenski, two US-based Morgan Stanley executives who helped to develop a global client base for TReFS. Jason Austin and Chris Bates, a lawyer Lex knew from business school, were also at Morgan Stanley – Bates shared a flat with Lex in the Isle of Dogs, then a relatively unfashionable area close to the bank's headquarters in Canary Wharf.)

The team eventually grew to about a dozen people, with Lex as leader. While he continued to meet frequently with David Brierwood – his mentor – Lex's reporting line was to Jane Guttridge, a tough, New York-based Morgan Stanley veteran. Guttridge's career had already passed its peak. She mostly left Lex to run with the TReFS business, while acting like a full-time cheerleader for the young Australian in the upper echelons of the bank.

LEX CERTAINLY STOOD out. When he first showed up at Morgan Stanley, as a very junior banker, he handed out his own, home-made business cards. And while most of the desk-bound bankers he worked alongside dressed casually, in chinos and open-collared shirts, Lex turned up in stiff, tight suits. His new colleagues joked that he looked like an undertaker.

A lot of what he wore was bespoke, from a tailor in Cheshire. Increasingly he also eyed Savile Row and Jermyn Street, the homes of high-end tailoring in London where top bankers had their suits cut and fashioned. He talked about buying £1,000 shoes as though no banker was complete without a pair.

Much of Lex's fashion sense came from a niche, tongue-in-cheek British magazine called *Chap*, which celebrated conservative styles like tweed and pocket squares. The magazine, and a book called *The Chap Manifesto*, became famous for a while because the publisher organized street protests when the preppy fast-fashion brand Abercrombie & Fitch planned to move into Savile Row. On weekends in the office, when other bankers would dress down, Lex would still wear a suit and tie. In rare moments of relaxation, usually back at his home in Cheshire, he wore garishly coloured trousers – purple, yellow or pink – and he almost never wore trainers, except when he was running.

His accent changed. Bundaberg drifted into the distant past and he began to acquire the clipped tones of the British upper class. Colleagues were often surprised to find out he was from Australia.

He was also fascinated by the British establishment.

'One day,' he told his TReFS team, 'I'm going to be knighted.'

At work, he had an acute focus on even the most boring details. He would ask specific, technical questions of the staff who worked in accounting or in technology. He wanted to know how the software worked. He wanted to know how TReFS would be accounted for. He was no whizz with computing or software but, compared to most colleagues, he was like a tech visionary in the stuffy Wall Street bank.

The TReFS team sat in a glass office, at one end of a huge floor dedicated to fixed income. Outside, the trading desks were buzzing with row after row of bankers working on mortgage-backed securities and other complicated investments – the alphabet soup of derivatives with acronyms like CDOs and ABCP that blew up when the financial crisis roiled the global economy and sent the financial sector into a tailspin.

Lex's team was a sideshow, but he was going after the bank's biggest corporate clients, including household names and big businesses. His pitch was very similar to the OzEcom and TRM blueprint developed by his one-time mentor, Robert Cleland. It went like this: Morgan Stanley's biggest corporate clients paid their suppliers ninety or 180 days after they submitted an invoice. That meant suppliers were out of pocket for a while, which could put them under some financial strain. The bank would step in and pay suppliers much earlier, but at a discount. The bank would collect the full invoiced amount later and it would fund this programme through the asset-backed commercial paper market – in effect, Lex would convert the clients' obligation to pay the invoices into securities that in theory could be traded like bonds. The whole thing would be wrapped up with a Morgan Stanley guarantee, and they'd buy credit protection – insurance that pays out if the client defaults on the loan – to hedge against the risk of a default.

The whole programme ran on a privately owned, third-party technology platform called PrimeRevenue that carried out most of the heavy lifting, processing the invoices and matching payments. Prime-Revenue was a relatively tiny tech start-up and Morgan Stanley was a key client for the firm. There was a sort of co-dependency. PrimeRevenue needed Morgan Stanley because the bank was its biggest client. Lex needed PrimeRevenue to make TReFS work. Culturally, though, the two organizations were miles apart, and the laid-back techies mocked Lex for his fake British accent, and his uptight behaviour.

The TReFS team remained small, but Lex acted as though they were already a big deal. He and his team would fly around the world, meeting with top-level executives at major companies in New York, Tokyo, Hong Kong, Sydney. Lex even bragged to colleagues that he might have the highest travel bill of any executive in the company.

TReFS had some success. Kingfisher, the home improvement

business, signed up, as did the huge UK supermarket chain Sainsbury's. Executives there saw the programme – known as 'Project Perceval' – as a logical, safe way to provide relatively cheap funding for their small suppliers. Lex even hired a video production crew to film Sainsbury's trading director Mike Coupe in a stilted, low-fi video touting the benefits to suppliers of 'improving your cash flow, your liquidity and improving your costs.' Morgan Stanley then paid to mail out the video on CD-ROM to hundreds of Sainsbury's suppliers. (A few years later, when Coupe was Sainsbury's CEO, he was famously caught on camera another time, singing 'We're in the money' while waiting for an interview about a planned merger with one of the store's rivals.)

Lex told colleagues he was the highest-paid Morgan Stanley associate in the world. Within months, he had been promoted to vice president. Within two years, he told some colleagues he'd been paid a million-pound bonus – incredibly quick even by the then excessive standards of the City.

He talked about changing finance for ever. The young, energetic team he'd forged found it easy to fall in behind the mission. But even at this early stage in Lex's career, some colleagues were also concerned that Lex's promises were running ahead of reality. He presented overly ambitious projections that didn't reflect what they were seeing on the ground in meetings with clients. Lex would frequently tell senior managers that this corporation or that big business was going to sign up to TReFS, when his colleagues knew they'd only held a preliminary meeting. It was wishful thinking. The client might sign up eventually, but Lex presented it with such bravado, with such a bold face, that anyone hearing him would think the deal was as good as done.

He was also proposing deals that were much more complicated than the simple supply chain finance model, relying on multiple layers of default protection or complex structures and funding methods. Often the programmes Lex conjured up fell into an accounting grey area, which appealed to some clients as they could shift debts off their balance sheet.

Still, the business was growing, and Lex's reputation in the bank was rising with it.

Then disaster hit.

The global financial crisis was borne out of lax mortgage lending in parts of the US, but its impact went around the world. One morning, in summer 2008, the TReFS team showed up to the office and the trading desks that mapped out their floor were more or less empty. Hundreds of fixed income staff found their security cards didn't work. They had been laid off overnight.

Lex's team had slipped through the net. He seized the moment. *We're still here because supply chain finance is the future of banking*, he said. *We're changing the world*. He was like the coach of an underdog sports team, rousing his players for a shot at the title. His mostly young TReFS team was impressed. In the midst of this huge banking crisis, Lex was coming out fighting.

In reality, his optimism was misplaced. A few months after the trading floor had been cleared out, TReFS was effectively finished too. As the crisis raged, a Chicago-based investment management company that ran a crucial part of the TReFS programme – the asset-backed commercial paper conduit – called to say they were pulling out. Their move was swift and decisive. For Morgan Stanley, exiting TReFS wouldn't be so straightforward. The bank couldn't just shut the programme off. That would leave some big customers in the lurch. Sainsbury's had quickly run up close to $1 billion in the TReFS programme, all of it financing the grocery chain's extensive network of suppliers. The financial crisis had taken on a deeply political flavour, and it would have been impolitic of the US bank to leave a major UK blue-chip company with such a headache. But the bank didn't want Lex's SCF loans to land on its balance sheet either – across Wall Street and the City, bankers were trying to shrink their balance sheet lending, not grow it.

Lex found an opportunity amid the meltdown, conjuring a complicated resolution. This involved shifting funds from one of Morgan

Stanley's subsidiaries – a specific type of deposit-taking banking subsidiary known as a Utah Industrial Bank. Banking authorities have strict rules about using customer deposits for investment banking activity, though Lex always insisted that he believed the plan didn't breach any regulations. He made it work, for a short time at least, and the investment bank was able to tap hundreds of millions of dollars of liquidity, he told colleagues later.

(Much later, a lawyer for Lex and his media spokesperson told me this story wasn't true. A Morgan Stanley spokesperson denied it too. But then, in an interview with me, Lex said on the record that he had in fact tapped the Utah Industrial Bank for funding and he insisted that there was no breach of any rules. When I went back to Morgan Stanley, the spokesperson again said it never happened.)

By February 2009, Lex's bosses needed a permanent solution. They launched a sales process and tried to find a buyer for the entire TReFS programme. A pitch deck for the sale was dubbed Project Cloud – a reference to a special purpose vehicle (SPV) called Thunder that had been set up to process the SCF programme. (SPVs are subsidiary companies, frequently used in structured finance, that perform a specific business activity.) The sales deck for Project Cloud said the business at that time had relationships with five clients, and about 500 suppliers, and that there was about $500 million of outstanding loans. The document explained that Thunder, which was sponsored by Morgan Stanley, bought the rights to debts that its clients owed to hundreds of their suppliers. The deck explained the relationship with PrimeRevenue. And it touted the 'opportunity to acquire [a] high-performing management team.'

There were no takers. Partly, other banks at this stage of the financial crisis had no more appetite than Morgan Stanley for making more loans. They also questioned the idea of buying the programme at all. What were they getting beyond a couple of problematic contracts? Also, what was so special about this management team? And didn't the technology really belong to PrimeRevenue anyway?

Another proposal came from the Wellcome Trust – a UK-based health charity that is supported by a multibillion-pound foundation. The trust's top management suggested it could fund the TReFS programme. But it had no expertise or experience of running a supply chain finance programme and ultimately the idea never took hold.

Bigwigs in Morgan Stanley found themselves in talks with UK authorities, including officials from the Bank of England, trying to figure out a solution to this delicate problem. Eventually, the central bank tweaked its own rules so that it could temporarily acquire some of the loans. Another arrangement was brokered: Royal Bank of Scotland, which was then owned by the government, effectively took on the loans to Lex's former supply chain finance clients in the UK. A similar arrangement saw Bank of America take on the US-based clients of the programme.

After TReFS dissolved, most of the team, including Lex, moved elsewhere.

For Lex, the end of the Morgan Stanley programme was yet another harsh lesson in the fickle nature of finance. His takeaway was that the bank funding model was dangerous. In the event of a crisis, the banks could simply pull away, leaving the whole SCF programme in trouble.

LEX'S FORMER MORGAN Stanley boss, Jane Guttridge, had jumped ship to Citigroup. The US banking behemoth was under the stewardship of CEO Vikram Pandit and his right-hand man John Havens – the two had previously run a hedge fund called Old Lane LLC that Citi bought in 2007. Within months of arriving at Citi, Pandit was appointed head of the entire bank as it too faced potential disaster. Citi had stumbled through the financial crisis like many of its peers. But under Pandit's leadership, it had survived the worst of the crisis and was soon back in hiring mode. Central banks and governments had stopped the bleeding by early 2009 and within months the flood of new money into the economy meant the good times were – sort of – back.

Guttridge, in a jargon-filled interview with a trade publication around this time, said that the appetite among clients for supply chain finance was taking off, 'driven by the need to improve returns on invested working capital and the search for global operational productivity improvements.' She hired Lex and several of the old TReFS team to tap into this growing demand.

Lex thought of Citi as the 'big gorilla' in the whole trade finance space. Unlike the investment banks that generated most of their revenue from trading and big M&A deals, such as Morgan Stanley, much of Citi's business involved managing the day-to-day business of its clients, including major corporations. In theory, this would be a dream match-up for Lex, giving him access to billions of dollars in global payments. In practice, the pairing was a mess.

Lex found Citi too bureaucratic, too rigid and too cumbersome to match his ambitions. The bank insisted that he only pitch the SCF programme to existing corporate customers – a vast group, but in Lex's view only a fraction of the potential market. He was thinking much bigger than that. Lex believed there were lots of smaller suppliers that should get access to SCF, but he had to ignore them because they fell outside Citi's range.

He clashed with several senior managers, including John Ahearn, the bank's then head of trade finance. Ahearn, a hard-nosed, tough US banker, had first grown wary of Greensill when Morgan Stanley had pitched him the TReFS business. The two continued to battle as Ahearn tried to keep Greensill within the parameters of Citi's rules, while Lex skirted round his boss to make his case to other top executives. Lex was particularly close to Havens, then the bank's chief operating officer, and he told friends and colleagues that Havens's office door was always open to him. Others perceived this as Lex pulling strings higher up the organization in order to avoid the bank's normal processes.

Ahearn, who was nominally Lex's boss, was particularly concerned that Greensill was pitching supply chain finance loans to riskier clients who might not be able to pay them back, and that he was planning to extend repayment terms for much longer periods than was normal. At one point, he said he was going to sign a supply chain finance deal with the Dutch electronics giant Philips. It would be a big win for Citi and for Lex personally. Philips was a huge name. Lex was touted by his cheerleaders for landing it. But the praise soon dissipated. It turned out the deal had been priced as though Citi was lending to the main corporate entity, when actually it was a loan to a Hungarian subsidiary of the firm. That was much less impressive, and the borrower would have had to have been charged a much higher rate for the loan. In the end, the deal didn't happen.

Lex was also earning a reputation as a lavish spender on the company's account. Citigroup, whose roots were in banking ordinary retail customers and mundane company accounts, was an entirely different culture to Morgan Stanley. In investment banking, a big expense account was often equated with high achievement – especially prior to the financial crisis. But in a bank like Citi, in the years following the crisis, managers kept a much tighter leash on their staff. Lex's boasts about having one of the highest American Express bills in the entire bank might have confirmed his lofty status at another bank, but at Citi they went down like a lead balloon.

One incident really stood out. In April 2010, when Lex had been at Citi for just a few months, he travelled to Copenhagen to meet a potential client. His travel plans were unexpectedly disrupted when the Icelandic volcano Eyjafjallajökull spouted ash high across swathes of northern Europe. Thousands of flights across the continent were grounded for days because of concerns the ash might damage their engines. Lex, like the rest of the world, was stuck. Not only that; he had no change of clothes. And he looked set to miss another important meeting back in the UK. Ever resourceful, he rented a car, bought a new suit and shirt, and made his way to the meeting via boat and on land. Despite the chaos and inconvenience, Lex told colleagues that the meeting went well and he won the client over. But when he later submitted an expense claim for about £4,000, mostly for the new emergency wardrobe change, Ahearn – apoplectic – refused to sign it off. That kind of lavish spending was anathema to the stringent management at Citi. When Lex retold the story to colleagues, he relayed it as though it was a kind of badge of honour.

A final straw came a few months later. Lex had managed to get the backing of the UK government for a new supply chain finance programme, run by Citi. The programme would aim to help small and medium businesses in the wake of the financial crisis. The UK government, Lex told his senior executives, had agreed to provide a kind of backstop for Citi's loans. If the bank needed to offload the loans quickly, the government would take them on. In theory, it sounded like a good proposition. The UK government support reduced Citi's cost of lending. However, Lex's bosses were puzzled. The first client to sign up was US grocery giant Walmart. The next client was the US computing business Dell. Why would the UK government support a US bank lending to huge US companies? Lex's explanation was complex and confusing. It involved swapping dollar transactions into pounds sterling and had no connection to the underlying objective of helping UK businesses. The structure might have been clever, but Lex's bosses were unimpressed. The whole thing seemed like an embarrassing accident waiting to happen, and in the end, Citi allowed the programme to fizzle out.

DURING HIS TIME at Citi, Lex Greensill also sat on a Bank of England committee on supply chain finance, starting in September 2009, that was looking at ways to get more money into the 'real' economy. Two dozen or so interested executives from across the big accounting and law firms, a couple of banks, supply chain technology platforms and insurers gathered once a month, often at London's Tower 42 office block.

The group was mostly middle managers. Lex usually seemed distracted and underwhelmed, as though the committee was a bit beneath his status. In May 2010, the committee issued a report that concluded the prospects for rapid expansion of SCF were limited – not at all what Lex believed. Funding was still restricted to a handful of banks. Investors either couldn't put money in, were wary of complex and uncertain regulation, or didn't see how they could generate a big enough return to make it worthwhile. The findings were unpopular with the SCF fans on the committee – three quarters of the group's members, including Lex, decided they wouldn't sign the report.

Lex's time with Citi was coming to a hasty end. It hadn't been a roaring success, though he'd been able to continue building out an impressive network of movers and shakers. Most significant among them was Maurice Thompson, renowned in the City and across Europe, who was head of Citigroup's UK business. Thompson was a fox-hunting aficionado and the High Sheriff of Leicestershire – an office that dates to Saxon times and today involves dressing up in a seventeenth-century uniform of dark velvet coat, breeches, buckled shoes and a sword. His support for Lex in the coming years was critical to the rise of Greensill.

For now, though, Lex's time with the titans of Wall Street was over. At Morgan Stanley, he had sweated over the business for years and the bank had abruptly ditched it when the financial crisis hit. At Citi, he was squeezed out by senior managers who, in his view, were unable to match his vision. The experience had confirmed that the banks were too slow, too conservative, too narrowly focused on a handful of clients and on maintaining the status quo. They were dinosaurs, waiting to be made extinct by a new breed of financial entrepreneurs playing by a different set of rules.

If Lex was going to become really rich, if he was going to fulfil his ambition to reinvent finance, he would have to do it on his own terms.

THREE

# Supplier Beware

Since the earliest days of human trade, buyers and sellers of goods have been pitted against each other. Suppliers want cash paid up front or on delivery. Buyers want to pay when it suits them. That was true for Mesopotamian farmers, fifteenth-century English weavers and American fur trappers. All wanted to be paid for their goods as soon as they were shipped or earlier. Often, merchants wanted to drag out payment until they'd sold the goods on again to their own customers. It's a deep flaw in the system of trade where it ought to be in everyone's best interests to keep the cash flowing.

For millennia, the 'factor' – a kind of banker that specializes in trade finance – played a critical role in bridging the divide. Factoring has underpinned local and global trade since well before Cosimo de' Medici created one of the first truly international banking empires, which expanded from Florence and Rome across all the great commercial centres of fifteenth-century Europe. It works because it is in everyone's best interests to have a healthy, smooth-running supply chain, with cash getting to where it's needed, when it's needed.

This is how factoring works: a supplier is owed money by its customers. These IOUs are called receivables, and until they're paid up, the supplier doesn't know how much they will eventually collect. Some customers will pay everything on time. Some will pay but maybe not for a while. And others might not pay at all. The factor buys the IOUs, or receivables, paying a small discount to the invoiced amount and then chases the customer for the full amount later. Sometimes the factor loses out if the customer never pays up. Mostly they make a small profit.

In the past few decades, factoring has evolved. Rapidly.

Starting in the 1980s, economies quickly globalized, seeking out cheaper workers and means of production. That led to more complex, longer supply chains, spanning several countries. There were more components, more suppliers, more transactions. The consultants McKinsey & Company estimate that a single car manufacturer such as Ford or Volkswagen might have 18,000 suppliers, spanning just about every continent on the planet. Production will grind to a halt if the suppliers are not in sync. Everyone in the long, twisting chain wants to be paid on time, to keep the machines running, to make sure workers keep showing up.

Banking is nothing if not innovative. A whole slew of financing techniques has also sprung up, with names like dynamic discounting, early payment discounts, accounts receivable financing, letters of credit.

A version of factoring called supply chain finance – SCF, or sometimes 'reverse factoring' – emerged within the last few decades. Some in the industry trace its beginnings to developments in the auto industry in the 1980s. Others say it started in Spain around the same time.

In 1998, a mid-ranking executive at Chase Manhattan bank filed a US patent, now lapsed, for a supply chain financing technique. The wannabe inventor was Roland Hartley-Urquhart, one of Lex's colleagues at Morgan Stanley, who'd run the US side of that business. He also became one of the first and longest employees at Greensill Capital. His 1998 patent explained SCF like this:

> A method for financing a supply of goods (a supply chain) from a supplier to a buyer in which the buyer has a lower cost of funds than the supplier . . . The buyer generates a purchase order for the goods which is forwarded to the supplier who in turn ships the goods to the buyer. The supplier sends an invoice to the buyer which stores the invoice in a database. The financing institution electronically accesses the database to retrieve the daily invoices. The financial institution then calculates the financing applicable to the shipped goods and forwards a payment to the supplier. Upon maturing of the financing, the buyer settles with the financial institution by remitting the gross proceeds.

There were versions of SCF popping up everywhere. Robert Cleland's OzEcom was in Australia, and TRM was in the UK. Whoever invented it, SCF involves a contortion of the original, simple approach to factoring. Instead of the supplier approaching the factor, it's the buyer of goods who makes the move.

Here's how it's explained in a July 2021 paper titled 'The determinants and consequences of reverse factoring: Early evidence from the UK' by Chuk, Lourie and Yoo of the University of California, Irvine:

> To illustrate with a brief stylized example, suppose that Procter & Gamble purchases certain raw materials from small and mid-sized local suppliers. Further suppose that a fictitious company XYZ Inc. is a small supplier that has recently sold some raw materials to Procter & Gamble for an invoice price of $100. In this fictitious example, Procter & Gamble would typically remit a cash payment of $100 to XYZ 60 days after receiving the raw materials from XYZ. Now suppose that Procter & Gamble offers a reverse factoring program [sic] using a bank as the financial intermediary, and XYZ has

decided to participate. Under reverse factoring, Procter & Gamble would pay the full $100 to the bank later, which is likely later than the typical payment period in the absence of reverse factoring (i.e., later than the 60 days in this example). In turn, the bank would pay XYZ earlier than 60 days, but the payment amount would be lower than the full invoice amount. For example, the bank might pay $98 to XYZ, such that the bank earns a $2 fee in exchange for facilitating the transaction and for bearing the risk of non-payment by Procter & Gamble.

Reverse factoring may be seen as a 'win-win'. The bank decides how much to charge for its service based on the credit rating of the buyer, not the supplier. Because the buyer tends to be a bigger company, it usually has a stronger credit rating, meaning that there is a lower risk that it will fail to pay up and the bank can provide cheaper financing.

The use of SCF has grown quickly. By 2017, about two-thirds of the biggest companies in Europe ran a supply chain finance programme, according to accountants PricewaterhouseCoopers (PwC). But there's room to grow further. For the most part, banks that offer SCF programmes have stuck to their investment grade corporate clients – big companies that are less likely to default on the loans. That's a tiny proportion of the companies that theoretically could become SCF customers.

McKinsey say that the use of SCF could grow at 20 per cent a year through 2024, and that there is a potential pool of annual revenue tied to SCF of $20 billion.

At the same time, rule changes after the financial crisis, and the tendency for banks to tighten up their balance sheets, led some banks to curtail their commitment to exactly this kind of business. That opened a gap for specialized firms, often using new technology, to enter the market.

*

ROBERT J. COMERFORD IS a partner with accountants Deloitte and previously a Professional Accounting Fellow in the Office of the Chief Accountant at the US Securities and Exchange Commission (SEC). He's not famous. He wasn't even especially senior at the SEC. But in the SCF world, a speech Comerford gave in 2003 at the thirty-first national conference of the Association of International Certified Professional Accountants is seminal. It is the Gettysburg Address of SCF.

In the speech, Comerford discussed 'certain transactions involving trade account payables' that were being used to circumvent existing rules on balance sheet disclosures. Comerford goes on to describe the transactions that have caused his consternation, and what he describes is a kind of SCF deal. The SEC, he said, believes that the substance of these transactions is that the buyer has borrowed money to pay its bills. The financing should be recorded as debt.

The speech is so important because one of the appealing things about SCF for many big companies is that it isn't debt. Proponents of this view argue that the financing is given to the small suppliers, who are getting their invoices paid early.

Remarkably, for years following Comerford's speech, there was little movement from the usual financial gatekeepers – the accountants and regulators and rating agencies. It sat in an accounting grey area. It wasn't clear how it affected the creditworthiness of a company. It wasn't clear if SCF was debt or not.

As the use of SCF grew and grew, the amount of financing that simply wasn't being recorded anywhere on anyone's balance sheet was growing and growing too. The accountants, regulators and other gatekeepers that guard global capital markets had started to worry about what might happen if this money stayed in the shadows.

In 2015, Moody's, the rating agency, issued a report on Spanish energy group Abengoa that said its 'large-scale reverse factoring programme has debt-like features . . . Moody's notes that the practice is likely widespread.'

Lack of disclosure rules on reverse factoring make it hard to measure, while the supposedly short-term nature of the financing means it can unwind quickly and leave a borrower suddenly facing a shortfall. A few months after that Moody's note, Abengoa was forced into a painful restructuring and narrowly avoided going bust, though only for a few years. It filed for insolvency in early 2021.

SCF burst into the headlines for the wrong reasons again in 2018. Carillion, the construction and facilities management company, collapsed into bankruptcy that year, in one of the biggest corporate failures in the UK's history. At its heart was a kind of SCF programme, promoted by the UK government and based partly on advice it received from Lex Greensill, known as the 'early payment facility'. Carillion had used the SCF programme to stretch out its payment periods to 120 days, giving suppliers the option to get their money within thirty days if they paid a fee to the banks behind the programme. The construction firm was building up debts that were hidden among ordinary trade creditors on its balance sheet – meaning it didn't affect the company's credit rating.

The same year, Fitch, another rating agency, also weighed in. Fitch said companies were using SCF as a 'loophole' to hide borrowings that 'may have negative credit implications.'

The SEC also began to sniff around. Since 2019, the US regulator has asked several big US companies about their use of reverse factoring, including Coca-Cola, Procter & Gamble and Boeing.

The Big Four accounting firms have piled in too. In October 2019, Ernst & Young (EY), Deloitte, PwC and KPMG took the unusual step of sending a joint letter to US accounting regulators, seeking guidance on how they should treat SCF in the accounts of companies they audited. A couple of years later, their collective prayers were answered. Sort of . . .

In September 2021, the Financial Accounting Standards Board, the authority for US accounting standards, proposed new rules for SCF. The proposal would require companies to disclose if they use

SCF, and details about the size and key terms of the programme. Finally, almost twenty years after Comerford's warning, it looked as if the gatekeepers might have come up with some rules.

Back in 2011, however, there were no obstacles in Lex's way. When his efforts to turn Citi and Morgan Stanley into giant SCF shops had run aground, Lex set up his own firm, Greensill Capital.

He added a few twists to the reverse factoring mix. For starters, he didn't have a giant balance sheet like the big banks had to fund all their deals, and he didn't want to rely on the vagaries of the asset-backed commercial paper market. Instead, he would tap other people's money in a more direct way.

Since the global financial crisis, central banks around the world had flooded the market with cash and forced down interest rates to try to get the global economy back up to speed. Lex bet he could tempt investors to fund his supply chain finance loans if he offered just a little more than they would get leaving their money in the bank. He sought out giant fund management houses that ran billions of dollars in investments for wealthy clients like company pension plans and super-rich individuals. He sold some of his supply chain finance loans, the best stuff, to big European and Japanese banks. He also tapped corporate treasury departments; the biggest global companies like Vodafone or Boeing often sat on big pools of cash that were not earning much. And he wanted a bank of his own that would collect deposits from customers and use them to pay for SCF loans.

The second twist he added was to wrap the whole scheme in insurance. Regulations prevented many investors from putting their money into all but the very safest investments. But Lex knew the companies he would have to lend to were not all top grade, especially at the start. After all, who would work with 'Greensill Capital'? The solution was to buy trade credit insurance. This is a type of insurance policy that pays out when there is a default on the loans Lex was planning to finance. If the loans made by Greensill Capital were covered by a policy from an insurer with a strong credit rating, then investors would treat the loans themselves as though they had a good rating too. That meant Greensill could access a much broader group of investors to fund the loans. It was reminiscent of the years leading up to the financial crisis, when pools of low-grade assets were mixed with better-rated investments and sold as low risk. Not wrong exactly, but you had to look closely to see what you were investing in.

The final Lex twist was to add new technology. In the wake of the financial crisis, there had been an explosion in new financial technology companies, or fintechs. Some of these were in the payments processing space, and included PrimeRevenue, Orbian, Taulia and Demica.

Lex was no techie. Instead, he hooked up with a series of other aspiring entrepreneurs who carried the bulk of the technology he needed to run the business. And then he liberally applied the fintech tag to Greensill Capital too.

To make it all work, Lex created a tangle of special purpose vehicles (SPVs), trusts, offshore companies and subsidiaries that each played a critical role. In essence, he'd taken one of the oldest, simplest forms of banking, and supercharged it for the twenty-first century.

Greensill Capital was up and running. But the seeds of Greensill's problems were sown. It was complex. It loaned money to the riskier end of the market. The clients in Greensill's reverse factoring programmes often didn't have great credit ratings. The funds Lex created masked low-grade corporate debts with insurance, which made it look as safe as putting money in the bank. And Greensill was touting itself as a hot new fintech, when in reality Greensill was a financial intermediary with an appetite for convoluted corporate chicanery.

FOUR

# Mixing Business and Politics

Lex Greensill's rise to the upper echelons of politics had begun at Morgan Stanley. The young Australian banker had landed at the bank's Canary Wharf offices with a vigorous work ethic, a firm belief in his own destiny, and the support of David Brierwood, one of the bank's top executives. He also landed at more or less the same time as another, far more vaunted outsider.

Jeremy Heywood was a seasoned economist and civil servant who'd worked the corridors of power under various governments since the 1980s. He ran the Treasury under Conservative and Labour Chancellors alike. He became Principal Private Secretary to Tony Blair – it is Whitehall folklore that when al-Qaeda terrorists flew hijacked planes into the World Trade Center in New York on 11 September 2001, Blair called Heywood, the one adviser he could truly trust in a moment of deep crisis, and asked: 'Are you sure there aren't any aeroplanes flying towards us?'

In the otherwise anonymous civil service organization, Heywood was a rock star. But in 2003, Heywood left the service. During the high-profile Hutton Inquiry into the death of Dr David Kelly, an expert in biological warfare and former UN weapons inspector in Iraq, Heywood acknowledged he had skirted normal procedures and not drawn up minutes for some key meetings. Shortly after, he quit Whitehall for the City, and joined Morgan Stanley's UK investment banking division.

The Wall Street firm is a colossus. Today, it has more than 60,000 staff worldwide with more than 5,000 in London. Like the other global banking giants, staff from one business unit don't necessarily mix with their colleagues in another part of the bank. This is partly by design and regulation, to protect the integrity of the bank's relationship with its clients. It's also partly because the investment bankers are often seen as a breed of alphas.

Heywood, the former civil servant, was different. He had made a career out of striding through the bureaucracy and red tape in government. He was always deeply curious too. And he spent some of his time at the bank meeting with a broad range of colleagues – grey-haired City veterans as well as eager new associates – across whatever business line or department fascinated him next. He was especially keen to meet people who worked on something innovative or unusual. One of those bankers was Lex Greensill, who was making waves with supply chain finance.

Supply chain finance was exactly the kind of esoteric business that piqued Heywood's interest. When he met with Lex, Heywood was intrigued by the potential for it to help small to medium-sized enterprises (SMEs). He thought Lex was interesting, clever, charismatic in a way, and deeply knowledgeable about the product he was working on.

Though Lex and Heywood were in different spheres, their paths crossed from time to time. At one point, a team of high-level Morgan Stanley bankers were pitching for business with Transport for London (TfL). Heywood was there, and somehow Lex had worked his way into the meeting too. At the end, one of the Morgan Stanley bankers – a well-connected capital markets guru named Piers

Harris – asked for a little more time with the TfL executives to explain the bank's supply chain finance programme. Lex introduced himself as Morgan Stanley's global head of supply chain finance. His colleagues were astonished – Lex had just made up a global title that gave him a massive promotion.

WITHIN A COUPLE of years, Lex and Heywood had both moved on. Heywood was summoned back to the civil service, first under Labour Prime Minister Gordon Brown, and then as a top bureaucrat serving the government of Tory PM David Cameron. Lex moved first to Citi, and then, in late 2011, he started his own firm, Greensill Capital.

The chance meeting of Heywood and Greensill at Morgan Stanley might have ended there, with Lex occasionally knocking on the door at the civil service, pitching supply chain finance programmes, invoking his brief relationship with the Whitehall mandarin to enhance his own reputation. But then the door opened wide.

The UK economy was struggling to recover from the impact of the financial crisis. The government of Cameron and Chancellor of the Exchequer George Osborne owned stakes in privatized banks and had forced through a package of austerity measures to drive down their costs. The Bank of England, like its peers around the world, was flooding the economy with cheap money. Yet there was barely a ripple. What else could be done?

This was the backdrop to the Breedon report, a months-long government-commissioned research project that looked into non-bank lending as a means of supporting SMEs. The project was set up by the Business Secretary, and the task force behind the report was led by Tim Breedon, then CEO of Legal & General, the giant insurance company. His team included half a dozen of the most powerful finance leaders in the UK, such as London Stock Exchange CEO Xavier Rolet and Dame Helen Alexander, the deputy chair of the Confederation of British Industry. In March 2012, Breedon's task force issued its findings, in a report headed 'Boosting Finance Options for Business'. For Lex Greensill, the fifty-page document was a gift from the political gods.

Breedon concluded that the financial crisis had shown UK businesses were too reliant on bank lending – the crisis had shown the danger of that approach, as banks had suddenly and ruthlessly backed away from clients in order to try to save themselves. The report said that 'there is a need for new mechanisms to support growth in the UK' – chief among these being SCF.

An entire section was devoted to a version of SCF and reverse factoring, with flow charts and a real-life example from Network Rail of how it could work.

Breedon specifically recommended that the government should, 'Explore how it can use its power as the biggest purchaser in the UK to encourage its own suppliers to adopt supply chain finance or similar schemes to support their suppliers; and work with banks, industry associations and professional bodies to accelerate adoption of supply chain finance.'

This was a green light – SCF was now official UK government policy, and expertise in this niche corner of the banking world was suddenly in demand.

By this time, Heywood was Cabinet Secretary, the highest-ranking official in the UK civil service. He had also been knighted earlier in the year. It was his job to ensure government policy was implemented. So, when Breedon asserted that the government should promote SCF, Heywood turned to an oddball banker he'd met at Morgan Stanley years earlier, SCF's passionate advocate, Lex Greensill.

GREENSILL HAD MET with several parts of government over the years, through his roles at Morgan Stanley and at Citi. By early 2012, before the Breedon report had even been released, Heywood helped

Lex get a role in Whitehall, on a short-term, unpaid basis to offer advice on supply chain finance. Lex had already left Citi and set up his own firm, Greensill Capital, though it was nascent at this point.

At first, Lex had no special access, no email address or pass to buildings. He was initially given three months inside the corridors of power. But anyone who knew Lex knew that it wouldn't end there. His initial three-month spell in Whitehall led to a longer one. He soon gained official IT and security access for the Cabinet Office and to Number 10 Downing Street. He carried a Number 10 business card and he had a Downing Street email address.

He began holding meetings inside Number 10 and other government buildings with contacts at tech platforms and in the insurance industry, and with big companies such as Vodafone and Carillion. Often, he'd try to impress guests with a tour of Number 10, whether they wanted one or not. Once, while showing a contact around the prime minister's residence, and intending to take his guest into the dining room, he instead walked straight into a broom cupboard.

The informal nature of his appointment could have been a hindrance. Lex turned it into an asset. He took on a kind of roving brief, seemingly turning up wherever he wanted. He met with officials in the Ministry of Defence and pitched the idea of using supply chain finance to pay for the maintenance of Voyager air-to-air refuelling planes and the construction of some new Eurofighter Typhoon jets. Another time, he suggested using supply chain finance to pay for a multibillion-pound nuclear submarine. Ultimately, these suggestions didn't go anywhere, though they did raise eyebrows among Whitehall staffers, who couldn't see what benefit Greensill's proposals offered.

Lex continued to work his way through government. He was a whirlwind. He met with officials at Her Majesty's Revenue & Customs, at the Highways Agency, the Department for Work and Pensions, the Department for Environment, Food and Rural Affairs, and Network Rail.

He eventually got somewhere, following meetings with officials at the Department of Health. Lex suggested a plan to finance payments made to independent pharmacies for prescription drugs. Many of these pharmacies were small businesses and they had to wait weeks to be reimbursed for the drugs they handed out to customers. Officials pushed back on Lex's idea, arguing that if there was a problem with late payments, then the government should just pay the pharmacies on time. Why did the government need someone else to finance its bill payments? Despite the resistance, the idea ended up in front of David Cameron, who signed off on the pharmacy plan. The programme went into effect, initially run by Lex's alma mater, Citibank. Later, the contract passed to Greensill Capital.

Although it's unclear whether Lex's work had any positive outcomes for the government, he began to reap the rewards of his time there. In 2014, he was appointed a Crown Representative – one of a select group of businesspeople advising the government on economics and trade.

He'd always coveted a formal British title. He'd told his colleagues on the internship programme at Morgan Stanley that he would be knighted. In September 2015, Lex's supporters in Whitehall began preparing the groundwork to have him rewarded in the Queen's Birthday Honours, the parade of gongs dished out by the government to those it favours. Heywood was keen to have Lex nominated for a CBE, one step below a knighthood. The rationale was that he had done years of unpaid work advising the government on supply chain finance.

Lex's nomination hit some resistance – there was opposition based on the view that Lex's free advice didn't merit such a top honour. Where was the hard proof that it resulted in anything much?

Lex told acquaintances that he had hired a consultancy based in Mayfair, London that helped wannabe award holders with their nominations and charged as much as £40,000 for services including writing applications, drafting letters of support, and face-to-face meetings to support their application.

In February 2017, a citation from Heywood's office in support of Lex's nomination said that 'over 3,000' pharmacies used the supply chain finance programme that Lex had helped set up in the UK, resulting in more than £3 billion in early payments, and savings to the government of about £100 million each year. The citation also claimed Greensill had 'a real impact on the UK economy and saved the taxpayer money especially in the Health and Defence areas.' (Later, a National Audit Office report largely debunked these claims.)

Sue Gray, the Cabinet Office's head of ethics, pushed back, saying Lex should settle for a lesser gong, the Order of the British Empire. In a heated email tug-of-war, Gray wrote that 'Lex must remain an OBE and while we can put him forward for a CBE it will be outrageous if he gets one'.

But the lobbying in Lex's favour was relentless. Eventually, the honours committee put his name forward in March 2017. A few months later, Lex's mother flew to the UK. Her son, Lex Greensill from Bundaberg, took her to Buckingham Palace. There, she watched Prince Charles award her son with a CBE.

IT'S HARD TO pinpoint exactly when Cameron's relationship with Greensill blossomed. The two had crossed paths for years. Lex had once met Samantha Cameron, who had previously been creative director of the upmarket stationery brand Smythson. Sam Cameron mocked Lex's flimsy Greensill business cards. Lex followed up by having Smythson make the cards for his fledgling firm Greensill Capital. It was an expensive extravagance for a start-up company and there was an echo of a famous episode in Bret Easton Ellis's postmodern novel *American Psycho* in which the psychotic banker at the heart of the tale seethes with anger when a rival presents him with a more expensive business card.

When Cameron joined Greensill Capital, in 2019, it hardly caused a stir at first. Just another former politician taking a private sector role. The former PM's motivation for joining the start-up wasn't hard to fathom. Many top politicians took highly paid jobs with financial companies. After leaving the prime minister's office, John Major became a chairman at the leading private equity firm Carlyle Group, while Tony Blair took on a role advising J.P. Morgan, the giant Wall Street bank. Cameron's own Chancellor, George Osborne, landed several jobs, with the global asset management giant BlackRock and later with the London boutique investment bank Robey Warshaw. Indeed, Osborne's vigorous and varied post-political career earned him the nickname 'Nine Jobs George'.

Cameron, though, took a different route, avoiding the kind of established big businesses his predecessors had favoured. Cameron had always been a fan of technology businesses and disruptive start-ups. Tech was cooler than Wall Street for starters. And although you could earn big bucks in banking and investment management, the rewards from holding equity in a hot new tech business could be far more handsome. Pick the right one, and it was like buying a winning lottery ticket.

At Greensill, Cameron was paid several hundred thousand pounds in salary and took home a bonus worth several hundred thousand more. His stock in the company would potentially pay out tens of millions of pounds, depending on what valuation Greensill could achieve. And he might not have to wait for an initial public offering (IPO) or sale of the company – unlike most of the other senior shareholders, part of Cameron's stock vested every year for three years, meaning he could cash out part of his holding worth millions of pounds. The former PM's main role was to lend credibility to the business and to open doors. He made introductions to top businesspeople and political leaders alike.

Government broadly became a talent pool that Lex frequently dipped into. He hired several former government staffers to Greensill Capital. Bill Crothers was the government's commercial chief – he'd appointed Lex as a Crown Representative – before he went to work for Greensill. Sean Hanafin was an adviser on supply chain finance between 2012 and 2014 – he joined Greensill in a senior role a few years later. David Brierwood, Lex's old mentor from Morgan Stanley, was a Crown Representative from 2014 to 2018, and he began working for Greensill Capital from 2014.

Lex also hired former UK Home Secretary David Blunkett and Australia's former Minister of Foreign Affairs, Julie Bishop.

How did he get the politicians on board? Some of them might have bought into Lex's claim that he was 'democratizing finance'. Typically, those closest to Greensill were given a major financial incentive. The firm was a big payer – salaries were sometimes double the norm. And Lex distributed shares liberally too.

One politician who turned him down was the late Paul Myners, the former UK Treasury minister under Gordon Brown, who passed away in early 2022. Myners was wary of Greensill – especially because of the potential conflicts attached to the politicians who were working for the firm – and raised questions about the company in the House of Lords, where he had a seat. He was also the chair of Edelman, a giant global public relations firm whose subsidiary, Smithfield, counted Greensill as a client. When a Smithfield PR executive set up a meeting between Lex and Myners to clear the air, it only did more damage. Within minutes of the meeting starting, Greensill offered Myners a seat on the board. The politician and businessman took this to be arrogant and a red flag – surely no one credible would pitch such an important role to a person they'd just met. Myners turned Greensill down – and continued to question the firm through his parliamentary role for years thereafter. Emails emerged later that appeared to show Myners on friendly terms with Greensill. But, in my experience, though he was always courteous, he was also highly suspicious of the Greensill business model.

Greensill knew that political connections helped him appear credible. He frequently boasted that he was a senior adviser to the US administration of Barack Obama, and that he'd been introduced to the president by David Cameron. There was even hard evidence – a photo showing Lex meeting Obama at a supply chain finance summit in Washington DC in 2014, sitting in the Greensill office. The reality was somewhat different. The meeting had come about after US Treasury officials working with small businesses asked their UK counterparts about the supply chain finance programmes that Lex had advised on. Lex visited the White House twice and met Obama just once, alongside dozens of other businesspeople. Cameron's spokespeople later denied he'd made any kind of personal introduction, and the White House never seriously followed up on Lex's proposals.

# FIVE

# Greensill Capital

Lex Greensill's work in government was getting him noticed and earning him status. But it wasn't making him rich.

Greensill Capital had launched in 2011, partly funded by watermelons. Lex and his youngest brother, Peter, had struck a deal that saw Peter – who was building a farming business – get a stake in Greensill Capital and Lex get access to some watermelon revenues to kickstart his company. But he needed more.

Lex gradually collected a coterie of wealthy patrons. Perhaps the most important of these, in money terms at least, was John Gorman, a US entrepreneur involved in property, financial services and agriculture. Gorman had been director at a Chicago-based bank and co-owned a construction company.

One of Gorman's businesses was selling farming equipment and supplies. He found himself pitching agricultural equipment to Peter, who explained what his brother Lex was up to. Gorman invited Lex to Florida, where he owned an expansive waterfront property. Lex turned on the charm and explained his vision of a global supply chain finance business. By the end of their meeting, instead of Gorman selling tractors to Greensill Farming Group, Lex had persuaded the veteran businessman to invest in Greensill Capital. The company's accounts show that Gorman, who joined the Greensill board, loaned the company about $24 million.

Others soon followed. Like Gorman, several of the early Greensill backers had Chicago connections.

David Solo is a quiet, introverted MIT graduate and computer scientist. He had started out at O'Connor Associates, a fabled Chicago options trading firm founded in the 1970s and renowned as a stable for maths whizzes, many of whom came to dominate derivatives trading in the decades that followed. O'Connor was bought in the late 1990s by Swiss Bank Corporation (which later became the giant Swiss bank UBS). There, for a time, Solo was a star and a protégé of the top management. He helped resolve the mess left behind by UBS's ill-fated investment in the hedge fund Long-Term Capital Management, whose near-collapse in 1998 sparked genuine fears of a global financial meltdown. He was also at the forefront of the development of the market for credit default swaps, a kind of financial contract that offers protection against the possibility a borrower will default on loan payments. A 2008 column in the *Financial Times* by the journalist John Gapper describes a meeting with Solo where he began drawing diagrams of how 'loans might be priced like swaps and options and be traded by banks and investors . . . There was no obvious reason banks had to make loans and hold them until maturity, taking the entire risk of borrowers defaulting. Instead, he and others in the credit derivatives market reasoned that banks could originate and trade debt, using swaps and options to transform it into securities. Banks would take less credit risk and use up less of their precious capital while investors would get a new way to make money. Everyone would be happy.'

A few years later, the same 'everyone wins' pitch was standard Greensill methodology. Solo had also accumulated a significant amount of personal wealth. At UBS, he had run Global Asset Management (GAM), an asset manager the bank owned that had been set up twenty-five years earlier by famed investor Gilbert de Botton, the father of author Alain de Botton. Over a few years, GAM was sold by UBS to another Swiss bank, Julius Baer, and then spun out of Julius Baer as a separate company. Solo and a couple of other senior GAM insiders made a fortune along the way.

He was an odd CEO. Incredibly shy, Solo hated the limelight and shunned large company-wide meetings. He was nicknamed the 'Phantom of the media', according to a profile on Swiss news site *Finews*. Equally, he was super-smart, perhaps one of the biggest brains in asset management. Solo's mind seemed to work faster than everyone else's. He seemed to know what you were about to say even before you said it. In September 2014, around the time he met Lex, GAM announced Solo was leaving the company.

Greensill's supply chain finance ideas were right in Solo's wheelhouse. He became a Greensill director and backed Lex financially too. Solo, a jazz fan, set up an offshore company called Ratamacue – named for one of the foundation techniques of jazz drumming – which gave Greensill a loan of about $10 million.

Another early backer was Patrick Allin, a Canadian tech entrepreneur and accountant. Allin worked at PricewaterhouseCoopers for years and then became co-founder and CEO of Textura, a Chicago-based business that sold billing software to the construction industry. He made a fortune when Textura first went public and then sold out to software giant Oracle for about $660 million. Along the way, Allin was also accused of securities fraud by a well-known stock researcher called Andrew Left who profits by making salacious accusations against companies while betting their stock price will fall. An article on Left's website, *Citron Research*, described the behaviour of Allin as '*The Wolf of Wall Street* meets *American Hustle* meets *The Sting*'. In particular, Left had taken issue with the way Textura had recorded revenue, and he called out Allin for not disclosing in his corporate bio that he had also been CEO at a failed company called Patron Systems. Textura and Allin had denied the allegations of wrongdoing, but the stock price took a beating. Allin was replaced as CEO in 2015 and left the company. When the Oracle acquisition happened, he still had stock worth tens of millions of dollars.

Mickey Carusillo was another ex-O'Connor trader. Carusillo had managed bond and equity trading before the Chicago firm was taken over. Since then, he'd spent decades amassing a fortune as a partner in a so-called proprietary trading firm. Carusillo appeared in a 2019 article in the US business magazine *Crain's* as he was trying to sell his 4,300 square foot Chicago apartment for $4.3 million. 'We're only using this place about four months out of the year,' he said, explaining that he and his wife spent most of their time at their Florida home. The Carusillos loaned about $10 million to Greensill, the company's accounts showed.

There was an additional loan of around $10 million from Ronald Ferrin, another Chicagoan and a connection of John Gorman's. The two were co-owners of a real-estate business called Fairmac Realty. Ferrin and Gorman had also once held a substantial stake in AMC Entertainment, the US movie theatre chain.

Other backers had met Greensill through his time at the banks. David Brierwood, who'd opened a path for Lex from Manchester Business School to Morgan Stanley, continued to be supportive. Brierwood had been a director at Greensill Capital since 2015; even before that, in 2014, his family had loaned Greensill about $10 million.

Maurice Thompson, the former head of Citigroup in the UK, was also on board. Thompson had become chairman of Greensill Capital. The accounts show that in 2014 he and his wife loaned the company about $7 million.

Many of these backers also invested in Greensill's equity too, putting millions more into Lex's company. By 2016, these Greensill fans had sunk about $100 million into the business in aggregate. Mainly through word of mouth and smooth networking, Lex had managed to accumulate a significant pool of funds.

*

IN THE YEARS immediately after the financial crisis, I came across many bankers who'd become disillusioned with the industry. The constant upward trajectory had ground to a sudden, bone-jangling halt. Occupy Wall Street protesters and images of laid-off bankers carrying files out of their former offices had perhaps left a mark deep in the consciousness. It was especially true for younger bankers. Many of them felt let down by the big banking corporations that squeezed all the juice out of their staff – albeit paying them handsomely – but weren't loyal when it mattered.

It was not exactly idealism or a spirit of fairness that drove them out. Rather some bankers began to believe that you could remake the financial world in a way that was more efficient and would take advantage of modern technology. There was a sense that this would be easier in a new financial start-up than in the legacy banks. And it might be possible to get a stake in one of these new businesses that could pay rich dividends down the line.

I knew lots of bankers who ditched their old roles and joined a start-up. There were a fair few senior executives who took a role at these new businesses too. It became a running joke that former CEOs of the biggest banks in the world were no longer playing golf. They were joining fintech company boards.

This was the world into which Greensill Capital was born. Lex had his backers – a collection of his former banking bosses and the wealthy Chicago connection. He also managed to persuade a handful of former colleagues to join the new company.

Roland Hartley-Urquhart – Lex's colleague at Morgan Stanley and Citi – was a relatively seasoned banker. Though he was well liked, Roland's career had mostly been in a much lower gear than Lex Greensill's. Nevertheless, Roland was fabulously wealthy. The American had neither earned nor inherited most of his fortune. He'd married it. Roland's wife was Jessica Nagle, who had co-founded the financial analytics company SNL Financial in 1987. SNL had grown from just a handful of employees in a New Jersey office block to having more than 3,000 staff around the world, and was eventually sold to McGraw Hill and Standard & Poor's for $2.2 billion. Nagle had become fabulously rich along the way. Roland and Jessica lived the high life, socializing on board yachts or at fashionable Hamptons parties. The couple were photographed in the society pages of coffee table magazines aimed at New York's elite. They were so rich, Greensill insiders joked, that even their dogs had accounts with private airplane company NetJets. Roland had never needed the roles at Morgan Stanley or Citi. Greensill was an opportunity to build something more meaningful.

Others had long-standing, personal connections to Lex. Chris Bates and Jason Austin were long-time colleagues, and about as close to true friends as anyone Lex knew. They were all in. Dave Skirzenski was another former Morgan Stanley and Citigroup colleague with a track record in trade finance. Jonathan Lane was an ambitious lawyer who gave up a career at Accenture to join Greensill Capital.

Lex had funding. And now he had a team.

Solo was especially helpful in opening doors with a couple of big asset managers. Thompson helped introduce Lex to the investor General Atlantic. The board might meet at Thompson's London club or they might get together at Hartley-Urquhart's house in the Hamptons. But Greensill was resolutely Lex's business. The board mostly waved through whatever Lex wanted. Brierwood, who had helped Lex make his first steps into banking, often turned up to board meetings with a guitar, and would strum it as the meeting rolled by.

IN THE EARLY years, Greensill Capital struggled. But you wouldn't necessarily know it. Greensill spent to impress. In London, Lex could often be found at the five-star Royal Horseguards Hotel, a plush site overlooking the Thames right around the corner from Parliament. (His family lived in northwest England.) The grand building, modelled on a French chateau, is a favourite spot for politicians to meet with businesspeople. Its construction in the late nineteenth century was also the focus of a famous fraudulent pyramid scheme perpetrated by a Liberal MP – a bad omen presumably missed by those who did business with Greensill back then.

Lex frequently held breakfast meetings at Horseguards. At this time, he often wore his Downing Street lanyard and almost always carried his two business cards: one with the UK government coat of arms on it, Lex's name and the words 'Senior Adviser Prime Minister's Office', and the other for Greensill Capital, which was about 50 per cent bigger than a normal business card. To those who asked why it was so big, Lex replied that the card had been made deliberately too large to slide down in a Rolodex, so it would stand out. Sometimes, when Lex was trying to hire someone, he'd even present them with a Greensill card made out in their name, as if to say: Look at what you could become.

Lex also became a trustee of the board of the Monteverdi Choir, a London-based choir and orchestra group. The Monteverdi promotes young musicians and classical music. It also serves as a networking platform for the establishment. Greensill board member David Brierwood was a trustee, as were various fund managers, private equity executives and senior bankers. Prince Charles is the group's patron. Greensill sometimes sponsored Monteverdi events, spending as much as £80,000, including at Buckingham Palace. It was part of the price of entry to the British social and cultural elite.

GREENSILL CAPITAL NEEDED an office. Lex secured a spot on the Strand – a few doors down from Coutts, the royal family's bank. The decor struck many visitors as odd. There were enormous paintings in baroque frames, lots of wood panelling, black wallpaper and black leather seats, and even a suit of armour and a long medieval pike. Lex wanted it to look like Rothschild, but many visitors thought it looked more like a theme park, or the distorted impression of a traditional City bank seen through the eyes of an unwitting outsider.

Greensill also opened an office in Gansevoort, in New York's trendy Meatpacking District. The former industrial area had once been a den of iniquity before it was transformed, from the 1990s onwards, into a centre for cool Manhattan fashion and design, with trendy restaurants and glamorous bars. By the time Greensill arrived, the hipsters had moved on to other parts of the city, but it was still an expensive location to set up shop. Unlike other start-ups, where packing boxes serve as stools, the Greensill Gansevoort office underwent a major renovation, with Roland's wife Jessica Nagle directing the work. Walls were taken down and the floorplan was redesigned. New artwork was acquired at a cost of tens of thousands of dollars. Visitors from the London office and elsewhere who flew into town stayed at the nearby Gansevoort, then one of the coolest and most expensive hotels in the area.

New starters at Greensill were well looked after too. Even the most junior staffers would fly business class on long-haul flights. Lex himself travelled mostly on a private aircraft. Even though the Greensill business was not yet profitable, in 2015 he spent about $4 million on a Piaggio P-180 private turboprop plane. Greensill Capital didn't have much business, but it looked the part.

# SIX

# Bottom Feeding

Lex had attracted some loyal staff. He had some heavy-hitting financial backers. He had developed the blueprint for supply chain finance over the decade he had spent at OzEcom, Morgan Stanley and Citi. He'd even begun to make deep connections inside the UK government. But he wasn't making much headway with Greensill Capital.

A handful of big banks sell trade finance, including Citigroup, HSBC and Italy's UniCredit. But there is a reason they only offer it to their biggest corporate clients. Trade finance, including supply chain finance, doesn't make much money. Often, the banks do it as a kind of loss leader – a business that doesn't make sense on its own, and may even be loss-making, but which has some value because it builds a deeper, more profitable connection with the client. Few of the banks offer it to risky clients – smaller companies like start-ups, or companies that operate in industries where cash flow isn't predictable. For the most part, that was the space where Greensill was forced to play. Lex wanted to join the big guns of global finance, but instead he was stuck with a series of misfiring deals.

One pair of related companies was important in Greensill's story for years: Tower Trade Group and BSi Steel.

BSi is a South African steel company founded in 1985 by an enterprising industrialist named William Battershill. It started out selling discount steel products to farmers – unwanted pipes and other metal objects. Twenty-five years later, after several acquisitions and reinventions, the company claimed to be 'one of the lowest cost large-scale steel distributors in Southern Africa', and operated in Zambia, Botswana and several other countries in the region.

BSi was also struggling to deal with difficult conditions in many of its key markets, as the global economy floundered and demand for its products was subdued. Battershill needed to lower BSi's costs. In 2012, he turned for help to Charles Reynolds, a Swiss-based British citizen from South Africa. Reynolds was a charismatic wheeler-dealer who had been in trade finance since the 1980s. Most recently, he'd operated a Hong Kong-based trade finance business alongside a smart, tech-focused New Zealander called Rob Barnes. Critically for what happens next, Barnes was also the founder and former CEO of PrimeRevenue, the technology company that Lex Greensill had relied upon to process invoices and payments for the Trade Receivable electronic Financing System (TReFS) programme at Morgan Stanley. Barnes had known Lex Greensill for years. Lex had even tried to hire Barnes to Greensill Capital. (A recurring theme at Greensill Capital is that Lex tried to hire every expert he came across – a smart strategy, though many, like Barnes, turned him down.)

Barnes was genuinely an expert in the modern forms of trade finance. He understood the technology well, and he understood funding and the value of trade credit insurance to the whole model. He wasn't a salesman. But he knew a good one – Lex.

Tower Trade was a joint venture set up by Barnes and Reynolds with BSi. Its primary purpose was to provide cheap trade finance, mostly to BSi but in theory to other potential clients too. Lex provided the funding, about $23 million of it. He also got trade credit insurance, partly from the giant insurer AIG. Initially, the model operated as a straightforward supply chain finance programme. It did exactly what Lex, Reynolds and Barnes had said it would, paying invoices more efficiently and lowering BSi's costs. But it didn't make much money.

Pretty soon, the relationship steered into more complex, and potentially more lucrative, waters. Greensill, Tower Trade and BSi invested in a mine in Chile. Another entity related to Tower Trade and BSi, called Sentinel Bridge, agreed to buy iron ore from the mine and hold it until there was a viable amount to ship. Sentinel had a separate contract to sell the ore to a third party. Greensill funded some of the mine's start-up costs and funded Sentinel's purchase of the ore.

BSi's accounts explain what happened next: 'The venture proved to be a costly failure due to a series of extraordinary events, including, inter alia, iron ore price drop of more than 60%, our only viable port damaged by a storm and not repaired to date, and finally, a spurious survey report by a world renowned survey agency, which led us to pay for 38,389 tons of iron ore that was never delivered to our stockpile.'

The mine was also implicated in an elaborate fraud, revealed in a filing made by the US Attorney's Office in the Southern District of Florida. A Miami-based conman named Navin Xavier had used false information and forged documents to convince nearly a hundred investors to hand over more than $29 million for a stake in the same Chilean mine. Instead of using the money to mine the ore, Xavier and his wife spent lavishly on jewellery, luxury vehicles and cosmetic surgery. 'Eventually,' according to the US Attorney, 'Xavier used new investor money to pay old investors in a Ponzi-like fashion before the scheme collapsed.' In 2017, Xavier was sentenced to fifteen years in prison.

For BSi, Tower Trade and Greensill, the whole investment had been like a business investment disaster movie where everything that could go wrong did go wrong. The mine was eventually put into liquidation, leaving Greensill and Sentinel to pursue their lost funds through the bankruptcy process and a multi-year legal case. The result was that Sentinel owed Greensill about $4.5 million – which Greensill agreed to roll indefinitely at a rate of about 2.25 per cent. BSi wrote down its entire $2.5 million investment.

The Tower Trade joint venture was proving to be a major headache for BSi. Some of Reynold's former clients, and their problems, were washing up in Tower Trade, and BSi's board and management were struggling to understand what they'd become involved in. Referring to a $14 million disputed loan to a denim trading company, for instance, the accounts said that, 'The flow of funds was extremely difficult to track' and noted ongoing delays and rising costs. It was typical of an incredibly messy relationship. In 2017, BSi's external auditor, Deloitte, said that a loan of about $15 million from BSi to Tower Trade might not ever be paid back and gave the company a qualified audit opinion – essentially one step short of refusing to sign off on the accounts altogether.

By then, Barnes had long since moved on. Greensill, though, was still there. Loans to Tower Trade and BSi would be a feature of Greensill's business for years to come.

In those early years, Lex was often reduced to bottom feeding the riskiest clients and pushing the boundaries on what could viably pass through a supply chain finance programme.

In 2012, he arranged a supply chain finance programme with the owners of Griffin Coal, a giant mine more than 200 kilometres south of Perth in Western Australia. Griffin, which was owned by an Indian company called Lanco, would submit supplier invoices and Greensill would pay them. Griffin then had to pay Greensill back later. It was standard stuff.

By 2013, though, Griffin's accounts showed that it had become entirely dependent on support from its Indian parent and the Greensill facility, according to a later Australian court judgement. The following year, Australian tax authorities froze all Griffin's bank accounts due to the non-payment of taxes. The company was in deep trouble. Yet later the same day, Greensill transferred A$2 million to Griffin to pay the tax bill. This wasn't a supply chain finance payment – it was a short-term loan to a financially troubled mining project to settle its problems with the tax authorities. If supply chain finance represented one of the safest, steadiest forms of corporate lending, this kind of transaction was just about the opposite.

Lex's relationship with Griffin didn't end there.

In April 2014, Lex told the mine's managers that he planned to visit and would more than double the capacity of the loan facility from around A$30 million to around A$75 million. The managers were optimistic, but the additional funding never arrived. A little later, Griffin hired a small contracting company called Carna to provide staff to run the mine. In internal emails, Griffin's bosses admitted that without Carna's staff, the mine would not be able to produce any coal at all. Soon after, though, Carna also got into financial difficulties and blamed Griffin, saying the company was failing to pay its bills on time.

Lex's solution to this was typical and established a pattern that he followed for years to come. Faced with a problem loan and a client that was in desperate financial trouble, Lex doubled down, entering a separate deal with Carna itself. Lex paid one of Carna's own suppliers about A$9.7 million, and Carna agreed to repay Greensill A$10 million later. This didn't solve anything at all. The flow of cash was sclerotic. Everyone involved was increasingly desperate for bigger and bigger loans that Greensill just couldn't finance. Carna collapsed a few months later, in 2015, with debts of about A$70 million, including about A$10 million owed to Greensill.

(The disagreements dragged on for several years, with lawsuits flying between Carna, Griffin, Lanco and others. In 2021, an Australian court ordered Griffin to pay Carna A$5.1 million, a decision that a local MP described as a nail in the coal miner's coffin.)

Griffin and the Chilean mine episodes should have flashed early warning signs to anyone looking at Greensill over the next few years. These were risky loans to vulnerable commodities companies. There were complex legal wrangles and convoluted financing structures. There were allegations of fraud and misconduct. There were borrowers who didn't pay their bills. And when things went wrong, Lex's instinct always was to double down on his problems.

He had a knack for being in the wrong place at the wrong time. Greensill was one of the lenders to Abengoa, a Spanish renewable energy and infrastructure company that ran into trouble in 2015. The company had gorged on about €9 billion of debt but was short of cash following an overly ambitious plan to expand around the globe. A supply chain finance programme arranged by Greensill had been one of the ways in which Abengoa's overall debt level was hidden from investors. When the company collapsed, Greensill was among dozens of creditors left trying to recover millions of dollars of soured loans.

The collapse of UK construction and facilities management company Carillion with about £7 billion in debt in 2018 was one of the biggest corporate failures ever in the UK. Greensill wasn't a lender to Carillion, but Lex had a cameo role in its ill-fated history. Lex had been prominent in the group of government advisers whose work had led to a broad push for UK companies to use SCF programmes. Carillion's executives even met with Greensill before setting up their own 'early payment facility'. - a version of SCF, which was central to the way Carillion's debts were largely hidden from investors prior to the company's demise.

TWO OTHER OF LEX'S long-term relationships that started in the early years of Greensill Capital were with Andy Ruhan and with Neil Hobday.

Ruhan was a British businessman and property developer. He had made a fortune from a series of big property deals – notably he'd been an early investor in data centres used by investment banks before selling out, and he'd then made more money buying and selling a chain of hotels. He flirted with tabloid fame in the early 2000s because of his flamboyant lifestyle. He drove racing cars and briefly sat on the board of the Lotus Formula One team. In 2002, the helicopter he was flying crashed in rural Hereford; Ruhan, badly injured, crawled through two fields to flag down a passing motorist. By the 2010s, his fame was in decline, and his personal life was also in freefall. In divorce proceedings, Ruhan gave his address as a yacht in the Mediterranean. His wife denied remarkable claims that she was questioned about a plot to murder him, while his lawyers denied that he was hiding money offshore to avoid giving it to her in a settlement.

Also in the 2017 divorce proceedings, the London court heard that Ruhan had once been 'phenomenally rich' and 'a highly successful businessman'. And they heard that he claimed to be insolvent 'to the tune of £2 million . . . as a result of virtually his entire fortune, some £200 million, being stolen from him in March 2014' by a group of 'treacherous' fraudsters.

Even as his fortunes apparently took a nosedive, Ruhan continued working on various property projects. His reach extended from the UK to the Middle East and the US, though his deals were often entangled in complex, years-long litigation. Sometimes he employed Hobday, another property developer, though with a less spectacular record than Ruhan's.

Greensill helped broker a lucrative property deal that generated a few million pounds in profit for Ruhan, and decent fees for himself too. He also got to know Hobday, who became a sort of deal originator for Lex, sniffing out companies that needed loans.

Lex's network of well-connected backers was helpful, and he started to make inroads with big-name investors and with clients who wanted to borrow money. Pacific Investment Management Company (PIMCO), the giant California-based company founded by 'Bond King' Bill Gross, did its first transaction with Greensill in 2014. Lloyds Bank also worked with Greensill from about 2015, and had more than £1 billion invested in Greensill supply chain finance loans. Sometimes clients were brought on in part through Taulia, the payments platform. Taulia was a bit like PrimeRevenue. It had the technology to process payments and invoices and run SCF programmes. Lex was able to secure funding for those programmes from banks or big asset managers. Greensill and Taulia together were working with Vodafone, Huawei, General Mills and the German chemicals company Henkel, for instance. Sometimes these deals could involve processing billions of dollars in transactions.

These were impressive big-name clients, and impressive funding partners too. But it was all a bit of a mirage. This business rarely produced much in the way of revenue and even less in terms of profit. But that didn't matter. While Greensill booked much of its revenue from loans to unknown smaller companies, projects and entrepreneurs, these deals with big businesses gave the firm the appearance of credibility and scale. It was as if there were two separate business models, mixed up together. One was a barely profitable blue-chip SCF business, and the other was making risky loans to financially troubled businesses. Nothing was straightforward.

Lex made some headway in Mexico after hiring Ricardo Ortiz, a trade finance specialist with connections in Latin America. Through Ortiz, Greensill was able to find a way into Pemex, the state-owned oil giant Petróleos Mexicanos. Pemex was struggling to deal with prolonged low oil prices and had pushed its supplier payment terms out from twenty days to 180 days. It was also seeking an SCF provider that could ease the pain for its suppliers. Greensill stepped up with a facility backed by the Mexican development bank Nacional Financiera (Nafin). The first transaction that went through the programme was a staggering $100 million with a single supplier. Soon other Pemex suppliers were asking to join the programme. Nafin and Greensill made $3 billion available to process these supplier payments. The deal was quickly lauded as a great success by Greensill's executives. On a podcast with industry publication Rigzone, Roland

Hartley-Urquhart gushed that Greensill was 'very excited about the prospects in Mexico', and that the deal with Pemex had revitalized small businesses in the Mexican oil industry. Greensill even won an award for one of the 'deals of the year' in influential trade finance publication *Global Trade Review*.

But the success didn't last. Within a few months, it was apparent Greensill didn't have the infrastructure or the technology to support such a large, complex programme. Its technology could only really handle a few suppliers at a time. Pemex's suppliers began complaining to the company about problems with payments that were putting a strain on their business. Eventually the oil company stopped the programme.

Another especially striking episode revolved around an Asian mobile-phone technology distribution business called Dragon Technology. Dragon worked with a Silicon Valley smartphone company called Obi Mobiles that focused on emerging markets, especially in India and the Middle East. Both firms were backed by Inflexionpoint, a private equity firm co-founded by John Sculley, the former CEO of Apple and Pepsi-Cola Co. Since leaving Apple in 1993, Sculley had become an influential tech investor, helping to grow and sell several tech-focused companies.

At one point, Sculley said in an interview in the Indian press, the Canadian government had approached him to buy BlackBerry. He thought its business model didn't work. There were too many staff and costs would be far too high. But it got him thinking about whether it would be possible to manufacture and distribute handsets much more cheaply.

The owners of Dragon and Obi planned to piggyback off Sculley's name to build a powerful, more profitable rival to some of the cheaper smartphones that were already successful in emerging markets like India and China. Sculley brought in some of his former staff from Apple to help with design and managing the process. Dragon would make the phones cheaply in Shenzhen, China, and Obi would sell them in places like the UAE, Indonesia and East Africa. Obi executives talked about selling two million handsets in India alone in their first year, with a rapid expansion thereafter.

To support the companies' ambitious plans, there was financing in place from HSBC.

Dragon's backers at Inflexionpoint were also introduced to Lex Greensill through a former Morgan Stanley connection. Over lunch in London with Sculley and several other Inflexionpoint and Dragon execs, Greensill pitched his SCF product as an innovative, cheaper source of funding. Lex was charismatic, enthusiastic – and convincing. Dragon signed up for tens of millions of dollars in Greensill funding. The facility renewed every few months; because it was always rolled over, it was positioned like a term loan, not SCF. It was funded partly by Greensill itself and then syndicated out to banks and others. The whole thing was also protected by trade credit insurance from AIG.

But the project did not go to plan. AIG's coverage of the Dragon deal had been short term, and the insurer decided not to renew it. They had seen defaults on several other Greensill transactions and some executives there were increasingly concerned about working with Lex. They felt he was pushing the boundaries of SCF. Their decision not to renew on Dragon was a big deal. It would mean the loan would be pulled too. Lex met with the AIG executives who had cut him off and asked about the coverage again. The insurance executives were clear – the coverage had ended. Lex's face went ashen white. This was potentially catastrophic.

Dragon ended up filing for bankruptcy in Singapore in September 2016.

Lex was able to negotiate a settlement that meant Greensill didn't follow Dragon into insolvency, but the incident was a sign of a much more significant long-term issue. AIG had seen several Greensill deals go wrong and had run out of patience. As the issues piled up, AIG resolved to cut all ties with Greensill. There were other insurers in the market, some with bigger trade credit insurance business than AIG. But Lex's reputation for taking on more risk and more complex transactions was spreading.

Some of the insurance agents started to do their own deeper due diligence on Lex's clients, asking Greensill to send over invoices and other documents to support the SCF programmes he'd set up. Sometimes all was OK. Other times, there were problems. Documents were harder to get hold of than they should have been. Sometimes there were problems with the invoices themselves. Lex was able to secure trade credit insurance for several more years, but his options were narrowing. Eventually, that would be critical to the demise of Greensill Capital.

At the end of December 2016, it was hard to imagine Greensill's business going much further. There were some big wins, with well-known companies investing in Greensill loans and taking financing from Greensill too. But this business was not profitable. There had been a series of embarrassing and costly stumbles. The whole thing seemed to rest on the financial support of a small band of wealthy individual investors. The accounts showed Greensill had racked up cumulative losses of $123 million. The firm appeared to be headed the same way as many of its clients. And yet, the seeds of a completely different trajectory, at least in the short term, were already sown.

# SEVEN

# Greensill Bank

Lex was excellent at spending other people's money, whether a government budget, or his employer's expense account, or funds from the wealthy patrons who'd backed his start-up.

But if he was to make his billionaire dream a reality, he'd need even more access to even more people's money.

That's where the bank came in. Lex didn't just want to disrupt the banks, he wanted to own one too.

In early 2012, investment bankers in the City were shopping around a German institution named NordFinanz Bank AG, known as NoFi. A pitchbook shared with potential buyers – a kind of sales document that bankers use for mergers and acquisitions – was doing the rounds in February and March 2012. NoFi was founded in 1927, in Bremen, at the height of the Weimar Republic. For most of its existence, the small bank had been a bit of a disaster, struggling from one near-collapse to the next and switching owners every few years. It had just a handful of branches and a few dozen staff. The bank took deposits from ordinary Germans, made loans to Germany's Mittelstand group of small businesses, and provided financing for mortgages and car buyers too. Since the 1960s, NoFi had also been a provider of factoring services.

Over the past few decades, NoFi had been passed from new owner to new owner. Each time, a different strategic plan was put in place, but the bank mostly languished. By the noughties, NoFi was unprofitable and unloved, a mashed-up and confusing collection of failed ambitions. It even owned a campsite, acquired when a client went bankrupt. The German regulator, BaFin, had ordered the bank to scale back its business. NoFi often operated under restrictions imposed by BaFin.

Despite all that, ownership of the bank had one big upside – the potential to use it to acquire deposits that could be invested in something more profitable.

From around 2010, NoFi had another new set of owners, led by Stefan Allesch-Taylor, a British entrepreneur and financier. Tall and self-assured, Allesch-Taylor is a serial board member, film producer, columnist for *The Times* newspaper, coffee roasting company boss, academic and philanthropist. As professor of the Practice of Entrepreneurship at King's College London, his views on starting and running a business are often sought out by journalists.

He once told the magazine *Gentleman's Journal* that the key traits to being a successful entrepreneur are to be ruthless, to have a vision, be good at reading other people, hustle constantly, respect others, and to be good with money – for this last one, he wrote, 'read really very, very mean with money . . . You wouldn't think so watching the "burn" of big tech companies or the staggering losses of others but remember the stats – only a tiny percentage of new companies survive. If you can't balance your monthly budget, it's going to be a problem. Every penny spent has to be thought about before you spend it.'

The other NoFi Bank owners were an eclectic bunch too. They included Robin Saunders, a US-born banker who had risen to prominence in London in the late 1990s when she was one of the top dealmakers in the City. Born in North Carolina and raised in Florida, Saunders graduated from Florida State University. After college, she went into finance and eventually joined Citigroup, where she worked on securitizing loans – turning them into securities that are sold to investors. In 1992, she moved to the UK and her career took off. She landed at Germany's WestLB bank, where she led a team trying to make a push into the City. Saunders embarked on a spree of deals across Europe. She worked on high-profile transactions for Bernie Ecclestone, the Formula One chief, and British retail titan Philip Green, and became a regular in the financial pages. The tabloids dubbed her the 'Queen of the City' and said she was worth hundreds of millions of pounds. Her fortieth birthday party, in 2002, had been a three-day event in Florence that reportedly cost £400,000, with 180 guests dining in a medieval palace and a thirteenth-century church.

Saunders' reputation took a hit when she was forced to leave WestLB after a television rental company she'd helped finance went into administration, helping to push the bank to a €1.7 billion loss. In 2004, she set up a private equity company called Clearbrook Capital, which is based in London's glamorous Mayfair district and counted the financier Lord Rothschild as a backer and Allesch-Taylor as a partner. A 2005 profile of Saunders included her notable quote: 'I'm not going to do a dumb deal.'

The other key NoFi owner was Andy Ruhan, the property developer, who was also a Greensill associate. Greensill had arranged deals for Andy and benefited from his largesse too.

The management team running NoFi for this group of owners had tried to reposition the bank once more, with a focus on leasing plant and machinery and lending to small businesses. Their plan was that NoFi could fill a vacuum left by other banks getting out of this kind of business in the years after the financial crisis. But the turnaround project was less than straightforward. Among the many complications, there were a bunch of dud clients, such as 1860 Munich,

Germany's oldest professional football team (the less glamorous cousin of giants Bayern Munich), which was in poor financial health. Dealing with clients like 1860 in the politically charged atmosphere of the early 2010s was a massive headache. With German regulators breathing down their necks, demanding additional capital and more, the shareholders just wanted to get out. So, in 2012, the pitchbook circulating in London outlined a plan to revive NoFi with an injection of about €28 million of new capital that would steady its fragile balance sheet.

Lex came across as insanely ambitious, and eager to own a bank. Desperate perhaps. He also seemed to be in awe of Saunders, the celebrity banker who was known for her lavish parties. Lex was a minnow dealing with a group of sharks. He was smart, not naive. But it was easy to persuade him to invest in NoFi. Greensill agreed to a deal, initially investing as a minor shareholder, and later, by 2014, acquiring control of the bank.

Lex eventually forked out over $25 million for a business that had net assets of just $10 million. It was worth it, almost.

Within a few months, the NoFi name was no more. Rebranded as Greensill Bank AG, the German business was added to the global Greensill corporate family. Its annual report declared a shift in strategy. The bank would no longer run current accounts. It would stop processing cash transactions. Instead, Greensill Bank started targeting larger, longer-term deposits. And it started to use those loans to fund supply chain finance deals sourced by Greensill Capital. The bank paid better interest rates than you could get pretty much anywhere else in Germany, and attracted deposits from customers, including a slew of German municipal governments. As many as fifty municipalities deposited hundreds of millions of euros with the bank. Places such as the industrial city of Osnabrück, Giessen, the capital of the state of Hesse, and the medieval town of Monheim am Rhein all put their funds into Greensill Bank.

Lex also beefed up the bank's credentials in moves that echo the way he courted respected names in London. He lured Eberhard Kieser to join Greensill Bank's board in 2017. Kieser was slick, smartly dressed, hard-nosed. He had previously been a board member of the Auditing Association of German Banks – a sort of industry group that is responsible for maintaining financial sector stability. He instinctively knew how the German banking regulators thought and acted.

The bank also got a credit rating from the Berlin-based rating agency Scope. The analysis was tough in places and noted concerns about the rapidly growing bank but ultimately Scope gave it an investment grade rating – essentially a stamp of approval. It didn't emerge till much later that the relationship was riddled with potential conflicts. First, Greensill signed an exclusive partnership agreement with a Scope subsidiary to provide ratings on its supply chain finance loans. Also, Maurice Thompson, the chairman of Greensill's own board, was an investor in Scope and sat on its board. (Scope's policies say that it won't issue a rating to a company if a member of its board has more than a 5 per cent stake in Scope – Thompson fell outside this threshold.)

At first, Greensill Bank was a drain on the company. Lex had to make sure the bank maintained certain balance sheet ratios to satisfy the German regulator. But that meant funnelling as much as $5 million a year from other parts of the business. My sources said Greensill shifted transactions into the bank to help with its profitability, so that a receivables financing deal that made about 2 per cent a year in Greensill Capital was moved into the bank at a yield of around 5 per cent a year. The shortfall was covered elsewhere in the Greensill group.

But over the next few years, as Greensill Capital itself attracted billions of dollars in new investment, Lex was able to turn the bank into a key part of his business. He poured hundreds of millions of dollars more in to bulk up the bank's balance sheet, which went from about €340 million in 2017 to €670 million the following year. By 2019, it was €3.8 billion.

That was crucial to the way Greensill would operate. With access to his own, significant balance sheet, Lex could move assets around more freely. He didn't have to persuade investors to buy the loans he was selling. He could simply park them in the bank. Lex could run his business like a giant shell game, like a street hustler, shifting dollar bills around, hiding them in front of your eyes. He could take problematic loans out of Greensill Capital, or out of the SCF funds that were already in the works, and hide them in the bank.

It seemed like a smart plan, but it was deeply flawed.

# EIGHT

# Global Asset Management

In September 2014, Alex Friedman replaced David Solo as CEO at Global Asset Management (GAM). Like Solo, Friedman was cerebral, and rather quiet for a CEO. But in other ways, the two were very different. Solo's early career had been in trading derivatives at Chicago's O'Connor & Associates. Friedman had been an elite mountaineer and climber, sponsored by major outdoor clothing brands, who only stopped after a couple of close calls on the mountains. He'd also been a White House Fellow in the Clinton administration and an assistant to the US Secretary of Defense. In business, he'd worked as a mergers and acquisitions banker, he'd been the CFO of the Bill & Melinda Gates Foundation and, since 2010, the global chief investment officer at UBS, overseeing more than $2 trillion in clients' money. Solo was a trader, fixated on clever ways to make more money. Friedman was methodical, more process-driven, a strategizer.

Though he and Solo had spent a lot of time discussing the business before it was handed over, Friedman was still surprised by what he found once he got inside. GAM was disjointed and dysfunctional.

It operated like a bunch of fiefdoms. There was one head office in London – on King Street in St James's, where Friedman spent most of his time – and another in Zurich. Teams in both locations were suspicious of one another and often sought to undermine their Swiss or UK cousins. Each of these locations ran separate, duplicate IT systems and human resources functions. It was like two totally different companies.

The structure was knottier still. There were offices in fifteen countries. Many of the staff in far-flung locations had been with GAM for decades and hadn't met with their senior managers in either Zurich or London. Across the company, managers were running more than 170 different investment strategies, often branded in completely different ways. Many of them were underperforming and going nowhere. There was no central department managing risk either, which meant that no one had a great handle on what risks the company was taking as a whole.

GAM had about 1,500 staff – three times as many as comparable businesses. Many tasks were still done manually, and antiquated IT systems often ran databases from the 1990s, written in code by staff who had long since left the company. In contrast to the hard-charging culture in much of the City, most staff rarely worked long hours. Few of them owned shares in the company and didn't appear to care that the stock price had been going nowhere for years. The frontline investment staff were more addicted to their bonuses, which were tied to the performance of their investments and the amount of assets they managed.

All of this had led to a situation where the investment teams often viewed themselves as independent units, operating loosely under the GAM umbrella. The way GAM was set up, individual portfolio managers ran their own strategies without reference to the CEO, who was not allowed to interfere or question their investment decisions.

GAM had also fallen foul of its main UK regulator, the Financial Conduct Authority. The FCA had expressed concern about documentation and practices on the equity trading side at GAM. The regulator had indicated they thought GAM was not cooperating with their inquiries about these problems. After Solo left, the FCA ordered a so-called Section 166 or Skilled Persons Review – a kind of special, independent audit that aims to root out inappropriate behaviour. It's a blemish on a company's record and puts the executives on notice that the regulator has its eye on them.

GAM's cost base was bloated and performance was not as good as in the past. But there were broader, external forces hurting GAM too. The whole industry was under pressure to reduce costs and justify their fees. The global investing environment was relatively benign, with low interest rates and weak economic growth everywhere. That made it harder for investment managers to truly stand out. Active managers like GAM – which charge higher fees because they aim to actively outdo benchmark indexes – were losing out to passive managers that just copy the market and charge clients less.

When Friedman reported his first set of annual results in early 2015, profits had fallen by about 16 per cent from the previous year. Just months into his tenure, the company appeared to be in trouble. He unveiled a plan to cut costs and simplify the organization. He'd also bring on board new people and some new investment strategies. Within eighteen months, there was a whole new management team, and hundreds of jobs had been cut to save money.

The changes were very disruptive. Assets continued to decline as the company shifted strategies. A couple of new businesses that Friedman had acquired were taking too long to integrate and dragged on the company's earnings. The staffing cuts damaged staff morale, especially in Switzerland. A hostile activist investor had bought a bunch of GAM shares and started jostling for Friedman to go. The share price, which had initially risen in Friedman's first six months, was soon down by about 50 per cent from its peak.

None of that, though, would prove nearly as significant as the affair the company was about to run into.

Months after leaving GAM, Solo had taken a stake in Greensill. And soon after that, he began pushing for GAM and Greensill to work together.

Solo had a close and long-standing connection to one of the key investment managers at GAM, a portfolio manager named Tim Haywood. He was one of the highest-profile investors in the City, whip-smart, convivial, well known to finance journalists and well liked by colleagues. Haywood ran GAM's biggest fund, the Absolute Return Bond Fund (ARBF), which courted investors from around the world, including the likes of the Chicago Police Pension Fund and the team that invested savings on behalf of all the municipal workers in Berlin. The fund's rules allowed Haywood to invest their money in a broad range of assets, including government, corporate and emerging market bonds, as well as pretty much anything else he liked the look of. He could also use complex derivatives to hedge the fund's performance or to juice its returns. As a senior, experienced manager with tenure at GAM, his informal role stretched well beyond managing his own fund. He had, for instance, designed some of the processes for managing risk at GAM – the checks and balances meant to prevent major missteps or stop individual portfolio managers getting out of line.

Haywood had a degree in chemical engineering from Edinburgh University and an MBA from Cranfield School of Management, one of the UK's top business schools. His father had been a farmer and Haywood owns a country estate in Rutland, in the east of England, known as Gunthorpe Hall. The property includes a large manor house and several holiday rental properties. He told acquaintances that when he wasn't working in the City, he loved to be on the farm.

After college, Haywood had spent more than two decades in the investment management industry, in Hong Kong and in London. He had a reputation for swinging for the fences as an investor. Colleagues sometimes referred to Haywood as Paul Tibbets – after the pilot of the infamous *Enola Gay* Superfortress bomber that dropped the atomic bomb on Hiroshima in 1945 – because of his tendency to drop big investing bombs.

Haywood also became something close to a City celebrity and liked to mingle with the rich and powerful. He planned to run for the largely honorary position of Lord Mayor of London. He sat on the board of St Paul's Girls' School, an elite private school in West London.

Solo and Haywood's connection ran deep. They had spent years bailing each other out.

In 2007, Haywood led a team of managers that established a hedge fund firm called Augustus Asset Managers, which they spun out of Swiss bank Julius Baer. The firm, named after the Roman emperor who succeeded Julius Caesar, started out well enough, and had accumulated $14 billion of client funds within a few months of launching. In the run-up to the global financial crisis, he made an early bet against US subprime mortgages, and made bumper returns. He told colleagues he was genuinely unhappy that the author Michael Lewis had not included him in his blockbuster book *The Big Short*. But performance stuttered thereafter, and investors pulled their money out as the crisis raged on. By 2009, Augustus was bleeding assets and its flagship fund was more or less closed down. Solo, then CEO of GAM, came to the rescue. GAM was itself owned by Julius Baer at that point (it was spun out later, enriching Solo and some other senior managers), and Solo agreed to buy Augustus back for a nominal sum.

A little later, Haywood returned the favour. Pre-financial crisis, Solo had taken a big investment in a US mortgage company called Carrington. The bet had soured fast when the mortgage market tanked. Haywood had helped Solo out by putting the Carrington investment into one of his better performing funds, where the losses on the mortgage company could be hidden from investor scrutiny.

Though Haywood's funds were focused on bonds, his heart always appeared to be in equities. It was hard to make a blockbuster investment in bonds, whereas a good equity trade could deliver the fabled 'ten bagger' – an investment that returned ten times what you paid for it. Between 2006 and 2011, Haywood entered a series of private equity-style investments that had been structured as debt securities. These deals, structured to comply with the bond fund Haywood managed, amounted to almost $200 million and involved investments in a series of seven or eight African businesses, including manufacturers of car parts, helicopters and electric meters. In the end, all the investments were a bust, though investors wouldn't have known it. GAM's other portfolio managers were having a stellar year, so Haywood's failed private equity investments were effectively hidden by the bigger picture.

Haywood eventually caught the bond bug, finding ways to make investing in bonds more exhilarating. In 2014, he told an interviewer that innovations like being able to buy credit protection or options on currencies meant 'the way you can express yourself in [bond trading] has become really quite manifold and that's exciting.'

After that big sub-prime trade, Haywood had struggled for a repeat win. The fund lost the confidence of many investors, with assets dropping from about $18 billion in 2013 to under $13 billion by the end of 2015. That decline was not just embarrassing: it had a direct impact on Haywood and his colleagues. The size of the bonus pool that many staff counted on for their big annual payout was tied to the amount of assets under management at the firm. The shrinking of Haywood's giant fund meant that the bonus pool for GAM's staff also took a big hit.

Some big investments he made with his own money didn't turn out well either. In 2015, he bought shares in a wood-chip fuel business for about £1 million and loaned the business about £1 million too, according to filings at Companies House. Within a couple of years, the company was in administration and Haywood lost everything, the filings show.

Solo knew Haywood wasn't afraid to place a big bet on assets that others thought were too illiquid or too risky to take on. He also knew Haywood had an appetite for innovative – riskier – trades. And by this time, he knew that Greensill needed to find a more stable, more flexible source of funding.

WITHIN A FEW months of Solo's departure from GAM, he'd introduced his old firm to Greensill. He messaged Friedman telling him he should meet with Lex, that he was impressive, well connected and had an interesting and potentially lucrative business model. They could be great partners, Solo thought. He told Friedman that he wouldn't be disappointed.

The new GAM chief invited Lex to his relaxed office in St James's. As always, Lex was formally dressed, in a tie and dark suit. He handed Friedman his UK government business card and introduced himself as working with Prime Minister Cameron's office and the US administration of Barack Obama.

Friedman was taken aback. It's highly unusual for a foreign, private sector business person to be an adviser to the US government, he said. Friedman had worked in US administration himself and had never seen an arrangement like that.

Yes, said Lex bluntly, it is highly unusual.

The inference was clear. Lex was staring Friedman down and claiming that he was indeed exceptional.

The meeting was tense. Lex appeared unhappy whenever he was really challenged. If he was questioned, he tended to push back hard, as if trying to prove he knew more about the subject at hand than Friedman. Friedman was not convinced that this was a person GAM should work with. He was particularly unsure about the role of Greensill Bank, wondering what its purpose was. He told Lex politely that he was declining to invest in Greensill.

But if he thought that would be the end of it, he would have been wrong. Within days, Friedman took an angry call from Solo. The former CEO called Friedman, screaming and swearing down the line. You're missing out on a huge opportunity, Solo told him. You don't understand what Lex is building. If you don't work with him, he'll take the opportunity elsewhere and everyone will know you turned it down.

Friedman knew Solo was an investor in Greensill and had a vested interest in the success of Lex's business – that was a warning sign that he should factor into Solo's 'advice' on the subject. Still, maybe he had a point, he conceded. Maybe he should give Lex another chance. Friedman second-guessed his previous decision. He set up another meeting with Lex, this time with the whole of GAM's senior management team, including legal counsel, the CFO and other top executives. If everyone else was on board, then Friedman would reverse his earlier call and allow the firm to work with Greensill.

Lex came back to GAM's office a few days later. He ran through his pitch again. Some of Friedman's colleagues asked about Greensill Bank. How did it fit into the Greensill structure? Why was it needed? Lex pushed back. They were looking at its role in Greensill all wrong. The bank really wasn't a concern. Lex refocused the group on his supply chain finance business. It was a winning strategy. That business was safe, steady, reliable. The GAM management team was broadly behind it. Friedman decided that if his legal counsel could take a deeper look into Greensill Capital and find nothing untoward, then maybe Solo was right after all.

Meanwhile, Solo himself had been lobbying for Lex. He had introduced Lex to Tim Haywood, and Haywood fell for him. Hard. They were similar in many ways. They came from farming stock. They enjoyed proximity to power and politics. And they had an unwavering belief in their own abilities. Greensill's esoteric investments also seemed perfectly designed to appeal to Haywood's sense that he was smarter than the average City money manager.

With Friedman essentially out of the way, Haywood began working with Lex. He dined with Greensill's board and executive committee at the historic, swanky – and somewhat stuffy – Royal Automobile Club on Pall Mall in London. He took flights on Greensill's private aircraft to Sardinia on vacation. He was a guest at a Greensill-sponsored performance of the Monteverdi Choir at Buckingham Palace. He took tickets from Greensill to Glyndebourne, the famed opera house set in the Sussex countryside south of London.

The result of their close relationship was that GAM's investment into Greensill's assets began flowing freely. Haywood's ARBF fund made its first investment in supply chain finance assets sourced by Greensill in October 2015. The deals started small. Initially they were simple SCF investments. But they grew, and changed, and morphed and became more complex, riskier and loaded with potential conflicts.

There was a series of investments tied to something called Laufer Ltd, a company incorporated in October 2016 whose sole shareholder was Lex Greensill. In all, over the next couple of years, Haywood invested more than $500 million in Laufer. This investment had allowed Lex to pay off loans to Greensill's wealthy backers. He had told Haywood that the giant private equity firm Blackstone wanted to work with Greensill if he agreed to drop other funding partners. Greensill was paying 10 per cent to 12 per cent on a bunch of loans to some of his shareholders – friends and family like Solo, Gorman and so on. If GAM refinanced those loans, at a cheaper rate, Lex would turn Blackstone down and stick with Haywood's firm.

Lex and Haywood also began working ever more closely with Sanjeev Gupta, a British-Indian industrialist. Gupta said he was aiming to build a global metals empire out of unloved businesses around the world. Haywood and Lex were keen to finance it. Haywood had invested in assets tied to Gupta starting in 2015. Over the next couple of years, he invested hundreds of millions of dollars more in Gupta's deals, all brokered by Greensill. Haywood bought securities tied to the purchase of an aluminium smelter and a power plant in Scotland. He invested in portable power units, known as Little Red Boxes (LRBs), that ran on biofuels, and which were supposed to take advantage of government subsidies. To long-time colleagues and investors in the ARBF fund, Haywood appeared to be besotted and beguiled by Gupta and Greensill. He flew around with them, visiting potential acquisitions and investments and shaking hands with top politicians.

During this period, Haywood also bought complex Greensill securities backed by aircraft leasing payments and by a loan to an offshore company that tied back to Andy Ruhan, the former owner of Greensill Bank. The loan, which Ruhan discussed with Haywood in GAM's office, was supposed to be backed by a stake in a New York skyscraper development.

Haywood and Lex had also launched a separate GAM Greensill supply chain finance fund (GGSCF), which exclusively bought securities backed by SCF loans made by Greensill. Initially, most of the loans went to Vodafone. Lex had worked with the telecoms company years earlier when they'd been a client of Citigroup.

The fund was filled with invoices from Vodafone's suppliers. Greensill paid these invoices early and at a discount and then reclaimed more from Vodafone later. A convoluted set-up saw Vodafone also become an investor in the fund. To the non-accountant it's hard to figure out the point of it. But there were significant benefits to Vodafone. The arrangement meant Vodafone was essentially profiting from having its suppliers choose between being paid a discount or being paid late. It also helped improve the look of Vodafone's balance sheet. (Normally, when a company pays its suppliers' invoices, it reduces its payables and cash balances by the same amount. Processing invoices through the fund results in a lower payables balance but cash just shifts into 'short-term investments'.)

Although nominally open to other borrowers and investors, Vodafone dominated the fund. The telecoms company was so important that executives at Greensill and GAM began referring to the fund in conversation and in emails as the 'Vodafund'.

Haywood also struck an unusual side arrangement with Lex that said if total assets in the Vodafund fell below $1 billion at the end of March 2017, Greensill would pay a fee of $1.25 million to GAM for each of the next four years. The arrangement, known as a fee ramp agreement, didn't provide any benefit to investors in any of GAM's funds. Instead, it was effectively a $5 million pledge to GAM itself.

By early 2017, the Vodafund had not grown as anticipated. Voda-fone's auditors were uneasy with the accounting benefit the company got from its dual role as investor and client, which restricted how big the fund could grow without the involvement of other partners. Haywood and Lex amended the fee ramp agreement so that the trigger date for payments to GAM was shifted to the end of September 2017. In the summer, Greensill also struck a complex deal with the Swiss branch of US agribusiness Bunge. The deal essentially saw GAM provide hundreds of millions of dollars in financing to Bunge, which it reinvested in the SCF fund. The transaction doubled the size of the Vodafund and dealt with the problem with Vodafone's auditors. (I came across the Bunge deal later, in part because of a strange reference to the $1.2 billion in Greensill's own accounts, which made it look as though Greensill itself had a huge stake in the GGSCF. When I asked Greensill about it, one senior executive who was rolled out to explain it to me initially tried to suggest it had something to do with insurance before simply acknowledging he didn't understand what had happened.)

As Haywood's involvement with Greensill deepened, it also started to raise eyebrows at GAM. The was some pushback from Haywood's colleagues, some of whom were reticent about putting more money into investments sourced from Greensill. When there was resistance, Solo, who still held some influence at GAM, came to the rescue. In a December 2016 email to a senior GAM investment manager, Solo made it clear that he had supported GAM's involvement with Greensill, and he touted his knowledge of trade and receivables financing. Greensill was selling practically risk-free investments, he wrote. He also pointed out that he was both an investor in Greensill and an investor in the GAM funds. It read like a brazen attempt to exert his influence, and an admission of his potential conflicted interest.

Still, within a couple of years, the GAM connection had transformed Greensill's business. Haywood had invested about $4 billion in Greensill's assets. It had allowed Greensill to largely pay off his wealthy backers. It had delivered crucial cash flow. It had established the idea of a dedicated SCF fund. And it meant Greensill was attracting interest from even larger pools of money.

Eventually assets from Greensill of all shapes and sizes came to dominate Haywood's ARBF fund. These investments were out of sight of the senior management team. But they were the cause of deep concern for one of Haywood's oldest colleagues.

NINE

# The Whistle-Blower

Tim Haywood had known Daniel Sheard for decades. The two worked together fresh out of university, at the London office of ANZ, the Australian bank. It was the late 1980s, and the City was booming after Margaret Thatcher's government delivered the 'Big Bang' – the wave of deregulation that transformed London into a modern financial capital.

At ANZ, Sheard worked on the fixed income team that invests in government and corporate bonds and similar financial instruments. Haywood was in equities. They occasionally swapped information about interest rates.

After ANZ, each went his own separate way for a few years. Sheard stayed in London. In the early 1990s, his career stumbled when he was censured by regulators for mispricing some investments. It was an embarrassing public chastening for Sheard early in his career and left a blemish on his reputation. Haywood left London and began to specialize in fixed income too. His work took him to Hong Kong before, eventually, he returned to the City to a role at the Swiss bank Julius Baer.

In 2006, Haywood was running a fund and looking for a co-manager. He met Sheard for a coffee at the Royal Exchange, a grand, sixteenth-century building next door to the Bank of England. Its central location and busy acoustics make the cafe there a classic venue for City types to meet and surreptitiously discuss job moves. Haywood's fund was doing well and the role was interesting. It would be fun to work with an old colleague again. Sheard agreed to join.

The two were a good match. Haywood was extremely confident and an intuitive investor. Sheard was more reticent and enjoyed the grunt work of digging through corporate filings and other minutiae. But Haywood's hunt for stellar returns also sometimes took him into areas that left Sheard feeling uncomfortable. Sometimes Haywood would take equity stakes in start-up businesses, a much riskier type of investment than the two fund managers typically aimed for. Often, he'd skirt normal documentation or credit analysis.

BY LATE 2015, the Absolute Return Bond Fund (ARBF) that Haywood and Sheard ran together was the faded jewel in the crown at Global Asset Management. Performance had dropped off in recent years, but it was still the economic driver of GAM's entire business.

That's when Haywood began investing with Greensill.

The normal investment procedure was that GAM's staff would look at an investment, do some research, and then contact a broker selling the asset. Once they'd decided to buy, two GAM managers had to sign off on the deal – the so-called 'Four Eyes Principle' is a common internal risk control process in investment management. At GAM the process was meant to be applied to every deal to ensure all deals were free of conflicts; everything was checked twice; no one could go rogue.

But the process for Greensill assets was different. Greensill had made the case that the existing GAM process was too slow and cumbersome to apply to supply chain finance, where settling invoices quickly was key. For SCF investments, speed was of the essence, and all the loans were short term. A new system was set up, exclusively for Greensill, so that Greensill would submit securities via its broker, Morgan Stanley. These would go straight to GAM, where only one sign-off would be required.

In emails to compliance and other staff in December 2015, Sheard challenged this approach. He was uncomfortable with circumventing normal process and pointed out that GAM 'has not undertaken ANY credit research or other Due Diligence on ANY of the Relevant Obligors.' (Obligors is essentially another name for the borrowers, and we will come to them in detail later.)

Sheard's correspondence sparked a series of replies and responses. But eventually, the discussion went quiet and everyone moved along. The numbers involved were small. The potential problems hypothetical. There was plenty of other work to be done and no one wanted to get sidetracked by the process around a few million dollars in a multibillion-dollar fund.

Lex also did his bit to allay any concerns. He came to GAM's office to meet with Haywood and some of the team. Seven or eight GAM staffers sat in a dingy second-floor meeting room while Lex ran through the features of his SCF investments. They were safe. They were liquid. They were short term. They were backed by real invoices for real transactions. Lex projected he'd bring in $10 billion in assets, which would generate tidy, reliable fees for the GAM team. Neither he nor Haywood mentioned that they were also working on a series of other funky loans, some to Sanjeev Gupta, others to Greensill itself, and yet more to other problematic business interests of Greensill's.

The pace of Haywood's Greensill investments continued to pick up. And so did Sheard's discomfort. Some of the investments appeared to have nothing to do with SCF, and Haywood's behaviour had become odd. He was out of the office a lot, often with Lex or Sanjeev Gupta. His colleagues at GAM joked about Tim's 'second job' working for Lex.

The Greensill deals were rapidly increasing in size. There were hundreds of millions of pounds loaned to Gupta for acquisitions he was making in Scotland. These were unusual in size and, because they were not very liquid, they couldn't easily be sold to someone else if GAM wanted to exit the investments. The Laufer deals were growing fast too. Haywood was also investing in aircraft lease payments that Greensill had put to him. In every case, Greensill was making significant fees – often millions of pounds per deal.

In the summer, Haywood began investing in more Greensill securities tied to Gupta, this time backed by biofuel generators. The numbers were huge – £250 million at a time. In August, Sheard and a couple of other senior managers asked Haywood for a meeting in GAM's St James's office. They told Haywood that the investments didn't smell right. They wanted him to get out of it. Haywood was annoyed and left the room. Shortly afterwards, Lex himself showed up in the GAM office and convened another meeting. He argued vehemently that the deal was a good one, GAM was getting well paid, there was no risk. The GAM sceptics were not convinced. After Lex left, they told Haywood again that they couldn't support the investment. Haywood made it clear he didn't care about their opinion.

In early August 2017, Sheard told Haywood that he couldn't continue. He would resign as a co-manager of the ARBF fund, though he'd stay at GAM. He wanted nothing to do with anything related to Greensill. Sheard sent an email to Haywood, GAM's CEO Alex Friedman and the CFO Richard McNamara. Haywood was shocked. He and Sheard had worked together for years. They'd known each other for decades. Sheard had been making noise about the Greensill investments for the past two years, but Haywood appeared to have been blindsided by his decision.

Over the next few weeks, there were a series of discussions at the top level of GAM about exactly what Sheard was complaining about. It was a mix of process (lack of due diligence, lack of analysis, lack of documentation), worries about the nature of the Greensill investments, and concerns that some of the Greensill securities just didn't fit with the rules of the ARBF fund. It was serious stuff, no doubt. But was it true? Or was it all just some kind of falling out between Sheard and Haywood? What was Sheard's motivation?

Haywood continued as though nothing had changed. Instead of selling down his Greensill investments, he held on to them. Haywood was not acting as if he'd just been outed in a major financial scandal.

By October, GAM's top management had enough reasons, based on Sheard's allegations, to make a move. They placed some restrictions on Haywood. He couldn't invest in new Greensill assets without a signature from Sheard, Friedman and another senior executive. But it hardly seemed to spook him at all. Two weeks after that rule was put in place, he renewed the Laufer investments, the complex securities that were effectively supporting Greensill itself.

In November, Sheard was supposed to fly with Haywood to Australia to market the ARBF and other funds to investors there. Although he'd resigned as co-manager, he still had a role in the funds. But Sheard just couldn't bring himself to make the trip. He couldn't in good conscience persuade investors to put their money into the funds when Haywood was still investing with Greensill and Gupta. Sheard told the firm he wouldn't be going. The implication was clear: we shouldn't be marketing these funds at all until we've cleaned them up. Remarkably, Haywood went anyway.

Around this time, a different narrative was taking hold. The office gossip was that Sheard was a troublemaker, trying to engineer his exit from the firm and to force a big payout. Even close colleagues questioned why he was creating such a fuss. Everyone knew he was stirring up trouble. If he had been so unhappy, why wait for so long, letting Haywood build such a big position with Greensill before kicking off? The answer to that, of course, was that Sheard had been raising his concerns all along, but no one had been listening. And besides, the scale of the Greensill investments had started off small and only grown incrementally. Haywood's Greensill investments were like a slowly boiling frog.

He spent most of the next few months working from home to avoid the antagonism. But in February, Sheard was in the office when a colleague dropped a couple of pages on his desk. They were critical documents that left Sheard dumbfounded. Haywood, working from home, appeared to have accidentally sent them to the office printer. The documents showed that he was planning to enter a complex 'put option' deal with Lex Greensill. If he went ahead, the deal would give Greensill the right to sell to GAM hundreds of millions of dollars of bonds tied to defaulted loans. In return, GAM was going to get a paltry sum of a few thousand pounds for taking on this risk.

It was an incredible discovery. Tim Haywood had been told not to do any more business with Greensill, yet this was evidence he was planning to do another massive deal. But it was worse than that. Many of the ARBF investors simply weren't allowed to invest in private option trades like this one, or buy defaulted assets, which this deal could force them to do. The deal made no economic sense – there was just not enough reward for the risk GAM's investors were taking on.

For Sheard, it was – another – final straw. With his lawyers, he went to the Financial Conduct Authority (FCA), bringing all the evidence he'd gathered over the past couple of years.

By involving the regulator, GAM would have to take his allegations seriously, Sheard and his lawyer reasoned. Something more substantial would surely have to happen. It did, but not necessarily in the way he might have expected. Sheard was questioned by the FCA's enforcement division, and by GAM's external counsel, which had been hired to investigate the allegations against Haywood. Sheard felt as though he himself was on trial. It wasn't clear that GAM's external law firm believed anything he was saying. Colleagues openly questioned his motivation too. His career and friendships were ruined.

A few months later, as the crisis blew through GAM's share price and made the firm front-page news, Sheard left the firm for ever.

WHISTLE-BLOWERS ARE a strange breed. I've worked with several of them. Sometimes they're true outsiders, whose otherness is what allows them to speak up. Sometimes they are so socially out of tune that they are oblivious to what will happen once they file a complaint. For the most part, blowing the whistle is a lonely, frustrating experience. But many whistle-blowers imagine they will be hailed as heroes for saving the company and are utterly disappointed when it doesn't work out that way. Sheard was not this kind of whistle-blower. He was acutely aware that if he blew the whistle on a star employee, the consequences for him and the firm could be brutal. Friends and colleagues would turn on him. Investors would pull their money out of the funds he ran with Haywood. GAM itself would almost certainly come under significant financial pressure. It might even go bust altogether. But he reasoned that – despite the fact it might wreak Armageddon on the firm and on his career – it was better than the alternative.

In the summer of 2016, a foreign exchange trader from HSBC had been arrested on fraud charges in the US while trying to board a transatlantic flight. A year later, the trader was found guilty and eventually given a prison sentence by a US court. The story weighed on Sheard. Some of the investors in the GAM funds were US pension funds, and he worried about the potential for US regulators to take an interest in what Haywood was up to with Greensill. The memory of his own earlier punishment for wrongdoing also lingered.

A little later, he was on a work trip to Frankfurt. Sitting on a bench near the city's opera house, Sheard took a call from a colleague. You must blow the whistle, the colleague told him. The colleague had been talking to a legal expert. If Sheard didn't blow the whistle, he could find himself in trouble for not speaking up.

Later, a couple of blogs that peddle finance scuttlebutt accused Sheard of being the 'villain' at GAM. 'Daniel Sheard is a short, driven individual who is highly competitive, a compulsive obsessive cyclist who likes to be around combative people', one of the blogs sniped. The blog's author alleged his motivation was jealousy over Haywood's bonuses and that Sheard had paid journalists to tell his version of events. None of this was sourced in a credible way. It looked like a hit-job, meant to undermine Sheard's version of events. I also heard later that Sheard was a special focus of Lex's ire. Lex talked about having him followed to see if he was leaking stories.

The decision to blow the whistle was a costly one, in just about every way. It was the toughest decision. It took a mental and financial toll. His reputation was dragged through the internet and more than one business news publication. He lost his job and incurred massive legal costs. In years to come, Sheard told people he wasn't sure if he had done the right thing, if all the trouble that followed was worth it. In the end, he had no choice.

After he was forced out of GAM, Sheard's career was essentially on permanent hold. He went into a kind of domestic retirement at his home in the north of England, where he grew cider apples and took days-long cycling trips. Meanwhile, his legal costs ran higher and higher. He was kept in limbo by the UK's finance regulators, who failed for years to make any kind of move or announcement about Haywood or Greensill. Sheard himself documented everything related to Greensill. He maintained file upon file related to Lex's business, well beyond the GAM affair. He was bound by confidentiality agreements that meant he couldn't speak to journalists or anyone else about what he knew. But he also had a presence on social media. For those of us who knew it, Sheard's social media posts became a fascinating source of insight into some of the key turning points of the next couple of years.

TEN

# Gupta Family Group

Sanjeev Gupta was born in Punjab, the son of an industrialist. He was sent to boarding school in England and went on to study economics at Trinity College, Cambridge. There, he set up a commodities trading business from his student halls of residence. He called the business Liberty House Group, and traded steel and rice and chemicals. Trinity booted him out of halls because he'd registered his business there. But he continued trading. Even then, he claims, he was making £1 million a day.

After Cambridge, Gupta continued to grow Liberty, setting up offices in Dubai, Singapore and Hong Kong. He got married – to his former company treasurer – and they started a family. As his personal wealth grew, he spent lavishly, collecting trophy properties in London, Sydney and Dubai, and vast estates in Scotland and Wales. He bought a private jet and a bank that he renamed Wyelands, also the name of the vast nineteenth-century country house and estate he owns in Monmouthshire. The BBC nicknamed Gupta the 'Man of Steel' and talked about him as the saviour of the country's metals industry.

By the early 2010s, he was well known and mostly well liked by banking and insurance executives. They wouldn't necessarily want to lend him money, but he was fun and charming, and always good for an expensive lunch in the City. He talked in grand terms about building a global metals conglomerate. He wanted to start producing steel in the UK and the US, and to do it in an environmentally friendly and sustainable way. And he planned to make this vision a reality with a series of bold acquisitions.

This kind of talk was interesting over dinner in Mayfair, but it was at odds with reality. The steel industry was struggling. Most Western facilities were too costly to run. Customers often paid late. Competition was too intense. Steel companies were in constant need of cash to keep the mills running. Nevertheless, the steel sector rolls in long cycles, and Gupta's supporters would say this was always a multi-year project.

Gupta made his move into the UK steel industry in 2013, when Liberty bought a mill in Newport, South Wales, from Mir Steel, a Russian-owned company. Funding for the deal came from a consortium of Dubai-based Indian investors.

What followed was a rapid series of acquisitions, processed through a spider's web of Liberty House companies. At every step, there was a big hurdle. The traditional banks were not keen to lend to steel businesses at all, let alone fund a whirlwind spree of acquisitions carried out by an unproven industrialist with few assets to his name.

That's where Greensill came in. When Gupta started, there were few other options in terms of traditional finance. So Greensill came as a breath of fresh air, Gupta told associates.

Lex and Sanjeev had for several years mixed in similar circles. Greensill had funded several commodities businesses, such as BSi Steel in South Africa or Griffin Coal in Australia. Both Greensill and Gupta were well known to the trade credit insurance industry too. They were both fiercely ambitious and talked frequently about disrupting established industries. Gupta realized that Lex's supply chain finance business could play a crucial role in building up his metals empire. If the big banks wouldn't lend to him, then maybe Lex could. He was so convinced that Gupta even took a stake in Greensill, acquiring a few thousand shares in the company in 2016 (though he sold the stake later the same year).

The two became close. Lex was enamoured of Gupta's ambition. 'I'm a big fan of what Sanjeev Gupta has been doing,' he told me once. 'I think exporting industrial jobs out of countries to Eastern Europe and China is not an awesome thing. If we can create jobs here, that's a cool thing. We are broadly always supportive of what Mr Gupta was trying to do, and we remain supportive of him as a matter of principle.'

Lex would often visit Gupta's office overlooking Sydney Harbour to discuss potential deals. Greensill executives attended lavish parties that Gupta threw at his mansions in Sydney and London. Sometimes Lex and Gupta would share a flight – both men owned private aircraft decked out in the same purple livery. The two were insatiable workaholics – often the best place to catch them was on board one of the planes, where they were invariably working free from the distractions you might get on the ground.

Gupta mirrored Lex's ongoing efforts to embed into the political and financial establishment. He hired as his right-hand man and chief dealmaker Jay Hambro, a former investment banker. Hambro, who had been educated at the elite Harrow School, was the scion of one of Europe's most elite banking dynasties. Gupta also lavished gifts and hospitality on Conservative politicians. His flat in Mayfair was next to 5 Hertford Street, a darkly lit, labyrinthine members' club favoured by Britain's political elite. He sponsored a squad of UK parliamentarians on a cricket-playing tour to Australia in 2017, where former Australian prime ministers watched their countrymen battle it out with their British political counterparts. The self-styled champion of 'green' steel even befriended Prince Charles, the ageing royal environmentalist, who appointed Gupta as an official ambassador for the UK Industrial Cadets programme, which aims to promote skills and training for the country's manufacturing industries.

Lex frequently told a story about how he brought Sanjeev to the Greensill family farm in Bundaberg early on in their relationship. The two men drove around the extensive agricultural property for hours. At one point, they sat at the top of a large hill overlooking the estate. As the sun came down across the Australian outback, Lex and Sanjeev outlined their plans for Greensill and Liberty House to carve out twin empires that would dominate the world's finance and steel industries.

For a while, there was a third member of their troupe. Lex and Sanjeev worked closely with Global Asset Management (GAM) fund manager Tim Haywood, in an interlocking triumvirate that appeared to benefit all three. Sanjeev had projects that needed financing. Lex had a start-up finance firm that needed deals to sell. Haywood had funds that needed higher-yielding assets.

OVER SEVERAL YEARS, Greensill and Gupta leaned on each other as they grew until, eventually, it was clear that if one stumbled, or withdrew his support for the other, the empires that both men were building would come tumbling down together.

Gupta began to call his business the GFG (short for the Gupta Family Group) Alliance. He acquired steel, aluminium and other assets across the UK, Europe, the US and Australia. In many cases, Greensill provided most or all of the funding. Gupta said the traditional banks were cheaper, but Greensill made lending decisions faster, and was much more flexible. He disliked the covenants that are usually attached to bank loans or bonds. Covenants often restrict a business owner's ability to buy assets or take on more debt. GFG paid high fees to Greensill, and though some of Gupta's executives questioned whether they were paying too much, it didn't really matter. The two companies were intertwined, mutually dependent.

By 2017, GFG accounted for more than two-thirds of all Greensill revenue. Greensill needed GFG for revenue – the interest and fees on the loans Greensill made to GFG. GFG needed Greensill for cash in the form of the loans Greensill extended. Still, some GFG executives and advisers were concerned. They pushed Gupta to diversify the group's source of funding beyond Greensill.

That wouldn't be easy. Gupta had a blemished reputation in the traditional banking sector. Some banks did work with GFG, but their relationships were fleeting and access to bank funding was a constant problem. At least four banks had already stopped working with Gupta since 2016, according to a Bloomberg News story, because of concerns about improprieties in the documentation provided by his company. The banks were SberBank from Russia, Australia's Macquarie and CWB, and ICBC Standard Bank, an Africa-focused Chinese bank. GFG told Bloomberg that its own internal investigation of the allegations of impropriety found no wrongdoing and none of the banks lost any money. But it was the kind of incident that left a stain that couldn't easily be washed away.

Other banks worried about GFG's over-reliance on short-term borrowings to fund his business. Short-term debt could be withdrawn quickly, which would leave GFG in distress and the banks potentially facing a default. Some financiers were concerned as to the viability of many of the group's assets and the convoluted network of related companies within the overall GFG structure. How could they be sure these businesses would generate enough cash to pay their loans off? What sort of collateral could be recovered in the event Gupta defaulted? Which creditor would be first in line if the business went into an insolvency process? The Gupta business network was just too murky for most bankers trying to answer questions like these.

By 2018, some of Gupta's top lieutenants persuaded him to try a new strategy. He should consolidate the various Liberty businesses into a single GFG conglomerate. GFG would have one set of financial accounts, which would give a clear picture of the entire business. With more transparency around the overall business, GFG could take out long-term debt with the banks and target an initial public offering of the company's shares. That would lead to more transparent reporting of GFG's financial position. And, finally, the company might untie itself from Greensill.

Gupta took some persuading. Listing the company's shares meant adhering to miles of red tape and costly reporting requirements. And reducing the group's reliance on short-term financing was all very well as a goal, but it was not going to be possible to reduce reliance on short-term debt until the company had something else to replace it with. Nevertheless, Gupta publicly said that he planned to list all, or part, of the business, in the UK, or Australia or the US – it depended on which day he said it and to whom.

In summer of 2019, he hired from accountants Grant Thornton a partner named Neil Barrell. At that point, GFG reportedly had annual revenue of more than $15 billion and 15,000 staff worldwide. Barrell had extensive experience dishing out strategic and operational advice to the steel, aluminium and automotive industries. He had previously advised GFG on its dealmaking spree. Barrell was hired to bring some order to the disparate businesses in the GFG group. He was also seen as someone who could take difficult decisions, even acknowledging problems with the business – a rare virtue in the GFG empire. Within a few months, he was promoted to chief operating officer, with a short-term focus of consolidating the GFG steel assets. At a conference in Italy, Gupta promised, 'Our integrated group will stretch around the world with a financial and governance structure suitable for an intercontinental business of our size.'

But in March, the project ground to a halt. Barrell died unexpectedly on a work trip. Gupta called it a 'devastating blow'. Without Barrell behind the plan, the whole idea of consolidating GFG went on hold. The Covid-19 pandemic had struck in earnest too. The future of the steel industry was unclear, and that suddenly became a much more pressing concern than promises of greater transparency: Gupta was more worried about keeping the business afloat than producing a set of consolidated accounts. The focus shifted. Inside GFG, senior management were only concerned with survival, including trying to get access to government funding for the under-pressure steel mills.

By then, Gupta had also come into the crosshairs of UK financial regulators. Wyelands, the bank Gupta owned, had been under investigation by the Prudential Regulation Authority in 2019. The PRA had become concerned that Wyelands had breached rules that limit the amount a bank can loan to related entities. In particular, the regulator found that Wyelands may have made loans to a series of entities that were apparently independent of Gupta, but which – on closer inspection – were connected to the steel magnate. When reporters at the *Financial Times* broke news of the PRA investigation, in early 2020, Gupta and Wyelands denied any wrongdoing and pledged their own, independent investigation. But much damage was already done. Heading into the Covid-19 pandemic, Gupta was under significant pressure. For Greensill, whose business leaned on Gupta so heavily, that was a major problem too.

# ELEVEN

# The Haywood Files

Top executives at Global Asset Management were not initially sure what to make of Daniel Sheard's allegations. In 2017, Alex Friedman and his team were dealing with the hostile activist investor, a broad restructuring plan, poor overall performance and integrating new acquisitions. They didn't appear to have grasped the seriousness of Sheard's allegations. Tim Haywood, the firm's star fund manager, seemed convinced he could make money from the Greensill investments. He even showed them that all was fine by selling a couple of Greensill assets at a profit (though it later turned out that he'd only sold them back to Greensill, and the deals never actually closed anyway).

By spring of 2018, GAM managers told Haywood that he couldn't enter any more transactions with Lex unless they were straightforward supply chain finance deals. They had also launched Project Dill, an investigation into Haywood's conduct. They hired two separate groups to conduct the probe. One of these was Bryan Cave Leighton Paisner (BCLP), a law firm, whose team was asked to look specifically into Haywood's conduct and whether he'd broken any rules. The other piece of the investigation was carried out by Prytania Solutions, a specialist firm that mostly assessed the value of the assets he'd bought from Greensill.

BCLP provided a draft set of findings early in the summer. The law firm said that Haywood appeared to have acted in good faith, and that he was motivated by getting a good return for the funds he managed. But they also found that he'd shown extremely bad judgement in taking flights on the Greensill private aircraft, and accepting other gifts. The lawyers also found that Haywood failed to carry out proper due diligence on his investments with Greensill, failed to create proper records of some of those investments and failed to comply with GAM's own procedures. He'd also communicated with Greensill through his private email, rather than company email. This had meant some of the Greensill trades were not visible to the broader team. Haywood might have acted in good faith, but the allegations about his behaviour included some serious evidence of misconduct.

Friedman and others became particularly concerned about a series of events they regarded as suspicious.

In one incident, recorded in telephone transcripts, a broker from Morgan Stanley who played a kind of middle-man role in selling Greensill-sourced assets to GAM, asked Haywood, 'the financials [accounts] are in two weeks. Do you want to hold off [making the investment] until you see the financials?' Haywood replied, 'No need. I trust Lex.'

Another time, Haywood put about $1 billion into investments sold by Greensill tied to Gupta. That was about 10 per cent of his entire fund – a huge amount of concentration for a supposedly diversified fund, and all of it concentrated in a single business tied to a controversial industrialist. And he did almost all of it in a two-week period in late August 2017, when most of the rest of the GAM management team was away on holiday. Some of the senior management team wondered aloud whether Haywood had deliberately timed the trades to avoid scrutiny.

On several occasions, Haywood made Greensill trades without getting proper signatures and didn't enter them into GAM's order management system that is meant to record all deals.

The ninety-two-page report from Prytania was more damning. Through a long-time source, I was able to get my hands on a copy. It was gold dust. The report went through all of Haywood's Greensill investments in meticulous detail. And its authors didn't hold back. My reading of it was that they were incredulous at the valuation of some of the investments. At other times, they appeared to be dumbfounded by the lack of due diligence or the speed with which Haywood had handed over hundreds of millions of dollars of investors' money to Greensill.

The report also clearly contradicted claims from Lex and his aggressive PR team that the GAM affair was an internal matter that had nothing to do with Greensill. For starters, it was clear that hardly any of the investments Haywood had made had anything to do with SCF or similar trade finance lending. That showed that a core piece of Lex's business was something altogether different to what he was saying in public. The report also showed in detail that many of the investments were highly risky – Lex must have known that they were a problem for Haywood's fund.

Above all, getting hold of a copy of the report gave me all the confidence I needed to keep pursuing this story. Something was wrong with Greensill and, now that I knew about it, I couldn't let it go.

Prytania was hired in early May and delivered their report two months later. They told GAM's management that there were major gaps in the data they'd been asked to look at. What they had found showed that Haywood's due diligence on the Greensill investments 'was not what it should have been and/or that the internal retention of documents is woefully short of adequate.' It said that one of his investments with Greensill 'appears to be little more than a "crap shoot".' Some of the Greensill assets were specifically forbidden, where individual investors in Haywood's funds had required all assets to have publicly available price quotes, or that the funds couldn't invest in complex structured credit products, for instance.

There were very specific concerns about several of Haywood's Greensill investments. One of these was called Steinway and related to British-Irish property developer Andy Ruhan, the former shareholder in Greensill Bank, who had declared himself bankrupt in divorce court proceedings. It was the Atlantic 57 deal that involved a stake in a New York skyscraper development.

The Prytania report's authors struggled to unearth everything they needed to see about this investment: 'We were informed by GAM that there was "very little to share"'.

The report said, 'We understand that the investment is effectively the purchase of a loan which was originally made by a (one time at least) billionaire (Andy Ruhan) to the developers of a "super scraper" in New York with extremely high-end living apartments on the top floors'.

Prytania's experts found that Haywood's due diligence into this transaction was severely lacking, and that it seemed unlikely he'd seen any documents related to the underlying loan.

They understood that Ruhan had invested $28 million in the building development and sold his interest to Haywood's Absolute Return Bond Fund (ARBF) for $18 million in October 2016. When it was not paid back a year later, the investment was rolled for another year at a higher value. In fact, the whole investment was far more complex even than that, and Ruhan's stake in it was disputed. The development sat at the corner of West Fifty-Seventh Street and Sixth Avenue, on a stretch known as 'Billionaire's Row', atop a former Steinway & Sons piano store. It had become the focus of a drawn-out legal dispute. A group of financiers, including renowned US real-estate developer Arthur Becker – the former husband of designer Vera Wang – had apparently purchased the site in 2013. The complex ownership of the site also involved a $21 million loan from a pair of Russian oligarchs, who had previously done business with Ruhan's

Formula One team. Their stake was allegedly routed through two entities registered in the British Virgin Islands called Grenda Investments and Atlantic 57 Consultancy, about which there was very little information anywhere, though Grenda was linked to Ruhan in court proceedings related to his divorce. (Haywood had also told colleagues at GAM that Ruhan had rights to property at an airfield owned by BAE Systems, which, he said, could be a source of value for the repayment of the Atlantic 57 loan. Prytania didn't refer to this, and my sources believe it was a red herring that didn't signify anything of value.)

The series of loans and investments were meant to pay off once the skyscraper was completed. But that's not what played out. Instead, the Steinway development was hit by massive cost overruns and long delays in construction. The owners and the lenders to the building development fell out. A real-estate investment firm that had provided a loan to the developers foreclosed on the property, meaning Ruhan and the other backers were wiped out. Litigation related to the development has dragged on for several years.

According to Prytania's report, GAM's own real-estate experts had advised against the deal and suggested GAM should 'prepare for a binary outcome', implying a fifty-fifty chance that the fund would lose its money on the deal.

(This loan was still sitting in the GAM fund when it was suspended. Later, I noticed the Atlantic 57 loan turned up in Greensill's Credit Suisse funds. After I asked the Swiss bank about it, the loan disappeared. But it still wasn't paid off. Eventually, it showed up in Greensill Bank when the firm filed for administration in early 2021. These could have all been different loans, though most likely each Atlantic 57 loan was simply paid off with a new one.)

Haywood had also invested $430 million in six deals brokered by Greensill tied to aircraft leasing payments. Five of those deals related to Norwegian Air, for whom Greensill had arranged the purchase of several Boeing 737 Max 8s. Lex had said in a press release at the time that the aircraft deals showed how Greensill combined 'capital, technology and expertise'. Greensill was particularly proud of the transactions, which were developed from a new insurance-based aircraft leasing programme established by Lex's insurance brokers at Marsh. Lex was especially pleased that Greensill had taken just six weeks to launch the deals. There was even a case study on the Greensill website, proclaiming the innovative transactions.

The Prytania report struck a different tone. It noted that Haywood had invested in the Norwegian Air deals when the airline was close to bankruptcy. The consultants suggested that the investment decision by Haywood was made too quickly, with no time for adequate due diligence. They found that the deals didn't pay enough, given the risks involved, and that the investment decision was likely entirely dependent on the associated insurance policies. Later, when aviation authorities around the world grounded all the 737 Max 8s because of a series of crashes, those Greensill press releases disappeared from the top of Greensill's site.

Another aircraft investment also raised some red flags. This time, Greensill had set up a special purpose entity, in Ireland, called 'Panamera Aviation Leasing XII DAC'. Panamera bought a Boeing cargo jet on behalf of a US-registered leasing group called Intrepid Aviation, which leased it on to a Russian air freight company that was part of the Volga Dnepr Group – an air transport operator with close ties to the government of Vladimir Putin in Moscow. Haywood invested about $170 million in Panamera. Prytania noted that selling this investment would be difficult given its size and the nature of the group that was ultimately leasing the plane.

Prytania also scrutinized the Laufer investments. Starting in October 2016, Haywood had invested in these securities that supported Greensill itself. Lex had written to other Greensill shareholders telling them that GAM was 'refinancing' the company. Over the next few months, Haywood had poured £311 million pounds into Greensill in a series of one-year loans. He'd also agreed that if Greensill couldn't repay the loans, the interest could be added to the total and the loan could be rolled over for five years to 2021. This was a highly unusual arrangement. Prytania's consultants also said that the return on this investment of about 5 per cent was less than half what it would expect. Effectively, Haywood was financing Greensill – a loss-making finance start-up – at well below market rate and with little protection if it defaulted on payments.

Other investments reviewed by Prytania included several tied to Gupta and brokered by Greensill.

These included the so-called Little Red Boxes (LRBs) – biofuel generators owned and operated by the SIMEC Group, which was owned by Parduman Gupta, Sanjeev's father, and which are part of the Gupta group of companies. In total, Haywood invested £650 million in securities tied to the LRBs, the report said. Greensill marketed the investments on the grounds that once the LRBs attained UK government accreditation, they would qualify for subsidies and could be sold to businesses as a backup power source. In theory, Haywood's funds stood to receive future flows until 2037 of more than £1 billion in total.

Prytania's consultants were shocked at 'the pace of acquisition of the assets, much of it over short time periods'. They found that Haywood appeared to have invested hundreds of millions of pounds within just a couple of weeks of being presented with the transaction. They wrote that 'we cannot comprehend how any significant [due diligence] was/could have been undertaken in that time frame.'

What made the investment even worse was that the LRBs never actually worked to the extent or in the way that was planned. At one point, Gupta Family Group (GFG) sales staff were urged to go out and persuade their contacts to buy an LRB, which were also known as 'GenSets'. But there were few takers. Instead, the LRBs mostly sat at a GFG site in Newport. From time to time, when potential buyers were shown the GenSets, a GFG staffer would hook one to a conventional generator and fire it up to show how they might, theoretically, operate.

(Eventually, SIMEC bought a biofuel specialist company called Fleetsolve to 'accelerate plans for the deployment of its biodiesel generators'. When I asked GFG about the LRBs in early 2020, a company spokesperson said that 'the business case for the GenSet bonds – based upon a range of third-party suppliers of fuels, on power prices and GenSet operating metrics – was robust, independently validated and shared fully and transparently with investors when issued.' The spokesperson also told me the GenSets 'have all been made operationally ready. The business plan has evolved since launch due to a number of external factors and all bond obligations have been met in full by SIMEC during that time.')

There were two large deals with GFG that Prytania looked at in detail. In the far Highlands of Scotland, on the scenic west coast, Gupta wanted to buy a group of assets from the giant mining company Rio Tinto. These consisted of an aluminium smelter and two hydroelectric power plants, all located near the tiny village of Kinlochleven and the region around it known as Lochaber. (Gupta had also acquired the 114,000-acre Jahama Highland Estates, a major location for grouse shooting, deer stalking and rural businesses.)

Gupta already had a relationship with the Scottish government, who had helped him pick up other assets in the past. The government in Holyrood wanted to support the continued operation of industrial facilities, especially in remote regions, to support the local economy and jobs. Gupta, Lex, Haywood and Jay Hambro schmoozed Scottish politicians to get their buy-in. The group of four dined with Scotland's Cabinet Secretary for Rural Economy, Fergus Ewing, at Cail Bruich, Glasgow's only Michelin-starred restaurant.

Starting in December 2016, Greensill set up a series of complex structures that provided financing for these deals. These were funnelled through Greensill's special purpose vehicles (SPVs) known by names such as Lagoon Park and Wickham – they were named for areas close to where Lex grew up in Bundaberg. In one case, the investments were backed by the promise that one Gupta-owned entity that ran the aluminium smelter would buy electricity from a hydroelectric power facility that was also owned by Gupta. If the Gupta-owned smelter failed to make the payments, the Scottish government agreed that it would cover the shortfall. Greensill and Haywood had claimed that guarantee made the investments effectively fail-safe.

All the investments tied to these convoluted transactions ran into several hundred million pounds. It was a staggering sum to have invested through a single broker, Greensill, into a single business owner, Gupta.

(In 2019, Reuters News Agency reported that there was evidence warranting further investigation that Greensill had given bond market investors false information regarding the Scottish government guarantees. Greensill responded by filing a claim for defamation in the High Court. In May 2020, Greensill lost a dispute about the meaning of the allegations made within the article.)

THE ATMOSPHERE AT GAM became fraught. None of the whistleblower's claims had been much of a secret. The dispute had been out in the open and dozens of people at the firm knew about it. It made for a tense period when work colleagues eyed one another with suspicion and worried about its future. At one point, Friedman's office was broken into. A couple of laptops and some files were stolen, though there was little evidence of damage and no breach of security. The incident was a mystery. Was it an inside job? They didn't know.

Haywood was operating under a dark cloud. The investigations were in full swing. Sheard had not been into work for some time, which had sent the rumour mill into high gear. Some big investors in the ARBF fund were getting wind of problems at GAM. Several of them decided to pull their money out. One big Australian pension fund manager visited the office in London. It was crawling with consultants and lawyers. Everyone seemed to be reluctant to talk. The fund manager met with Haywood and told him they were out – about $90 million was yanked from the fund in one go. Haywood practically begged them not to do it, but they were in no mood to change their view. The whole place seemed toxic. Within days, other fund managers followed, and Australian institutions alone had yanked several hundred million dollars out of Haywood's fund.

In May 2018, GAM's senior managers were increasingly nervous about the relationship between Haywood and Lex. Haywood was still doing new business with both Lex and Greensill, months after he'd been told to wind down his Greensill investments. Instead of reducing his Greensill investments, he appeared to be ramping up. By then, there was also evidence that Haywood had not entered Greensill deals into GAM's internal systems, had failed to disclose some Greensill deals at all, and documentation relating to at least one big deal had been stuffed into a locked drawer rather than disclosed to his concerned senior managers. Haywood later defended his conduct, saying that there were certain terms of the investments that couldn't be inputted directly into the company's record keeping systems. Nevertheless, at the time of the investigation, GAM's lawyers advised the firm's senior management that Haywood's conduct was problematic and that he was risking enormous sums of client money to keep the Greensill relationship alive. On this advice, Haywood's authority to make any transactions was pulled entirely.

In the summer of 2018, GAM's management shared the Project Dill findings with the Financial Conduct Authority (FCA). GAM was already under scrutiny from the regulator because of the Section 166 Skilled Persons Review related to the FCA's previous concerns about the firm's processes. This new admission about issues with the firm's star fund manager was highly embarrassing, but there was no option other than full transparency with the FCA.

Friedman and the rest of GAM's management and board were

unanimous that Haywood had to go. But they also worried that the departure of a well-known fund manager would spark a run on his funds, with grim consequences for the entire company. They debated whether to let him retire quietly and run down his funds in a more orderly fashion. That would be difficult, because many of the Greensill investments weren't very liquid – there was no ready market where they could sell the investments quickly. Friedman and the rest of the top team also felt caught between the rules that protect whistleblowers and the employment law that curtailed their ability to deal with Haywood.

GAM's management felt that the regulator made it clear their first responsibility was to protect investors in Haywood's funds. GAM's shareholders, its staff – they were a lower priority. They unanimously agreed to have Haywood retire, and if he resisted, they would suspend him, pending a fuller investigation that would likely lead to him being fired.

On a call in late July 2018, GAM's top management team laid out their proposal to the FCA, and their concerns about the damage that could unfold if Haywood's departure was sudden and public. A few days later, the FCA and GAM's executives exchanged emailed letters.

Karen Jones, a manager in the supervision unit of the FCA, explained the regulator's position. 'We note the concerns you expressed on our call regarding the possibility of fund volatility, diminution in value or adverse effects on liquidity of Greensill-issued assets as a result of customers/markets learning of a suspension of [Tim Haywood] and/or related circumstances. You indicated that potential adverse impact on customers from such developments may lead GAM to favour a retirement option for TH. To be clear, we do not agree that appropriate action in relation to serious misconduct should be compromised. Rather . . . we expect appropriately robust action.'

GAM's own internal head of compliance, Natalie Baylis, had only recently joined from the FCA. In her view, she told the rest of the management team, this was as stern and direct as the regulator gets. The message they wanted to convey was to get rid of Haywood, or the entire management team and board might be held responsible for his wrongdoing. The FCA's Jones had sent her letter to GAM on Friday 27 July. GAM suspended Haywood the following Tuesday.

The announcement said that an internal investigation had found issues with Haywood's conduct and pointed to concerns about procedures and record keeping. It also said the investigation 'has not raised concerns regarding [Haywood's] honesty.'

But the result was as predictable as it was sudden. Investors immediately began pulling their money from Haywood's funds. GAM was forced to 'gate' – block investors from taking their money out – to stop a full-blown run. Even funds that had nothing to do with Haywood were hit, as suddenly investors feared a knock-on effect on the rest of GAM's business. Its share price tanked. Management was in turmoil. By November 2018, Friedman and several others were gone. GAM was forced to cut 10 per cent of its staff.

The ARBF fund was liquidated, though it took until late summer 2019 to sell all the illiquid Greensill assets. Some of them soon popped up again elsewhere.

When Haywood was suspended in the summer of 2018, he still had a lot of friends and supporters at GAM. He had been, in many ways, top dog in the firm's London office. He managed the most amount of money. He was confident and popular. His detractors – Sheard and, to some degree, Friedman – were much quieter figures. It wasn't hard to find former colleagues of Haywood's who'd say the whole thing had been blown out of proportion. Haywood himself hired a big-name PR firm that was more than willing to push the line, parroted by Lex and his own media relations man, James Doran, that the real issue was one of jealousy; that Sheard had grown envious of Haywood's success and his bonus.

It's possible Lex and Haywood even began to believe it themselves.

The FCA, which had privately put some pressure on GAM to deal harshly with Haywood, based on the evidence of his behaviour and his investments in Greensill, was doing nothing in public to suggest they were aware of any wrongdoing. Instead, the regulator remained silent.

Then, in February, GAM announced it had fired Haywood. 'In certain instances, Haywood may have failed, in our judgement, to conduct or evidence sufficient due diligence on some of the investments that were made, or make accessible internal records of documents relating to these . . . Following the conclusion of the investigation and disciplinary proceedings [Haywood] has now been dismissed from the company for gross misconduct.'

Haywood didn't walk away quietly. He told journalists that GAM had made him a 'scapegoat' and that he intended to appeal the decision to fire him.

'I dispute many of the findings, while noting the majority of allegations have been dropped,' he said in emails to reporters.

Two months later, in early May, Haywood staged a bizarre moment of theatre. The former portfolio manager bought shares in GAM, which theoretically gave him the right to attend the company's annual shareholder meeting. He caught a flight from London to Switzerland. He made his way to the Park Hyatt, on Beethoven-Strasse on the shores of Lake Zurich. And he attempted to walk into the GAM shareholder meeting taking place that day. There, he would have been able to ask difficult questions and vote against the company's results. Instead, he was turned away at the door. GAM claimed Haywood had failed to complete a 'straightforward' shareholder registration process correctly. Haywood claimed that it was another example of GAM singling him out for mistreatment.

'No other shareholders were barred from attending,' he complained to journalists. 'I have been treated unfairly yet again.'

In July, GAM's new management team sought to put an end to the public name-calling. A year after it had first suspended Haywood, the Swiss firm said in a statement that it had finally completed its investigations and another tribunal that investigated how it was all handled.

'GAM is focused on the future of the business, and while it stands by its finding of gross misconduct, it has agreed with Tim Haywood that neither party will pursue the other based on current facts.'

It was a head scratcher for those of us following the story closely. Haywood and his PR team were left to interpret it in their own way, claiming that he had a case for unfair dismissal, but that it was too expensive to pursue it.

In truth, the whole episode had finished Haywood's career. It could have been just as bad for Lex. His major source of funding had suddenly, sharply dried up completely. At that point, Greensill's business could have died in an instant. But somehow, Lex avoided defeat.

# TWELVE

# General Atlantic

General Atlantic (GA) was launched in 1980 by Chuck Feeney, an American billionaire who'd made his fortune and then given much of it away. He was a forward-thinking businessman, who'd helped create the whole notion of duty-free shopping, and then profited from it enormously. Feeney was also a secret philanthropist, whose $8 billion-plus in undercover charitable donations earned him the nickname 'the James Bond of philanthropy'.

New York-based GA is no charity, though it has a reputation as one of the less rapacious firms in an industry known for aggressive investing techniques and short-term profiteering. GA today manages more than $80 billion and its clients include wealthy individuals and massive global pension funds. It aims to spot up-and-coming companies, buy stakes in them while they're still relatively small, help them grow and then list the company's shares on a public stock exchange or sell them on to another investor at a higher price. It looks for companies led by 'visionary' founders – like Feeney – with fast-growing businesses.

GA also focuses its investments around particular themes. When the team finds a company that fits into one of its themes, they dig and dig until they decide whether to invest. That decision is taken at an investment committee meeting, where partners of the firm grill the founders of the company that they're thinking of backing. It's a multi-layered process designed to filter out all but the best businesses to bet on.

Private equity firms like GA have seen their resources explode in recent years. By the late 2010s, they were sitting on $2.5 trillion in cash, and struggling to find places to invest. For businesses looking for investment from so-called PE firms, there was so much money sloshing around.

GA's youthful European chief, Gabe Caillaux, a former Merrill Lynch banker, was already an old hand in the industry, having joined the firm in 2004. He once told one of my Dow Jones colleagues in an interview that too many private equity firms relied on the 'trick' of financial engineering to generate returns, and that wasn't sustainable. The implication was that you needed brains, not just pots of cash, to make an investment pay off. Under Caillaux's leadership, GA in Europe had a stellar track record. Several companies he'd invested in had listed their shares, netting his firm enormous profits.

GA's London-based finance-focused team had for years been looking at the supply chain finance sector, which was beginning to take off. The prospects were compelling. McKinsey & Company said that the overall universe of payments that could run on SCF pro-grammes was in the trillions of dollars, but only a tiny fraction of the world's payments had so far been tapped by SCF providers. GA's view was that the traditional banks did a poor job of serving the market. There were a few small disruptors who were looking to do things differently.

From about late 2016, GA began homing in on Lex. He was a regular panellist at trade finance conferences and stood out as more charismatic and bolder than the techies and middle-ranking trade bankers who shared the stage. He also had impressive connections in government. GA also knew Maurice Thompson and David Brier-wood, the ex-Citi and Morgan Stanley bigwigs who sat on Greensill's board.

Caillaux's team began digging deeper into Greensill and courting him at the same time. They introduced Lex to companies that were in their orbit that could potentially benefit from SCF. It was a way to help Lex build the business, while also finding out a bit more about how he worked. Gabe met with Lex every three or four months for breakfast and a catch-up. As the relationship grew, GA spoke to insurers and bankers who worked with Lex. They talked to technology platform owners who provided technology to Greensill. They spoke to Tim Haywood at GAM before his funds blew up; he was gushing, unequivocally positive about the Greensill business and Lex's smarts.

In early 2018, Lex told his suitors that he would be open to them buying an equity stake. To GA, it sounded like a typical founder who'd decided that this was the right moment to seek more funds to grow his business. GA didn't know that persuading them to invest had suddenly become critical. At GAM, Haywood's position was looking increasingly untenable and senior executives were starting to put a block on more Greensill investments. In March 2018, Lex had phoned a senior manager at GAM, furious that the firm was refusing to roll over a $10 million loan – a relatively small sum, but Greensill was hanging by a thread. In that context, of course, Lex was suddenly open to an equity investment from GA. His business was in trouble. He'd take any money he could get.

Around the same time, Lex made some quick decisions to dress up the Greensill accounts. He made a loan to Tower Trade so that it could take a bunch of problem loans off Greensill's balance sheet. The effect was to disguise some bad assets – loans that were overdue and looked as if they couldn't be repaid – with one new loan.

Lex also owed Neil Hobday a fee he'd been promised for introducing deals to Greensill. Ahead of the potential GA investment, Lex promised Hobday stock and paid him about £400,000 up front, plus a consulting fee of £15,000 a month for several years. In Greensill's accounts, the stock wasn't recorded, and the lump sum was booked as a loan.

The effect of these moves was to make Greensill's accounts look better so that GA would put a higher value on Lex's business. Oblivious to Greensill's predicament and his accounting manoeuvres, GA began its due diligence process in earnest.

There were red flags. Caillaux and his colleagues noticed that much of Greensill's business was concentrated in loans to a single businessman, Sanjeev Gupta. Here, they took some comfort from conversations with government sources, who told them Sanjeev was a preferred bidder for UK steel assets.

They were also concerned that Greensill seemed to be burning through cash at an alarming rate, even for a hot start-up. They noted that Greensill had a lower-tier audit firm in the UK and a tiny auditor in Australia too – that would have to change if they were going to get any bigger. There were worries about Greensill's technology – it wasn't up to scratch. Lex liked to say Greensill was a fintech. But GA's team felt a $50–$60 million tech action plan, aided by a top consultant like Bain or Boston Consulting, was needed to bring the firm's technology up to the right level. They also thought Greensill's finance and accounting function was lightweight – not unusual for a new, fast-growing company – and that a lot of the business (too much) ran through Lex personally. These were all the sorts of problems GA's executives thought they could fix, assuming they had a willing founder to work with, who would listen to advice, even when it was critical.

Was Lex that kind of founder?

On that, GA had less clarity. There were certain markers that Caillaux and the team fixated on. Lex already had a private plane at this point, which raised some eyebrows. It was unusual for a small firm to have its own aircraft. Gabe questioned Lex about it, telling him that it could be bad for his reputation, and that he could instead get a membership with NetJets, or some other aircraft-on-demand service. Lex pushed back: 'Watch me work for a few months, see how much work I do on board the plane, and then let's talk about it again.'

After issues with Tim Haywood began to emerge at GAM, GA also talked to some contacts there. Was there a Greensill problem? No, the issues were focused on Haywood, the wayward portfolio manager, his poor due diligence and record keeping. It was also partly a dispute between two colleagues who'd fallen out.

GA's due diligence on Lex's character threw up several naysayers. Insurers who'd been burnt by Lex, and competitors in the SCF space who said he was stretching the business model into places it didn't belong. At times his business seemed too good to be true, and that was usually a sign that something was wrong.

Still, Caillaux's team couldn't tell how much of the criticism was real and how much was the jealous sniping of former colleagues or rivals who had missed out on Greensill's success. GA kept pushing for hard evidence of fraud or that Lex had broken rules. In the absence of any, the GA team believed the criticism just sounded like sour grapes.

Some of the people GA asked about Lex Greensill during their due diligence thought they were talking in confidence. Somehow Lex found out what they had said. When he did, he left an angry message with one of them, accusing this person of 'throwing a hand grenade' into his deal.

He needn't have been concerned. The grenade didn't explode. Caillaux put Greensill in front of GA's investment committee. Lex took part in a lengthy pitch. There was some pushback. Some partners questioned Lex's character. He was undoubtedly driven and charismatic, even visionary perhaps. But he seemed to be in a rush and he thought he knew all the answers already. Could they work with him to fix the business? Would he toe the line? Could he be reined in? Would he listen to valid criticism and make adjustments to his business?

These were all very valid questions. Lex had been impatient for success since OzEcom. He'd pushed boundaries throughout his career. He'd covered over bad loans and other problems since the founding of Greensill Capital. But big private equity firms like GA stake their reputations on their ability to mould difficult businesses into winners.

In the end, GA's committee decided to back Greensill. Lex was a disruptor. That upset some people. His business had some governance issues. That was not untypical of firms that were doubling in size every year or so. He was headstrong, but that was often the case with visionary leaders.

GA stumped up $250 million for an approximate 14 per cent stake in Greensill in July 2018. Whatever the internal doubts at GA, externally their investment was a ringing endorsement for Lex. He had the backing of one of the world's premier investors. And his company was valued at about $1.7 billion.

In a story in *The Wall Street Journal*, Lex said he hoped his firm would now expand into new markets where GA had an established presence, including Brazil, India and China.

Bill Ford, the CEO of GA, touted Lex's credentials: 'We're trying to lever technology to transform the financial services space, and in effect, fill voids that have been left behind by the large banks. Lex is nothing if not ambitious. We made this investment based on their growth story.'

If GA's executives also hoped they could shape Lex, initial signs were not positive. Within days of securing GA's investment, Lex splashed out on a new plane. At a cost of tens of millions of dollars, he told colleagues, Lex had upgraded his short-haul private aircraft for a bigger model, capable of flying longer journeys. Then he went on a victory lap around the globe, visiting potential business partners along the way, showing off his new plane and his elevated status.

What was left of the money hardly went towards the ambitious emerging market strategy Lex had outlined in the pages of the *Journal*. The GA investment landed just as things were blowing up at GAM, so some of the cash was spent bailing out of Haywood's funds, buying back loans Haywood had made to Greensill itself. After that, and after the much-needed tech upgrade, there wasn't much left for an expansion into emerging markets.

Lex saw another benefit of GA's backing. Less than twenty-four hours after that *Wall Street Journal* story landed, Lex emailed it on to an insurance industry executive who had previously turned Greensill away. 'I'm not sure if you saw our news yesterday,' Lex wrote. 'It would be great if this development would allow us to jointly reassess working together.'

The insurer, who'd been burnt by Lex in the past, declined his offer. It hardly mattered to Lex. He'd got GA on board, and it couldn't have come at a more critical time.

THIRTEEN

# The Bailout

It was April 2019, almost nine months since Global Asset Management had gated the funds run by Tim Haywood.

Friedman and his team had taken the drastic action to prevent investors withdrawing their money the previous summer to avoid a run on the funds. But now, Friedman and several others were gone. Haywood was gone. Sheard was long gone.

GAM was under the stewardship of David Jacob, who had been a non-executive director on the firm's board since 2017. Jacob was a veteran of the asset management industry, and not without his own baggage. Back in 2001, he had been fired from a senior role at Merrill Lynch when a currency trader who worked for him had allegedly shifted trading profits around to favour some clients over others. Since then, he'd been blemish-free in a handful of senior roles at City asset management companies. When he took on the role of CEO at GAM, he said he would do it on an interim basis only. He was a safe but unexciting choice: exactly what the firm needed. It was bleeding cash following the Haywood revelations, and its share price and reputation were in the gutter.

Jacob's priorities had to be: to calm the nerves of investors; to rebuild the business; to offload the remaining Greensill assets still stuck in Haywood's funds, and to return money to clients.

On the first of these, he spoke to all the firm's biggest investors, explaining that the Haywood problem was contained. It didn't go beyond the funds Haywood had managed. There was no systemic issue. Some of the distributors of GAM's funds – including the giant bank Credit Suisse – were given access to the firm's files, including some files on Greensill and the Haywood funds, in order to quell their concerns. Credit Suisse had initially put all of GAM's funds on a red list, not just Haywood's funds, meaning it wouldn't sell them to clients, but gradually gave them the green light after conducting their own due diligence on GAM.

Jacob also began to look for a new, permanent CEO. He'd promised his family he would only hold the role temporarily. And he began laying off staff to get costs down. So far, so straightforward.

Selling down the Haywood–Greensill investments was not so easy.

Despite what Lex said in public, there was no ready market for a whole lot of what was in there. A loan to a property developer backed by a stake in a disputed building. Bonds backed by cash flows from biofuel generators that didn't work. An investment tied to a Russian-owned cargo plane. Where were the ready buyers for this stuff, especially now that it was tainted with the smell of financial wrongdoing?

GAM was also facing another dilemma. The poor quality of the assets, their true value and the lack of a market for them was outlined in excruciating detail in the Prytania report that backed up Sheard's claims. But the more GAM said about it, the lower the firm's chances of selling the assets to another buyer without incurring a big loss. It's a dilemma many investors can find themselves in when they buy a dud. The more honest you are about the bad investment you bought, the less likely it is that you can pass it off to someone else.

The previous summer, GAM had set a deadline of 31 March 2019 to sell down the assets. Autumn, winter, spring all passed. There was a series of intense phone calls between GAM and Greensill. Lex dialled in from London. Jacob and GAM's lawyers were on the phone from Zurich. Lex was angry, always on edge, always demanding. It was a strange – and implausible – position for him to adopt given Greensill's central role in the whole mess. He might have been more cooperative, made more of an effort to appear accommodating. But the situation was also desperate for Greensill. The assets Lex had sold Haywood were stranded in his gated funds. If they couldn't be shifted elsewhere, then eventually GAM would be forced to try to collect on the loans to Atlantic 57, Gupta and others. And then they might discover that those borrowers simply didn't have the money to pay back. For Greensill, the situation was existential and Lex was fuming.

He seemed especially furious about stories in the media that focused attention on Greensill. These kinds of stories don't help us get the right value for the assets you want us to sell, he told GAM's team. What are you going to do to stop journalists from writing about us? he demanded. It was another strange response to the situation. There was nothing anyone – not even Lex's PR guy, James Doran – could do to stop journalists from attempting to sniff out the problems at the core of the whole affair.

Jacob remained calm. The only thing that mattered was liquidating the Haywood funds on the best possible terms. But that was not going as planned.

By April, Jacob had to acknowledge GAM had missed the deadline. In public, he was stoic. In a statement when the firm announced its results that month, he said he was focused on rebuilding GAM and thanked clients for their patience. The hard work to sell the assets at a good price was ongoing, he said.

The reality was still more complex. Almost all the asset sales were complicated. Greensill had been able to access other sources of funds – Greensill Bank, for instance – to clean up some of the problem assets. He was able to use cash from nascent funds he had recently opened with Credit Suisse and the new equity he had from GA. These sources essentially helped him bail out the Atlantic 57/ Ruhan loans and the loans Haywood had made to effectively fund Greensill itself.

He also tapped Morgan Stanley. The bank for several years had acted as a kind of regulated intermediary between Greensill and the investors in the securities he created. Morgan Stanley provided investors with pricing information and other data about the investments that Greensill sold. Lex turned to the bank again in his moment of need. Morgan Stanley used a special purpose vehicle (SPV) to repackage about £220 million of Greensill-arranged bonds related to Gupta businesses held in the GAM funds. The bank then sold them on to their own clients.

The Panamera assets, backed by lease payments tied to a Russian-owned cargo plane, had been put up for auction by GAM in late 2018. Greensill had surprised GAM's managers by coming up with the highest bid. His plan, apparently, was to take the assets off GAM's books at the same value he'd sold it to them, and then pass it on to another buyer. In reality, after winning the bid, the transaction stalled for eight or nine months as Greensill struggled to find another taker who wasn't put off by the Russian connection.

The most challenging assets to deal with, though, were the Little Red Boxes – the 'LRB' biofuel generators. GAM was sitting on £650 million worth of securities tied to years of cash flows from these boxes, but those cash flows were looking far from certain given the LRBs weren't yet working. Who would be willing to buy assets like this? Lex came up with the answer. He had somehow persuaded Gupta to buy back the LRB bonds.

At GAM, this was cause for optimism, but how could Gupta afford it?

Lex was already working on a new, ambitious Gupta Family Group (GFG) deal. Sanjeev Gupta had been eyeing a group of steel-making assets across Europe. These businesses were owned by the giant Indian steel company ArcelorMittal, which was under pressure from European regulators to sell down part of its business over concerns about competition. There were few buyers. Chinese steel companies had the funding, but they were tough competitors of Mittal. Few other businesses had the scale, funding or appetite to take the facilities on.

Gupta was willing, but he would need funding. The steel businesses would cost €740 million. European regulators demanded that it couldn't all be paid for with debt. Gupta scrambled to grab cash from around the GFG empire, using facilities he owned in Australia and elsewhere to raise more funds there, and then funnelling it into the European acquisition. Europe's regulators were satisfied. Then, having bought the steelmaking facilities – in Romania, and the Czech Republic and elsewhere – for €740 million, Gupta used them to secure €2.2 billion in new loans from Greensill. And with that trick of financial engineering, he had enough to buy back the LRBs from GAM.

As this dizzying alchemy was taking place, Jacob, the temporary GAM CEO, had been sweating on whether Gupta would come through on his new deadline for closing the funds in mid-July.

There was little contact from Gupta or Greensill. In typical Gupta–Greensill style, the deal was arranged informally, not much more than a nod and a handshake. Jacob was getting concerned. He even suggested that if Gupta and Greensill wouldn't hurry up and buy the assets back, then maybe GAM would put them up for sale in the open market. Then the world would decide how much loans to Gupta were really worth.

The sale of the LRBs was dragging on and on with nothing happening. When the money suddenly turned up in the summer of 2019, it was a huge relief, though at first GAM wasn't sure whether to make an announcement. Typically, the buyer sends instructions on how and where to transfer the bonds. But there were no instructions from Greensill or Gupta. It was highly unusual, though it was also typical of the shambolic nature of dealing with Greensill and GFG. Eventually, GAM figured out a way to make the transfer although no instructions ever arrived.

In July 2019, GAM announced that it had finally sold the last of the ARBF assets. In the firm's London office, it was cause for celebration. Greensill and Gupta were finally someone else's problem. Some of the senior investment managers – former colleagues of both Sheard and Haywood – pulled out bottles of champagne and popped the corks into the ceiling of their St James's office.

At Greensill, there was celebrating too. Many of Lex's top executives had thought the GAM affair would bring the company crashing down. The fact it hadn't done so went a long way to helping secure Lex's reputation for always finding a way out of a hole, no matter how deep and dark. For Lex's supporters, his Houdini act only proved Lex's special genius.

# FOURTEEN

# The Swiss Bank

Even before the arrangement with GAM and Tim Haywood had begun blowing up, Lex had already started working on an alternative source of other people's money, and it would dwarf what he got from GAM.

David Solo, the robotic banking guru and Greensill shareholder, had connections running through the core of the Swiss banking world. He introduced Lex to top executives at Credit Suisse, one of the biggest banks on the planet.

Lex rolled out his sales pitch. Supply chain finance was not only a 'fairer' type of banking, it was also safe. The loans were short term, liquid, diversified. They were backed by millions of invoices, flying between thousands of companies, many of them giant, global businesses.

For added safety, the funds could be wrapped in trade credit insurance. It would cost a bit. But even if borrowers defaulted, the investors would still get paid. It was almost too good to be true.

Lex's timing was on the money. In the years after the financial crisis, the biggest banks in the world were undergoing a major strategic upheaval. New regulations had made some old business lines obsolete, inefficient or unprofitable. Uneven rules around the world also tipped the balance so that US investment banks were winning out against banks in Europe, even on their own patch. Ultra-low interest rates set by central banks – a blunt instrument meant to boost economic activity – also tilted business lines in or out of favour, as did emerging technologies. The shifting global balance of economic power, from West to East, played a role too.

Most of the pre-crisis finance giants were going through some kind of overhaul. Credit Suisse was no different. In March 2015, the bank hired the charismatic French-Ivorian executive Tidjane Thiam as its CEO. Thiam was deeply intellectual and a former minister in the government of the Ivory Coast. He was an ultra-bright star of the finance world, with a Bill Clintonesque ability to engage audiences large and small.

Thiam had risen through the ranks at UK insurance giants Aviva and Prudential, which made him a slightly odd choice for CEO of a Swiss bank. He was an outsider, and he came armed with an outsider's perspective on the bank's predicament. He was also frequently blunt and direct.

One of his first aims at Credit Suisse was to rid the bank of a deserved reputation for sleepwalking from one scandal to another under his predecessors. The bank had paid huge fines for missteps, including helping some rich US clients evade taxes and for misselling mortgage securities.

'It's as though you guys have been shitting everywhere,' he told some senior managers shortly after taking over. He extended the metaphor. 'I'm going to clean up all that mess. I'm going to put in new toilets – the best, modern Japanese-style toilets with flashing lights and music. And then your job is to make sure people stop defecating on the floor and start using the toilets.'

His plan was to have a small number of key executives running major business lines, directly accountable to the CEO. It was a highly personalized structure, with Thiam at the summit. Over the next few years, the CEO himself was up way past midnight every evening, poring over daily profit and loss accounts sent from New York. The system was meant to ensure information flowed right to the top, that Thiam would have oversight of everything. But in some cases, it had the opposite effect, with staff fearful of sending problems up the chain. There was a perception that anything unusual, or in which the rewards came with a significant amount of risk, would be stamped on by Thiam. One particularly fraught relationship was with Iqbal Khan, Credit Suisse's wealth management chief. Khan and Thiam clashed frequently, with Thiam trying to curb the wealth management unit's appetite for selling riskier, but potentially higher-yielding, investments to its clients.

Thiam had pledged to shift the focus at Credit Suisse from investment banking to wealth management. But he wanted it to be safe, steady, not taking unnecessary risks. He would tip the balance of the bank's revenue away from dealmaking and one-off transactions towards long-term, repeatable fees. He also encouraged his bankers to target hungry young entrepreneurs, who could amass their own fortunes. The right entrepreneurs were little gold mines, just waiting to be tapped. These people could become a huge source of fees – for private bankers, the smooth-talking schmoozers who act as personal financial planners to the bank's ultra-wealthy clients; and for the investment bankers, who made money from helping to arrange loans and equity investments that new businesses need to keep growing.

Lex Greensill, with his burgeoning finance business, was right in the Credit Suisse sweet spot. Here was an ambitious entrepreneur with a track record of attracting waves of cash. He would be a lucrative personal client; Credit Suisse assigned Shane Galligan, their top private banker in Australia, to look after him. Lex was also building a major business that needed all the usual corporate finance services the bank could provide, such as loans and cash management. Finally, Greensill Capital was growing fast, which meant it was raising money, either privately, or potentially through a big initial public offering (IPO). There were huge advisory fees to be made in meeting Lex's debt and equity fundraising plans. In short, Greensill equalled fees galore for everyone.

There were other factors at play. For one, Galligan, the private banker who personally worked with most of Australia's billionaires, also counted Sanjeev Gupta as a client. The bank had provided Gupta with a mortgage on his A$35 million Sydney mansion. Lex also had on his side a deep inside connection at Credit Suisse. David Solo, the American banker who had been one of Greensill's earliest backers, had become the chairman of Systematic Investment Management AG, a quantitative investment business that was funded by Credit Suisse and which counted on its board Michel Degen, the head of Credit Suisse asset management for Switzerland, Europe, the Middle East and Africa. Solo's link to Degen proved critical in getting Credit Suisse's backing for Greensill. (Systematic Investment Management, known as SIMAG, was supposed to conjure up investment ideas that could survive any market crisis, using physics, complex self-organizing systems, and behavioural science. Instead, it struggled to cope with the turmoil of the global pandemic. In October 2020, Solo left the business and Credit Suisse folded it into another fund.)

There were Greensill sceptics at Credit Suisse, for sure. Bankers who worked with insurance companies that had dealt with Lex had heard of his reputation for pushing the boundaries and for lending to borrowers who defaulted all too often. They knew about what had happened at Tower Trade and Dragon and elsewhere. Others with connections at GAM had heard some of the inside stories about what happened with Haywood and his Greensill investments. Some bankers on the trade finance desk were also well aware of Lex's growing reputation for writing deals that seemed to hide the true nature of the dangers involved or accepting levels of risk that were not compatible with a highly regulated financial institution. Some of them spoke up.

But Greensill – Lex and the business – were too good a fit for the new direction at Credit Suisse. None of the concerns carried enough weight to block the Greensill pitch.

The Swiss bank started with a single Greensill fund in 2017. In a glossy magazine the bank published that year and distributed to its high-net-worth clients, Credit Suisse executives gushed over the promise of supply chain finance. The article, headed 'Good Mood Included', emphasized that these were safe, reliable investments with a broad benefit to investors and corporate clients alike.

SCF funds were 'short-term, low-risk investments that feature attractive returns', according to Luc Mathys, the head of fixed income in Europe, Middle East and Africa. Lukas Haas, the portfolio manager of the funds, said they 'have a term structure similar to low-risk money market instruments.' Eric Varvel, the bank's global head of asset management, wrote about how SCF could help clients of the bank 'gain an edge through this innovative concept', while investors could 'invest their funds on a short-term basis, similar to the money market, and achieve attractive returns.'

The glowing endorsements from some of the most senior bankers didn't end there.

A full-page chart explained 'How Buyers, Suppliers and Investors Benefit'. The benefits apparently included reduced risk of bankruptcy, greater transparency, more liquidity. None of them really turned out to be true. At least not in the case of the Greensill funds.

The article included an example to illustrate how the funds worked.

Imagine a supplier delivers goods valued at $10 million, and sends an invoice to the buyer demanding payment in three months. The buyer approves the invoice to Greensill and provides a promise to pay the $10 million in three months. The supplier then sells the debt it is owed – the trade receivable – to Greensill for $9.9 million, which is paid immediately. Greensill transfers the trade receivable to an SPV that creates and issues a note, which is bought by the SCF fund.

Insurance covers the risk of a default. And after ninety days, the buyer pays the agreed $10 million into the SPV. When the note is due, the SPV pays out to the fund. Bingo.

The magazine even included a full-page photo of Lex, grinning like *Time* magazine's person of the year, in a dark blue suit, crisp white shirt and perfectly knotted crystal-blue tie. His bio included the MBA, the law qualification, his stints at Morgan Stanley and Citi and in the UK government. It also said: 'He advised both Downing Street and the White House on the launch of their own supply chain finance initiatives.'

Lex talked gushingly of democratizing finance, of having small businesses close to his heart, though he also said that clients were typically large multinational companies. The returns on offer are 'hugely attractive', he said, as are 'the short duration and insurance cover of the underlying notes.'

The article said that Greensill Capital had started out with 'a seasoned team of specialists' and had grown to more than 160 staff in London, New York, Chicago, Frankfurt, Sydney and Mexico City. They had loaned more than $25 billion to companies in more than forty countries. What it didn't say was that Greensill Capital at that point had racked up accumulated losses of more than $100 million.

With the full support of the Swiss bank, interest in the funds swelled. The bank, with Greensill, launched another, and another, and eventually a fourth fund. By the end of 2019, there was about $10 billion of client money in Credit Suisse's SCF funds, which all invested exclusively in assets sourced by Greensill. The bank was making tens of millions of dollars in fees, and the claims that Mathys, Haas, Varvel and Lex himself made in the glossy magazine were echoed in marketing materials distributed to potential clients too.

Credit Suisse fact sheets scored the funds as a 1 or 2 on a scale of 1 to 7, where 1 is the safest. The fact sheets said that investors could withdraw their money weekly or monthly, depending on the fund, with just a few days' notice. The larger funds that mostly stuck to investment-grade borrowers – big, safe companies that were very unlikely to default – offered a meagre return of 0.8 per cent to 1.5 per cent more than the benchmark short-term interest rates, while a so-called 'high income' fund that worked with riskier borrowers offered returns of 3.5 per cent above the benchmark.

More marketing materials that Credit Suisse bankers shared with potential investors said the funds had 'multiple layers of protection', with the investments secured by claims against the borrower and in some cases guaranteed by a broad group of insurance companies.

A promotional document said that 'all the supply chain programs [sic] undergo a rigorous onboarding process including legal and risk checks', and that the investments 'have to meet predetermined criteria concerning e.g., credit risk . . . otherwise the trades are rejected by the portfolio manager.'

There were risks – the funds 'may at certain times have a relatively high exposure to a small number of obligors' and 'there is no guarantee that either the obligor or the associated insurance contract pays in full and on time.'

But several pages of charts with dotted lines and arrows flying back and forth tying SPVs to underlying obligations indicated to any reader that Credit Suisse and Greensill were smart. Greensill, the document points out, was backed by giant, global investors. Investors could get their money back with just a few days' notice. What could possibly go wrong?

IN INTERVIEW AFTER interview, Credit Suisse executives were always clear that the funds were only ever sold to qualified investors – conjuring up the image of sophisticated pension funds or sovereign wealth funds with armies of accountants and experts managing money on behalf of an entire company or country. Or super-wealthy individuals who can afford to hire the best advisers, and who ought to know what they're getting into. Some of the investors in the Credit

Suisse funds even took a long hard look at Greensill itself, spending months combing over its accounts and business practices before committing to the funds. So sympathy was likely to be in short supply for this group of clients. If the funds they invested in got into trouble, well, they would only have themselves to blame.

But the reality was different. Many of the investors in the funds were not sophisticated and didn't have the resources to carry out their own detailed due diligence. Few of them could possibly have understood the risks inherent in the insurance arrangements of the funds or the true nature of some of the underlying borrowers.

Some pension funds, especially smaller ones, are staffed by accountants who don't have specialist expertise in complex financial instruments. They rely on outside advisers – including their bankers – to help them wade through a confusing landscape of legal and financial chicanery. Greensill's web of SPVs and insurance contracts was nothing if not complex. Several big pension funds and institutional investors refused to put money into Greensill investments on those grounds alone – reams and reams of complex legal documentation just to make a few basis points more than you'd get from keeping your money in cash? It just wasn't worth the hassle, or the risk that there was something hidden deep in the legalese jargon.

The bank's individual private clients are heavily reliant on the advice they get from their expert banker to make those sorts of decisions. These people are not always financially sophisticated, even if they've personally made a lot of money. Some of these investors may be entrepreneurs who have run complex businesses. But there are plenty of others who have inherited their money or earned it in a world far from finance.

While some of the investors were certainly big institutions, most investors on average had a stake closer to just a few million dollars. These are still large sums to ordinary people. But an investor with a few million dollars could be a small-time entrepreneur, or might have inherited a windfall, or they could have sold a property in

London or Paris and need somewhere safe to park the funds for a few weeks. It is unlikely people like this would have their own team of super-charged financial experts poring over every detail of Greensill, the underlying obligors, or the minutiae of the relevant trade credit insurance documents. They relied on their private banker for that.

Many of these people are looking for somewhere to preserve their savings and come to a bank like Credit Suisse precisely because they are seeking good advice. Often, they have been introduced by a friend or business associate to a private banker over dinner at a nice restaurant. Sometimes, they're invited to the banker's home. The banker talks about the Swiss bank's funds and asks questions about the prospective client's investing 'style'.

The Middle East became a key market for selling the Greensill funds. Credit Suisse has an extensive network of private bankers in the region. Some of those clients were persuaded to take out loans to generate bigger returns for their stake in the funds. Sometimes they were told to borrow as much as 60 per cent more than they had invested in cash. Wealthy clients of the bank can borrow money at a low interest rate and invest it into a fund that pays a slightly higher rate. That way they're effectively getting paid for nothing, though if the investments go bad, they're on the hook for their own investment plus the total of the loan. It's a way to juice the potential reward, though at some considerable risk.

There were, the bank told clients, three layers of protection. First, the investments were backed by actual receivables payments, meaning that there was something tangible to hang the loans on. Second, there was due diligence on the obligors, to ensure they were sound businesses able to pay back the money they received. And third, there was trade credit insurance that would pay out in the event of a default. What's more, all these loans were very short term, another sign that they were relatively safe compared to other investments.

With such a safe investment, a client could be persuaded to put all their cash and similar investments into the funds.

But clients who read through the marketing materials could miss the role of Greensill, might fail to grasp that Greensill was the policy-holder on the crucial trade credit insurance, and not understand that Credit Suisse was doing very little due diligence of its own on the loans it was making, or on the businesses of the underlying obligors.

Investors could hardly have known that Credit Suisse had dele-gated practically all the decisions related to the funds to Greensill. They couldn't know that Greensill was taking their money and making long-term loans to speculative businesses. There was little to indicate that most of the trade credit insurance – billed as a crucial protection for investors – was sourced from a single, small Australian insurance provider courted by Lex himself.

From the investors' perspective, they put their money into Credit Suisse funds. In reality, they'd invested in Greensill funds that hid behind a credible Swiss veneer.

For a while, the funds performed as advertised. Until it all went wrong.

FIFTEEN

# Hodor

The first time I heard Lex Greensill's name was in January 2019. I was a senior editor at Dow Jones, owner of *The Wall Street Journal* and a London-based banking publication called *Financial News*. I didn't edit much and I did even less reporting. Mostly I 'strategized': trying to come up with ideas to improve our journalism and increase our readership.

A long-time source called me out of the blue. The source had something confidential to share and wanted to meet.

I worked with a lot of great reporters at the *Journal*. They were typically tenacious and incredibly thick-skinned. They badgered sources into submission. My style was a bit different. I didn't push sources very hard. I got on their side. I probably missed stories because of this approach. This was one of the rare occasions where my more subtle style paid off.

The source – an experienced executive who asked that I never use their name in public – had information about a scandal that had been bubbling for months in the financial press. We met for a walk on a windy morning on Primrose Hill in north London.

I knew that Swiss-based firm Global Asset Management Holding was in trouble. GAM was not a household name, but it looked after tens of billions of dollars for clients – big pension funds and super-wealthy individuals. I also knew that GAM had suspended one of its star employees, the high-flying City executive Tim Haywood, after a whistle-blower had made allegations about his behaviour. The suspension had spooked investors and GAM had been forced to close the fund. Shareholders had dumped GAM's shares. The company's CEO had been pushed out, and its general counsel and other executives had also gone.

All of that was well known in financial circles. But my source promised proof that GAM's hand had been forced by the Financial Conduct Authority (FCA), the UK's top financial regulator. The source showed me email correspondence that backed up this claim. GAM had shared details of its investigation into the whistle-blower's allegations with the FCA, and the regulator had been so concerned about Haywood's conduct and some of his investments that it demanded tough action. The information seemed less exciting to me than to the source. But what really piqued my interest was that all the investments at the centre of the affair were in assets generated by a little-known start-up finance firm called Greensill Capital.

I wasn't sure whether anyone would care too much about the FCA's role in pushing GAM's hand. After all, given the nature of the allegations against Haywood, it seemed logical that they should ask for tough action. Nevertheless, this was new information about an ongoing major scandal. Haywood and some of his colleagues at GAM were fairly media savvy, and there was a narrative that the whistle-blower was an embittered rival, and that GAM's executives had been hasty, pedantic, imperilling the firm over a couple of technical missteps. That wasn't what the correspondence I had seen indicated at all. And then there was Greensill.

I decided to write something up in *Financial News*. Before we published, in mid-February, I called Greensill's public relations executive, a New York-based former journalist named James Doran, to see if he wanted to comment. It was the start of a tumultuous relationship. Barrel-chested and over six feet tall, with short red hair and a goatee beard, Doran was a bombastic and erratic combatant. He had worked at *The Times* as Wall Street bureau chief, at *Scotland on Sunday* and at a Dubai-based paper called *The National*. Several of my colleagues and journalism friends knew him, and they all had stories to tell. He was widely known as a newsroom bully, who frequently yelled at junior reporters and had reduced colleagues to tears on many occasions. He also had a reputation for pushing the envelope on stories – several journalists I knew jokingly referred to him as 'The Fiction Editor' because, allegedly, he had a flexible approach to reported facts.

My first interaction with Doran was fractious. 'Why were we mentioning Greensill?' he barked down the phone. 'This was GAM's problem, not Greensill's.' I told him I could note in the story if he didn't want to comment and we moved on.

It might have ended at that point. But the story about the regulator forcing GAM's hand struck a chord with a certain cohort of readers. Other sources came out of the woodwork. One proved to be critical to the next couple of years of my life, a crucial source with detailed information about Greensill. The source wanted to know about the correspondence I'd seen between GAM and the FCA. I was careful in what I shared. Just enough to keep the conversation going, but not so much that I might compromise my arrangement with the person who had shown me the correspondence in the first place. By the end of an hour or so, I had established a terrific sourcing relationship, the best of my career. With this help, I began digging deeper and deeper into Greensill. I cracked a couple of other key source connections and started to build a picture of this hot new finance company that had brought a significant financial player, GAM, to its knees. And I began work on a story about Greensill itself.

From the start, I had been asking Doran for a meeting with Lex.

I repeated the request every few days. He usually replied that he would set something up, some time far into the future. By late March, my story was coming together. I had details about Lex's background, his time at Morgan Stanley and Citigroup, and the founding of Greensill Capital. The picture that emerged was of an aggressive, impatient risk-taker, who had some success at the banks but ultimately didn't fit into their highly regulated, bureaucratic confines. His business, Greensill, had almost collapsed until he formed a relationship with Haywood, who had used money from GAM's investors to prop it up.

At Dow Jones, our practice is that we run critical details of our stories past people we are going to mention before publication. The idea is that they get a chance to tell us their side. It's called the 'no surprises rule'. When I went to Doran, in early April, with the key details about my story, all hell broke loose.

I knew a lot about Lex at this stage. But what I didn't know was that Greensill was already deep into talks with the SoftBank Vision Fund, a mammoth $100 billion pool of investor cash tied to Japanese conglomerate SoftBank Group. The Vision Fund was shaking up the rules when it came to investing in new tech companies. Its sheer size meant it could outbid just about anyone. And its core approach was to buy huge stakes in lots of fast-growing companies, knowing that some would be duds and some would pay off big time. Typically, they made decisions fast, and in poured the money.

Vision Fund analysts had identified Greensill as a potential investment in early March and were already quickly moving towards a decision on whether to invest.

By the time I went to Doran with my list of questions, I was in a race against time. I just didn't know it. Doran, Lex and the inner circle at the top of Greensill – including legal counsel Jonathan Lane – had one aim: to delay my story coming out until after they'd secured funding from SoftBank.

Their approach was not subtle. First, Doran called me in

mid-April. I took his call in one of the soundproof booths in our office near London Bridge, next to the Shard. Doran was at rage level ten, screaming at me down the phone. I was unprofessional, he said. I was listening to disgruntled employees who shouldn't be talking. I was on shaky legal ground and they would hit me with a lawsuit.

His arguments were scattergun and misdirected. There was no legitimate way he could know who I was talking to. If anything, his aggressive approach – and the weakness of his counterarguments – indicated I was on to something. The last thing Doran and Lex Greensill seemed to want was anyone sniffing around their business.

I was confident in my reporting and stood my ground. Next, I sent Doran all the information about Lex we planned to publish. This was late April. The response came from Jonathan Lane. An emailed letter to Dow Jones's lawyers accused me of being vindictive and driving a false narrative about Greensill. It threatened further legal action if we went ahead with our story and said that I was unprofessional to run a story on Lex without talking to him. This was maddening. I'd been asking for a meeting with him for weeks. But I agreed with our lawyers we'd hold off if Lex would talk with us within a few days. Doran promised to set it up.

Days passed, and there was no meeting. What followed was a game of cat and mouse. Doran would set a date for a call with Lex, and when the date rolled round a few days later, Lex would be unavailable, too busy, in the wrong time zone. And then the cycle would start all over again. A date with Lex was booked then cancelled several times. In early May, we decided to push out the story. We had given Greensill plenty of time. We gave them a final hard deadline for Lex to talk. If it was so important to him and our story was so wrong, then surely he could talk. That's when Greensill pulled out the big guns. They sent a threatening letter from Schillings, the lawyers who represented privacy cases for the likes of disgraced cyclist Lance Armstrong and controversial retail tycoon Philip Green. It was a supremely aggressive missive, but also seemed to be full of misunderstandings about what we planned to publish. Perhaps that reflected what Lex and Doran had told Schillings, or maybe it was a kind of public relations misdirection strategy that was beyond my understanding. It held us up again.

However, by this time, our lawyers were emboldened as I'd walked them through every inch of the story. We finally decided to hit publish. The story landed on the front page of *Financial News* on Monday 6 May 2019. There was not a single call from Doran or Schillings or Lane or Lex. Not a single correction. The story was one of our best-read articles for months. It was flying around social media. I had won. At least, that's what I thought.

The real celebrations were in Greensill's offices across London on the Strand. In truth, I'd lost the race I didn't know I had entered. SoftBank's Vision Fund had wrapped up its incredibly fast due diligence process only a few days earlier. My victory lasted barely a week before Greensill announced it had secured a gargantuan $800 million investment from the Vision Fund. Later, Doran told colleagues that he was the most valuable employee at the firm because he had held back my story until after the Vision Fund was committed to Greensill. He compared himself to Hodor, a character in the HBO TV series *Game of Thrones*, who holds back a massive wooden door to prevent demons from getting through. Though, in the end, Hodor is consumed by the demons.

# SIXTEEN

# The Vision Fund

General Atlantic's investment in Greensill had put Lex on the radar of SoftBank Group Corp's Vision Fund, one of the biggest guns of global investing. It's a rule of high finance that if one big financial firm does a deal, others will probably assume that their rivals did their work properly and follow suit.

Masayoshi Son, the CEO of giant Japanese conglomerate Soft-Bank, had launched the $100 billion Vision Fund in 2017. He staked about $28 billion of SoftBank's own money; Saudi Arabia's sovereign wealth fund put up another $35 billion and about $15 billion came from Mubadala Investment Company, Abu Dhabi's wealth fund. The rest came from a collection of businesses and major global investors. Within a few months, the Vision Fund became the most powerful technology investor in the world.

At its head was a former Deutsche Bank executive named Rajeev Misra. Raised in Delhi, Misra studied at the Massachusetts Institute of Technology before embarking on a career on Wall Street. At Deutsche Bank, he had run a team of credit traders who profited from the crash in the US sub-prime mortgage market. He had developed a strong personal bond with Masayoshi Son since 2006, when he raised $16 billion in debt SoftBank needed for a large acquisition – the deal had helped make the SoftBank CEO a multibillionaire.

Misra joined SoftBank in 2014. His rise to the top of the Vision Fund was described in scintillating detail by my former colleagues at *The Wall Street Journal* in an article that alleged Misra employed a series of dirty tricks to undermine his rivals for the role. Misra and SoftBank denied the allegations.

The Vision Fund chief certainly has an unusual style. It is well known that he shuffles around his office in London's glamorous Mayfair district in bare feet, playing with strings of beads while encouraging his team to make hundreds of investments, often betting enormous sums on a chosen start-up at lightning pace. Sometimes the approach pays off. Sometimes it doesn't.

A report by an external consultant in 2018 found that there were few controls at the Vision Fund and staff were encouraged to gamble with the fund's money to enhance their own personal reputations. That culture has delivered a patchy track record. The fund has made billions from investments in cab service Uber and food delivery company Doordash. Its investment in WeWork, however, was a spectacular dud. SoftBank invested about $18.5 billion in WeWork. Then in 2019 the shared office business imploded when it was forced to drop a planned public offering of its shares after investors balked at its valuation and the antics of its flamboyant CEO Adam Neumann.

Meanwhile, Greensill's profile was rising after the General Atlantic investment.

In mid-March 2019, some junior Vision Fund executives working for Misra had their first brief meetings with Lex in New York and then with David Solo in San Francisco. On 26 March, the SoftBank team met with Greensill again. This time, it was a full day of talks with Lex, David Cameron and other members of the Greensill management team in London. The team liked what they found. They reported to Misra that Lex Greensill was worth his attention.

At first Misra was sceptical. He had seen Greensill's name mentioned in stories about what was happening at GAM, whose headquarters were just around the corner from the Vision Fund office. He was wary of investing in a company that was entangled in an ongoing financial affair. There were plenty of other businesses to go after. Why invest money, or time, in one that was already caught up in scandal? He didn't need the hassle. His team argued the GAM affair would pass and leave no lasting impact on Greensill. Greensill would survive and move on, a better company. They could also take some comfort that General Atlantic was already on board. Surely GA wouldn't have backed Greensill if there was any deeper impropriety?

Misra agreed to meet Lex in person.

A few days later, on Thursday 28 March, Lex came to the Vision Fund office. For Lex, this was a huge opportunity. Given the Vision Fund's reputation for largesse, this was a chance to seal an enormous funding round. Having GA on board brought credibility and helped clear some of the problem loans. Having the Vision Fund invest would make Lex and his brother Peter and some of the others extraordinarily rich.

He came to the meeting flanked by his chief of staff, Daniel Shuttleworth, and Bart Ras, a Dutch trade finance specialist who'd joined the firm in 2016 and was evangelical about supply chain finance. Neither was a heavy hitter. Ras and Shuttleworth were the chorus line. This was Lex's show.

The pitch was well honed. Lex retold his engaging personal tale, about his childhood on the farm near Bundaberg and his parents' problems with late payments. He preached the magic of supply chain financing. He talked about an NHS payments scheme that helped pharmaceutical supplies run more efficiently through the system. He outlined his plans to fund workers getting their salaries paid early too.

Misra was impressed. Like GA, the Vision Fund had looked at other supply chain finance firms. There was a compelling case for the entire sector. Greensill was the market leader. But the GAM issue still nagged. Misra bluntly quizzed Lex. Is this GAM problem going to come back to Greensill? No, said Lex. It's an internal GAM matter. Do I have your word that there is no way this comes back to Greensill, asked Misra. Yes, said Lex, you have my word. Misra was on board.

Lex's response to the direct questioning on GAM was beyond optimistic. Despite what he told the Vision Fund chief, Greensill lay at the heart of the scandal at GAM. Lex's firm wasn't some innocent bystander caught up in another company's affair. Greensill was the crux of the affair. But his responses to Misra, who held the key to vast riches, worked.

The following Thursday, Lex Greensill and David Cameron flew halfway round the planet to Tokyo. They bundled themselves into waiting cars and zipped across the city to SoftBank's imposing head-quarters. If the first meeting with Misra had got Lex officially in the door, then this meeting, in Japan, was critical. There were some of the same Vision Fund staff they'd met with before. But critically, Lex and Cameron also met with SoftBank CEO Masayoshi Son himself.

Son is one of the most powerful, and unconventional, investors in the world. He encourages the Vision Fund to invest huge sums of money on companies, so long as they can promise to shoot for the moon. He also compensates his top executives handsomely. Many of the senior lieutenants in SoftBank earn tens of millions of dollars a year. He wants them to identify fast-growing markets or industries, and then invest in the biggest, best or most aggressive businesses in that market. Often, Son invests more money than the start-up com-panies said they needed.

Cameron's role at the Tokyo meeting was mainly ornamental. He didn't contribute much detail about supply chain finance or deal terms. But he spoke passionately about the vision for Greensill. The company's future was exciting. It planned to change the way finance happened around the world.

Lex delivered his finely tuned pitch once more. He came across as ambitious, determined, a disruptor who would change banking for ever. He wasn't content with running a few billion dollars of supply chain finance programmes. Lex wanted to finance every single receivable in the world.

This was exactly what Masayoshi Son wanted to hear. Greensill was dealing with $31 billion worth of transactions already, but it could be handling $385 billion in just a few years. Revenue was $204 million today. It could be $2 billion by 2025. This was exponential growth.

The Japanese billionaire was impressed. This kind of business, this kind of growth, was exactly why the Vision Fund had been created.

Over the next few weeks, Vision Fund executives met with Greensill four more times. They had dinner with Lex and Gabe Caillaux from General Atlantic. Vision Fund people called several of Greensill's clients and major partners.

A SoftBank lawyer talked to GAM's new management regime, including the interim CEO David Jacob. The SoftBank lawyer reported back that – as far as they could tell – there was no risk of any blowback to Greensill. Greensill executives were not accused of wrongdoing and appeared to have no knowledge of ex-GAM portfolio manager Tim Haywood's activities. The lawyer also echoed a line that Lex frequently offered up – that none of GAM's investors lost money on the Greensill assets. This was an incredibly narrow assessment.

The Vision Fund spoke to Credit Suisse. The Japanese conglomerate was a lucrative client of the Swiss bank. Credit Suisse had worked as a financial adviser to the Vision Fund, helping to raise funds for some of its portfolio companies, including through an initial public offering (IPO). Masayoshi Son had also borrowed from Credit Suisse for decades, pledging his shares in SoftBank as collateral for billions of dollars of loans. Credit Suisse's Michel Degen endorsed Greensill wholeheartedly. The bank had about $4 billion of client money invested in Greensill's loans. They were planning on pitching to more clients in Asia and across Europe soon. They expected the funds to grow to $10 billion in a few years, maybe $15 billion.

SoftBank also spoke with Sanjeev Gupta. Greensill is exceptional, he told the SoftBank team. They're faster and more innovative than the banks. They're more expensive, but they are far more efficient and responsive to the needs of GFG. Gupta's response was hugely supportive of Greensill. Of course it was.

SoftBank spoke with a couple of dozen partners, clients, investors and others who worked with Greensill. But what struck me later was that nobody from the Vision Fund talked to Sheard, the whistleblower, or to Friedman, the former GAM CEO. They had not looked at the underlying assets that were at the heart of GAM's demise. They did not talk to the company that was by far Greensill's biggest insurance provider. They did not speak with some of Greensill's biggest customers, who were the company's main sources of revenue. These omissions are striking. SoftBank's research missed several key Greensill relationships that turned out to be major problems.

Whereas GA had courted Lex for years, the Vision Fund team made their decision at typically lightning speed. The outcome was the same. From start to finish, it had taken about eight weeks for the Vision Fund to decide to invest $800 million into Lex's business. A press release said the money was going to be invested in new technologies and to expand in emerging markets. But that wasn't really true. Lex immediately sent about $400 million to build up Greensill Bank's balance sheet. About $135 million would support initiatives in new geographical markets, or to acquire new businesses or develop technology. The rest would be used to buy shares from existing investors. For that, the Vision Fund got about 22 per cent of the company – Greensill was now valued at about $3.5 billion. Lex and his brother Peter owned more than a third of the shares, and they'd just become billionaires, at least on paper.

FOR THE NEXT few months, Lex's star shone brightly. He became a kind of finance start-up celebrity, a regular guest on business news television shows. He cultivated a relationship with Sky television's Ian King and with Sky News business reporter Mark Kleinman.

More importantly, he cultivated a personal connection to Masayoshi Son. SoftBank insiders felt Lex was spending more time with Masa than just about anyone else. The Australian followed his new mentor to Washington DC, Jakarta, Tokyo . . . just about wherever he went. He was like Son's shadow. The two talked most days by phone. And while everyone else referred to him as Masa, Lex insisted on the more formal 'Son-san' because, he said, it was disrespectful to call him Masa.

On a Vision Fund web page, Greensill said Masa was a 'partner and a mentor': 'He has worked with us, and particularly with me, to think about our core business and how we can actually take that core business and tackle other inequalities and other challenges that exist in the global market.'

The appreciation went in both directions. At internal SoftBank events, Son put Lex on a pedestal alongside other stars of the Vision Fund, especially WeWork founder Adam Neumann, who was still then in favour, and Ritesh Agarwal, the head of India's OYO Hotels. The three were featured in a presentation to SoftBank shareholders that referred to them as pioneers of artificial intelligence leading 'the biggest revolution in human history'.

Son also pointed to Greensill as an example of how portfolio companies could benefit from the network effect they could achieve by working together – the so-called 'Cluster of No. 1' strategy. Vision Fund insiders found that Greensill's name was frequently invoked by Son in meetings, often as a solution to financing problems at other portfolio companies. A Vision Fund company needed more cash? Greensill can get it. A portfolio company has trouble in its supply chain? Greensill will make it more efficient.

Lex's unrestrained ambition also played to Masa's most fanciful projects. One plan, nicknamed Project Olympus, involved lending billions of dollars to WeWork. *Wall Street Journal* reporters Eliot Brown and Maureen Farrell described what happened next in their book on WeWork, *The Cult of We*. According to their version of events, Son had asked WeWork CEO Neumann to fly to Tokyo for a meeting in August 2019. Neumann thought Son might ask him to call off the planned WeWork IPO – which was looking tougher every day – or offer to make a large investment. But he was taken by surprise when Son instead introduced Lex Greensill, touting him as the solution to WeWork's pending cash crunch. The WeWork CEO and his team were immediately sceptical that Greensill could really provide the funds, and they were concerned about potential conflicts of interest, given SoftBank's recent investment in Greensill. Neumann and his staff mockingly referred to Lex as 'Lex Luthor'; he refused the offer of Greensill's help.

By then, Greensill had quite clearly become the most favoured of Masa's flock of tech founders. In October 2019, just a few months after its first investment in Greensill, the Vision Fund poured another $655 million into the firm. Colin Fan, a former Deutsche Bank executive who was the SoftBank lead on the Greensill investment, said in a press release that Greensill was 'transforming global business access to working capital through its innovative business model.'

This time around, almost all the Vision Fund financing went to pay out existing shareholders. Lex and his brother Peter were the biggest beneficiaries. But others had hit the jackpot too. Lex told some of his staff that one early employee who had since left the firm was demanding Greensill pay out on about $100 million worth of shares. Lex said he paid the money, but only after extracting a fee of about 13 per cent, or $13 million.

Lex boasted frequently of his closeness to Masa. In November 2019, SoftBank held a conference for CFOs and CEOs of Vision Fund portfolio companies at The Ritz-Carlton hotel in Half Moon Bay, California. Greensill was treated like a guest of honour, and at one point he was invited on stage to provide lessons about finance to the other attendees. He also told associates there that Masa was personally mentoring him.

Not everyone at the Vision Fund was impressed. Some considered him arrogant. He was also racking up huge costs. Greensill was hiring rapidly, and it wasn't always clear why. Over the next twelve months or so, staff levels doubled to about 1,000. He was also one of only two portfolio company founders who were thought to have their own private jets. The other was Adam Neumann. But whereas Neumann was renowned for smoking marijuana and partying on board his jet, as *The Wall Street Journal* had reported in September 2019, you were more likely to get English tea and dry business talk on Greensill's planes. He was all flash without the fun.

In early 2020, though, Lex's reputation was still soaring. At the World Economic Forum in Davos that January, he was frequently by Masa's side, as the Japanese tech titan met with world leaders. Lex had arrived at Davos without proper winter footwear – a no-no on the slippery streets, where the footsteps of the global elite turn the snow and ice into a skating rink. Lex got his personal assistant to buy dozens of pairs of snow-worthy shoes and bring them to David Solo's Davos apartment, where Lex was staying for the duration of the conference. Too busy to visit a shoe shop, Lex effectively had his assistant bring the shop to him. He spent the rest of the week riding on Masa's coat-tails and following David Cameron around.

The next month, he followed Son to Jakarta. Masa was working on one of his grandest plans yet, to finance the construction of an entirely new capital for Indonesia. He had announced the project the previous summer. It would involve building a new city on a site in a sparsely populated region of Borneo. The city would boast futuristic educational establishments, medical facilities and transport systems. It would be four times the size of the current capital, Jakarta, which is polluted, congested with traffic, and sinking because of the over-extraction of groundwater.

The new capital would be super-wired for new tech, and citizens would pay a subscription to live there. And the whole thing would be financed by Lex Greensill.

Lex was the 'money guy', Son told Indonesia's president Joko Widodo, according to local TV footage. In front of other SoftBank executives, Masa asked Lex directly about his capacity to pay for the plans. Are you good for $100 billion on the new Indonesia capital? Yes, I'm good for $100 billion, Lex replied. Then he turned to Eric Varvel, the head of wealth management at Credit Suisse, who was also in attendance. Are we good for the money? Yes, said Varvel, if Greensill can arrange the deal, Credit Suisse would place $100 billion with its clients. For Masa, the new capital fantasy would be a reality built with Lex's money.

Masa Son was Lex's latest and most effective mentor. He followed in the footsteps of the likes of Robert Cleland at OzEcom, David Brierwood at Morgan Stanley, Jeremy Heywood in the UK government. Yet, within just a few months, the relationship would almost completely collapse.

# SEVENTEEN

# Lex and Me

I first met Lex on a windy day in September 2019. By then, he was a billionaire and I was an annoying journalist who kept writing stories that pointed out odd conflicts of interest and other problems with Greensill Capital. He told some of the senior executives at Greensill that he hated me because I had it in for him. In truth, I just thought there was something interesting going on at Greensill. Greensill seemed like a company that was either going to be massive one day, or was going to blow up.

Almost every time I asked James Doran or Credit Suisse or anyone to do with Greensill a tough question, the answer either didn't make sense, contradicted an earlier answer, or was provably false. And so I kept on asking.

That first meeting was arranged by Lex's external 'flak' – what journalists call PR advisers, because they are hit with all the missiles thrown by reporters. The flak had thought it would be a good idea for us to have a one-to-one connection. Maybe, in person, Lex would see that I didn't have a vendetta. And maybe, in person, I would get a better understanding of the magic that had bewitched so many more important people. I had certainly been trying to talk to Lex for months, so I agreed immediately.

Greensill's office is on the Strand, more or less opposite the Savoy hotel. It's a quintessentially London location for a business headquarters. At least, it would be if you had missed the past four or five decades. Most financial firms are in the City or Canary Wharf. Mayfair – with all its Michelin stars and cool bars – is the premium choice for hedge funds. The hottest new tech start-ups are in converted warehouses or co-working spaces in Shoreditch, surrounded by hipster coffee shops. Greensill, which aspires to be something like all these types of businesses, is located in one of the most touristy, most uncool parts of central London.

I was very keen to see inside the infamous Greensill office. I had heard it looked like a cross between a stuffy London gentlemen's club and a medieval theme park, with dark wood, leather chairs, Old Masters in baroque gold-leaf frames, and even a suit of armour on display. But I was to be disappointed. By the time I got there, Lex had completely refurbished. It was a bland corporate office with off-white walls and conventional furnishing. It was exceptionally quiet. The only decor of note was a framed copy of Lex's CBE certificate. Later, I heard that Lex had caught wind of people mocking the office's former look and ordered a change. He'd also decided that Greensill's branding should be fintech, not investment bank, so the medieval armour had to go.

My meeting got off to a bad start. The bombastic former journalist James Doran changed the rules of engagement at the last minute. The meeting had been billed as 'on the record', meaning I could publish everything Lex said, but Doran decided he wanted to make it completely off the record. It was a lame stunt. I was already in the room and Doran knew that it would be hard for me to walk away.

I'd had several run-ins with Greensill and Doran already. The whole 'Hodor' incident – when Doran had held back my story until after the Vision Fund had committed to Greensill – was still fresh in my mind. Another time, Doran, myself and a colleague of mine who had known him for years met for a coffee in Pret a Manger on Borough High Street. Doran had been visiting our office with Lex, who had been interviewed by Sky TV's Ian King, whose studio was in the same building as our office. I spotted Doran on the way out of the office and persuaded him to come for a coffee with us. It started out amicably enough – some small talk, a few questions about the TV interview. But when I asked him slightly more probing questions about the SoftBank investment, Doran started yelling at the top of his voice in the busy fast-food restaurant, accusing me of being unprofessional and threatening that I had to stop challenging the company if I didn't want to ruin my career. I looked at my colleague, who seemed to be in a state of bemused shock. I asked Doran if he still wanted the coffee. It was a surreal moment when I didn't know whether to laugh or leave. In the end, we sat down for an awkward thirty-minute chat.

In the meeting at Greensill's office on the Strand, we negotiated a truce of sorts. We could talk on background but determine later what was on the record. In the end, I sent a transcript back to Doran and told him I considered it was all on the record – I figured he was too lazy to go through it in fine detail at that stage. That turned out to be a good assumption, as he agreed to my terms, and I ended up with two hours of Lex on Lex.

The Australian financier began with the same story I'd heard many times about growing up on the farm. There were a few details other journalists hadn't reported, but it was the traditional backstory.

He talked about OzEcom. 'I went and worked in a start-up company that tried to do what we now call supply chain finance [SCF] and that company went bust. I was just an employee. I did actually put A$250,000 of my own money in, and I lost it all, which I have to say was really quite painful. But also that pain meant that I was like a dog with a bone and I didn't want to let it slip.'

He was friendly enough, and talked in a measured manner, frequently repeating my name. 'What you have to understand,

Duncan . . . you see, Duncan . . . And then, Duncan . . .' It came across like a crass attempt to appear charming. It seemed to me more like someone trying too hard to impose their control over the conversation. My sources who knew Lex described him in almost equal measure as impressive and charismatic, or false and superficial. Some of them say he's a pathological liar. I definitely didn't find him charismatic.

He also used a strange kind of pseudo-banker-speak, mixed with the kind of phrases an executive at a hip technology firm might use. It felt learned, studied, as if he was trying too hard. For instance, when he talked about his early banking career, he said, 'I thought Morgan Stanley was a way cooler brand than Rothschild, so I picked Morgan Stanley's bid.' Citigroup, he said, were 'the big gorillas in the space.'

He also backtracked entirely on points that had come up in my earlier reporting. For instance, when funding dried up for the SCF programme at Morgan Stanley, he now said, 'Fortunately, and you raised it in one of your articles, Morgan Stanley's bank in Utah, and this was perfectly within their authorizations to do, said, "We've got this, we'll do this, we've been looking for things that are compliant with the bank rules to be able to buy", and so they funded the programme but, at the same time, they basically said, "Guys you need to find a better way to finance your business."'

When I'd tried to publish that a few months earlier, Greensill had said it wasn't true, as had Morgan Stanley.

Despite the quirks, and the backflips, he did seem refreshingly honest about the early years of Greensill Capital. The plan after leaving Citi, he said, was to try a version of OzEcom back in Australia, focused on farmers, and expand from there. It was tough going.

'We didn't have big backers. We didn't have banks providing us with a balance sheet or anything like that when we started, so consequently we needed to pay the bills, and we did business with companies that were of a poorer credit rating . . . The truth is in growing our business we screwed up a few times.'

Lex talked about the shock of finding 'crappier' companies that 'are quite happy to screw you.'

He also said something that struck me as odd. 'When you look at our financial statements, you will see that we took a number of hits [but] if you removed our credit losses . . . we have always been profitable at an operating level.' That was like saying, we were always profitable, except for our losses. Was this the kind of charismatic sales talk that so many smart people had bought into?

He told me about how much he personally had on the line.

'I am considered the controlling shareholder [of Greensill Bank]. Each year, I have to freshly sign a guarantee to the German Deposit Protection Authority for 100 per cent of the deposits, personally, in the event that they ever have to pay out under the deposit protection insurance . . . So trust me, I quite like living in the house that I live in and I like driving the car that I drive.'

Lex even told me that he agreed with the critics of SCF who said it was a way for big corporations to hide the true extent of their borrowings.

'It's an odd thing to me that rating agencies have ever said that somehow a trade obligation is somehow different to money you borrowed from a bank, or from a bondholder. That's insane; it's still a dollar that you owe someone.'

It was an extraordinary admission that seemed to run counter to the rationale for recent years of rapid growth in SCF. He went on.

'Saying that because you owe it to a supplier, somehow that's not really a debt is, frankly, a nonsense . . . but so long as rating agencies want to maintain the fiction that a real trade creditor that is not supported by some special supply chain finance promise that's being made to a bank is non-debt, then companies are going to want to make use of that.'

OK, so it's a nonsense, but you can make money out of it.

Lex made some astonishing claims: 2.3 million companies relied on Greensill every day; Greensill funds the receivables on 51 per cent of all containerized seaborne freight in the world. These claims and others were incredibly hard to prove.

Eventually, we got to more challenging ground.

I pushed Lex on the loans to a series of odd clients – companies like Tower Trade and Atlantic 57 Consultancy, which had received tens of millions of dollars from funds that Greensill managed. Even a cursory look through their accounts would tell you that some of these companies had next to no ability to pay those loans back. Many of them also had personal connections to Lex. I asked him at length about Sanjeev Gupta.

At first, Lex brushed aside my questions. 'We can't talk about clients.' But the more I probed, the more tense the meeting became.

Lex was agitated. He said I was torturing him with the questions. He and James Doran insisted that it was unfair to ask about facts that I only knew about because they were more transparent than other providers of SCF, though I pointed out that they had to be more transparent because they were selling their SCF programme through regulated funds that were sold to investors.

Eventually, it was clear that no real answers were forthcoming. Lex's face reddened and he slammed his fist on the table. 'There's nothing wrong with doing business with friends,' he spat out. 'If you're going to keep insinuating otherwise, then this meeting is over.' He slammed his fist on the table again. As far as I was concerned, there was no point in continuing the meeting if I couldn't ask difficult questions.

THE MEETING HAD been full of interesting details. And I had a better sense of who Lex really was. But there were so many more questions than answers. I wrote a series of scoops in *The Wall Street Journal*, with my colleague Julie Steinberg, and in other Dow Jones publications like *Financial News* and *Barron's*. Other reporters were also writing stories about Lex. But for some reason, Greensill insiders told me, my name really needled him.

In November 2019, at a SoftBank event in California, Lex was guest of honour. Right before he was due on stage in front of dozens of other CEOs whose companies were backed by SoftBank, Lex found out that my colleague, Eric Savitz, a columnist at *Barron's*, was in the room. Savitz is a great reporter. He is also a good guy. Lex stormed over and demanded Savitz leave. Savitz didn't even know who Greensill was then. It was an angry confrontation that was only smoothed over after SoftBank media relations people intervened and persuaded Lex to continue.

It was a little later, in February 2020, when my bag was stolen from my car as I met my family for a meal near Oxford Street. A few months after that, Greensill insiders told me that Lex and Doran did have a private investigator on a kind of permanent retainer. Lex had also talked openly about having Daniel Sheard – the whistle-blower – followed, to see whether he was talking to any reporters. I couldn't be sure about the break-in. Maybe the whole thing was a sign of my paranoia as I dealt with this complex, confusing company, where getting to the truth seemed so incredibly difficult.

# EIGHTEEN

# The Obligors

After my first run-ins with Lex and Credit Suisse, I became more methodical. Every time Credit Suisse published documents related to the supply chain finance funds, I would read through them thoroughly, call round my well-informed sources and check what other information was available to the public. And then I would call Credit Suisse with a list of questions.

Mostly, these were focused on the 'obligors' – what bankers call the companies to which they make supply chain finance loans. Just to be clear, Greensill would often dispute that these were loans at all – they would make the case that they had paid some invoices on behalf of a client and that the client then had to pay them back. They hadn't directly loaned funds to the client at all, they would insist. But, in the real world, in terms that any normal human would understand, the client owed money to Greensill. Most people would understand that it was a loan. I guess 'obligor' is a reference to the client's obligation to repay the funds.

At Credit Suisse, the portfolio managers had to publish – every six months – detailed information about the performance of the funds and the loans they held. This information was often delayed, so that by the time the information was public, it might be several months out of date. It wasn't perfect, but it was a good place to start. They also published monthly summary updates about the funds. These were much timelier, although they were also less detailed. They showed who the top ten obligors were, based on the proportion of the funds loaned to each of them. You could work backwards to figure out how big the loans were. These monthly updates also showed which were the biggest insurance companies providing coverage to the funds.

Some of the obligors were huge, well-known companies that you'd expect to find in big supply chain finance programmes run by traditional banks – the likes of Coca-Cola, Vodafone or General Mills. Others were not. Some of them were start-up businesses themselves, with little to no cash flow. Some were other small trade finance businesses that offered a service similar to Greensill. Others were tiny companies that had a personal connection to Lex. Why did any of this matter? Because this wasn't Lex's money. It was money that Credit Suisse's clients had entrusted to the bank, and which the bank had handed over to Greensill.

Some of these loans, I asked about time and time again.

One that drew my attention early on was the loan to Atlantic 57 Consultancy. This was the same British Virgin Islands company that I had seen in the GAM funds. It was the vehicle through which the businessman Andy Ruhan had held a disputed stake in a Manhattan skyscraper.

Ruhan himself had several links to Lex over the years, through his stake in the predecessor to Greensill Bank, for instance. Greensill had allocated about $30 million of Credit Suisse's clients' money to Atlantic 57. It was clear Lex had used money from Credit Suisse to buy this loan out of the GAM funds. Not long after I asked Credit Suisse about Atlantic 57, the loan disappeared out of the funds – later, when Greensill's business had collapsed, I found documents showing it had been moved to Greensill Bank. This was a loan that never got paid back. Lex just shuffled it from one fund to the next.

Some other loans just didn't look like supply chain finance at all.

Primevere, a subsidiary of the UK retailer Shop Direct, was loaned about £80 million out of the funds. Its published accounts, listed on Companies House, said, 'The principal activity of the company is the ownership management of an investment property in the East Midlands that is currently under construction.' The Credit Suisse funds were paying for the construction of a warehouse. That might be a perfectly reasonable project to lend money to, but it's not supply chain finance. It has a different risk profile and the lender should charge a different rate for the loan.

The Food Revolution Group, a loss-making juice company in Australia, received a loan of A\$9 million. Its accounts referred to a 'working capital and term loan facility' from Greensill which 'has no maturity' – in other words, it was not a supply chain finance loan.

There were other obligors that just struck me as outright odd.

Greensill loaned more than £60 million from the Credit Suisse funds to various related entities loosely aggregated under the banner of the Catfoss group, a mini conglomerate of small businesses run out of the north of England. These were the companies introduced by Neil Hobday, the former associate of Andy Ruhan. One of the Catfoss companies managed a loss-making waste-processing plant in Gateshead in the northeast of England. Others dealt in modular buildings used at NHS hospitals. Another affiliated company called CHBG Limited was loaned about £15 million just weeks after it was incorporated. I found out later that Catfoss was frequently one of the biggest sources of revenue for Greensill in any given quarterly reporting period. By 2018, Catfoss was Greensill's third-biggest single client by revenue. Greensill recorded about \$20 million in revenue from Catfoss. In practice, though, it was less clear that Catfoss was such a great client. Staff at Greensill were constantly concerned that the firm couldn't pay back the loans Lex had made to the company. Often it seemed like when one loan came to an end, it was simply replaced with a new one. At the same time that Lex Greensill was claiming Greensill was a multibillion-dollar business with relationships with some of the biggest companies in the world, the company was in fact getting a major slice of its revenue from an obscure company called Catfoss.

Another strange borrower was R.W. Chelsea Holdings, the umbrella company for the UK- and Cyprus-based Chelsea Group, a collection of businesses that mostly provide security services in dangerous environments. The company sprang out of something called Hart, a private military-style security business started by Richard Bethell, the 6th Baron Westbury. Bethell is a former officer in the Scots Guards and the Special Air Service, the British special forces. He hit the gossip pages of UK tabloids in 2018 when the lawyer Cherie Blair, the wife of former prime minister Tony Blair, represented him in court after he was evicted from a multimillion-pound villa he was renting in Cyprus.

Chelsea Holdings had started out as a private military contractor providing protection to businesses in the Horn of Africa and other hotspots. Over the years, it had expanded into other security-related services such as crisis management for kidnap or extortion situations, or private security on board private jets. It also runs a secure accommodation camp at an airport in Mogadishu, Somalia, known euphemistically as 'Chelsea Village'. The company also runs a similar facility at an airport in Afghanistan.

The Credit Suisse funds loaned Bethell's business about $12 million. Like many of the other loans, this was rolled over, month after month, quarter after quarter.

Another obligor that stood out was Special Needs Group, a small company based in Chester, whose website said it provided 'bespoke, personalised services, including digital and finance solutions for school-age students who have learning disabilities . . .' Special Needs received about £9 million from the funds. The loans seemed strange.

The company's accounts appeared to show that it was only starting up – there was not yet much of an ongoing business to speak of. Also, some of the loans appeared to relate to a property, not supply chain finance. When I asked Lex about this loan, he responded by asking, didn't I think it was a good thing to support a school for children with special needs? This was hardly the point – and nor did I think Lex was lending out money for charitable reasons. Bloomberg News later showed that the owner of the company, a lawyer named Barnabas Borbely, was Lex Greensill's neighbour.

Yet another odd obligor was Kerry Leeds Investments. The Credit Suisse documents showed this company had received about £13 million pounds from the funds in late 2019 or early 2020. The documents also showed that the money didn't have to be paid back until 2023 – that's a much longer period than normal for supply chain finance. When I dug into it, there were further twists. Kerry Leeds had previously been called MIS Motorsport, which was a tiny specialist insurance business that offered coverage for race and rally car drivers. The company's sole director was Dermot Hanafin – cousin of Sean Hanafin, one Greensill's top executives. Its accounts, filed at Companies House, showed no balance sheet and no profit. Tracing Dermot Hanafin and the business links, I came across another company called Kerry Ireland Investments. Companies House documents showed that this company was only set up in 2019, and that Greensill Capital had a claim on all its assets (though there was little evidence the company had any assets to speak of).

Later, in September 2021, Credit Suisse published a document that showed the Kerry Leeds loan was still outstanding, months after the funds had collapsed. The same document showed that another company called Laidir owed about $12 million to the funds too – Laidir also deals in specialist insurance, including motorsport, and shares senior management personnel with Kerry Ireland Investments. Credit Suisse continued to refuse to talk to me about these entangled loans.

There was nothing to suggest these loans to companies like Special Needs, R.W. Chelsea and Kerry Leeds were improperly handled. It's not uncommon for finance firms to deal with other businesses within their personal networks, especially if potential conflicts are out in the open. But even if you assumed these loans were all above board, they were a million miles away from the big business, blue-chip supply chain finance programme that Credit Suisse promoted to its clients. Some of the loans were more like small business lending, or even venture capital-style investments in start-up companies.

There were so many odd loans. At times, I'd limit my questions for Credit Suisse and Greensill to just a handful, in order to make the whole process more manageable, so they couldn't use the volume of information I was asking about as an excuse not to respond. Often the result was disappointing, nonetheless. Greensill would say that they couldn't comment on the funds, as that was Credit Suisse's purview. Credit Suisse would say they couldn't comment on individual obligors.

One group of obligors I came back to over and over were the other finance companies that seemed to operate in the same space as Greensill itself. These included Tower Trade Group – which was connected to BSi Steel – and another related company called Deal Partners. Between them, they received tens of millions of dollars of Credit Suisse's clients' money. This was the same group that Lex had worked with way back at the start of Greensill Capital in a series of deals that had often turned sour.

There were various links between directors and other senior management at BSi, Tower Trade and Deal Partners. These were easy to prove. Charles Reynolds, the Swiss-based South African trade finance veteran bridged Tower Trade and Deal Partners, where he sat on the board. Rob Barnes, the former PrimeRevenue chief was also there at the founding of both companies. There were other senior managers and directors who worked for Deal Partners and Tower Trade. The accounts of BSi referenced loans with Tower Trade and their various joint ventures. Though there was no indication in the Credit Suisse funds of the connection, it was clear this group of companies was very closely related.

There had been a gap of a few years when Greensill and Tower Trade didn't do any business – the Tower Trade team felt that Lex had gone stratospheric after the injection of money from General Atlantic, and that their business was no longer a major partner. There were no Tower Trade, Deal Partners or BSi transactions funnelled through GAM and Haywood. But that changed once Lex had the Credit Suisse funds to play with. He had more money and needed more obligors. The group of people connected to Tower Trade had originated deals for Lex in the past and he returned to them again.

There had been personnel changes at Tower Trade. The CEO was now Tom de la Rue, scion of the famous money printing dynasty and formerly Prince Harry's commanding officer in the Army Air Corps. No longer flying Apache attack helicopters, de la Rue was forging a career in working capital financing. The royal connection, the military past, the establishment heritage – de la Rue was exactly the kind of person Lex loved to have in his network. By the time I started looking at Tower Trade, the connection to Greensill clearly ran deep. On Tower Trade's website, the articles that appeared under the heading 'Latest News and Insights' were all cut and pasted from news releases on Greensill's own website. It was as though Tower Trade itself was a subsidiary of Greensill.

Tower Trade, Deal Partners and BSi combined were getting something like $80 million of financing from the Credit Suisse funds. My sources told me that the companies never had any contact with the Swiss bank and there was no documentation linking them to Credit Suisse either. Their relationship was with Greensill Capital.

When I got in touch with the CEO of BSi, William Battershill, he replied that Greensill had been a 'valued and trusted funder' for the past ten years, and that all the financing went through the Tower Trade platform. I was able to find out that Tower Trade itself worked with a variety of obligors in places like Singapore, the Middle East and Monte Carlo.

At Deal Partners, the picture was even murkier.

When I first tried to contact executives there, one of them responded by email in a way that was highly unusual in my experience as a journalist. The source wrote back saying: 'You're asking a lot of questions and we have not met, if you want to win a Pulitzer prize, it does not come for free!'

The source said they knew Lex, Tower Trade and Deal Partners, and said they could tell me a lot about how it all fitted together. But they added, 'I trust you understand, there are no free lunches in the world of financial services.'

It wasn't the last time someone I contacted for this story asked for money in return for information. It would have been a huge breach of ethics to have gone along with a request like that and I immediately declined. Still, there was plenty of information to be gleaned if you kept digging.

Deal Partners was set up in 2011 as an Enterprise Investment Scheme (EIS) – a type of tax-efficient investment vehicle typically sold to wealthy people in the UK. Investors in EISs benefit from tax breaks because the schemes take their money and provide financing to sectors that the government wants to boost, such as small businesses. The tax relief is available on investments up to £1 million per year and the investors typically must leave their money in the scheme for several years.

A minimum stake in the Deal Partners EIS was £50,000, and the money had to be parked there for a minimum of three years. Investors were told they'd make upwards of 6 per cent a year. By 2018, Deal Partners accounts showed it had raised about £8 million from a few dozen investors.

Deal Partners' management said they used the funds to finance trade between small and medium businesses. In more candid moments, though, the management team at Deal Partners told colleagues and acquaintances that the company operated as a kind of safety net for underperforming assets in Tower Trade – loans that were not getting paid back on time could be shifted into Deal Partners where they would, in theory, be restructured into longer-term borrowings. But Deal Partners had failed to return anything like what was promised. Defaults were much higher than expected. A lot of the investors were deeply unhappy. At a shareholder meeting, Reynolds promised they could wind up the company and return their funds in 2019.

But that's only a part of the picture. The Credit Suisse fund documents showed that Greensill had loaned Deal Partners more than $50 million in financing – as much as ten times its annual revenue. It was an extraordinary sum, especially as the company's auditors had issued a qualified audit report citing concerns about £2.9 million in debts that were overdue and might not ever be collected.

Greensill had registered a charge over all of Deal Partners' assets, meaning Greensill would own Deal Partners if it defaulted on the loan payments. The Deal Partners charge document also linked the Greensill funding to a separate transaction altogether, a 2018 supply chain finance deal that Greensill had arranged involving the sale of tens of millions of dollars' worth of mobile phone handsets from Chinese telecoms companies Huawei Technologies and ZTE to a Malaysian business called UMobile. The two Chinese firms are quite well known, not least because they operate under sanctions by US authorities, who allege that both represent a national security threat.

When I asked Credit Suisse about this obligor, they rebuffed my questions as usual. Greensill said in an email that 'the involvement of Deal Partners in this transaction was because they are well placed to manage contracts where tangible inventory is involved' and noted that UMobile had met all payments.

But there was more to it. My sources told me that Deal Partners had provided a way for Greensill to repackage the Chinese-Malaysian deals so that they could be stuffed into the Credit Suisse funds. The underlying SCF loans with the Asia-based companies were for several years. But Greensill reprocessed the loans through one of its own special purpose vehicles (SPVs) and through Deal Partners to make the debt look like short-term financing. In return, Deal Partners was paid a service fee by Greensill. There was no way investors in Credit Suisse's funds could have been expected to know this. None of this ever appeared in Deal Partners' accounts – their shareholders were oblivious to the notion that documentation at Credit Suisse showed their company had borrowed $50 million from the Swiss bank's funds.

Deal Partners eventually filed for administration in 2021. A report produced by the company's administrators said that several of the companies that had been loaned money by Deal Partners were unlikely to repay their debts, including a Spanish clothing company and a South African shoe manufacturer. Each had borrowed millions of pounds and both were now out of business. The administrators estimated that only about 10 per cent of the total amount Deal Partners had loaned out could be recovered, and that would be swallowed up by fees associated with the winding up, outstanding tax bills, staff costs, and paying off other creditors to the company – including Tower Trade, which was owed more than £400,000.

Tellingly, the administrators' report also included several years of balance sheets. At no point was there a loan from Greensill or Credit Suisse of $50 million, or anything like it. The administrators also noted that Greensill Capital had registered a charge over Deal Partners' assets, but that they didn't believe Greensill was owed any funds.

The whole Tower Trade/Deal Partners set-up was dizzying. It was also completely at odds with the super-safe, steady investments that Credit Suisse pitched to its clients. It represented layer upon layer of complex transactions, which ended up with loans to sanctioned companies or tiny offshore entities that didn't pay back what they had borrowed. There was also nothing in the Credit Suisse fund documents to show that Tower Trade, Deal Partners and BSi were all entangled with one another.

One of the biggest black holes of all was in the so-called 'multi-obligor programmes'. These were described as packages of financing to different obligors. In all cases, they were named after areas or streets in or around Bundaberg, where Lex grew up – a reflection of how much Lex was still involved in the details of the business. There was Rasmussen, Seaview, Rehbein, Fairymead and Bingera – all of them would be known to the Bundaberg townsfolk. At Credit Suisse, they added up to hundreds of millions of dollars of additional financing. And though the documentation suggested it was for a varied group of obligors, in fact the lending in these programmes was often tied to a single business – most of those businesses were part of the Gupta Family Group (GFG) Alliance.

I was building a clearer picture of Lex's business. While Lex claimed to have relationships with massive global businesses, in fact he was making dozens of loans to a collection of friends, family and assorted acquaintances. Many of them were much riskier businesses than the supply chain finance funds that he purported to lend to. And many of the loans were long term, not short term. Some of the loans were more like equity investments that the recipient was never expected to pay back.

IN SEPTEMBER 2019, I flew to Zurich to meet with Credit Suisse's head of fixed income, Luc Mathys, and the portfolio manager running the Greensill funds, Lukas Haas. It was a warm, sunny day on Paradeplatz, the small square where the bastions of Swiss banking are headquartered. Compared to the giant, monolithic offices of the big banks in New York or London, the Swiss banking headquarters seem incredibly parochial and far less busy. It's a cosy, hushed world.

Inside the lobby of the bank's offices, I was met by a media relations person I had talked to many times before. My footsteps echoed down the marble corridors as we made our way to a meeting room. In addition to coffee, there was a bowl full of tiny Swiss chocolates.

Mathys and Haas arrived a few moments later. It was clear they didn't want to be there and couldn't seem to understand why they should spend any time explaining themselves to a lowly reporter. Mathys huffed and puffed through our meeting. I found out later that they had wanted the bank to sue us to try to stop us writing any stories about the funds.

As soon as we sat down, they asked that we treat certain answers to my questions as off the record, meaning I couldn't attribute what they said to them in any stories. It is a standard though annoying practice among big corporations, especially for difficult interviews. Typically, the executives and PR people say it helps them talk more freely without worrying about getting minor details wrong or breaking any promises of client confidentiality. Often, they're just trying to avoid being held accountable for what they tell us.

In this case, Haas and Mathys hardly gave me any answers to a series of questions. I asked why they had bought assets from the collapsed GAM funds and I pointed to the Atlantic 57 loan to Andy Ruhan, which was right there in the Credit Suisse documents. I asked why the funds invested in a series of small businesses with very little money, or none at all, that were personally connected to Lex Greensill. I asked about the loans to Gupta and to Catfoss and to Baron Westbury and his bunch of ex-UK Special Forces operatives and former mercenaries. I asked about the loans to Tower Trade and Deal Partners.

I also asked why so much of the trade credit insurance that protected the funds from defaults was provided by a relatively small Australian insurer called Insurance Australia Group (IAG). About 40 per cent of the insurance came from a unit of IAG known as The Bond and Credit Company (TBCC). Again, they declined to comment, although I was able to write a story a little later saying the bank's executives planned to implement a new policy that would limit the amount of coverage provided by a single insurer to just 20 per cent.

Still, I quickly realized the interview was pointless. There was nothing to report even off the record, as the two bankers essentially refused to engage with my questions. Mathys looked as if he might explode with rage, and Haas, who was more nervous, smirked and mostly 'no commented' his way through the interview. My sense was that I may have known more about what was in the funds than they did.

There was plenty of evidence that the bank wasn't really managing the funds at all. Credit Suisse hardly even hid that fact – a presentation to investors said all the loans met certain predetermined requirements for eligibility, but that the Swiss bank's portfolio managers did not 'exercise full discretionary investment management duties' in respect of the loans.

Fund documents were frequently strewn with errors. At one point, I asked a Credit Suisse spokesperson why all the loans mentioned in an investor update document appeared to mature on the same date. The bank promptly yanked the document off its website and told me the dates were wrong. I took this to indicate a really sloppy attitude from the bank's managers, who were supposed to be running the funds but in fact were delegating almost all that work to Greensill.

Crucially, Haas and Mathys returned time and again to the idea that the steady performance of the funds and the money flowing in was sufficient evidence that there was nothing wrong. But this was a flawed explanation. Money was flowing in because Credit Suisse's bankers encouraged it to flow in. Performance was steady because the funds didn't have to recognize when loans went bad – instead, they could just roll the loan over. It was a kind of 'extend and pretend' approach.

More than one Credit Suisse executive later told me it was the definition of a Ponzi scheme.

The only way the funds would be forced to show their true performance was if investors withdrew so much money, so quickly, that Greensill would have to liquidate its assets, revealing which loans had gone bad or could not be repaid in a hurry. Under any other circumstances, so long as money kept rolling in, Lex could write up whatever performance he wanted.

So long as the money kept rolling in.

# NINETEEN

# The Big Time

By late 2019, Lex had definitively hit the big time.

Greensill Capital was a 'Unicorn' – a private start-up company valued at more than $1 billion. (The term was meant to indicate the rarity of these ventures, but unicorns were flourishing, in part thanks to a flood of money in the market, and the largesse of investors like SoftBank's Vision Fund.)

Lex himself was a billionaire too, at least on paper. And though a large chunk of his wealth was tied up in Greensill Capital stock, Lex and his brother Peter had also taken hundreds of millions of dollars of cash out of the company.

The trappings of wealth followed. Greensill Capital had not one but four private aircraft – two Piaggios, a Dassault Falcon, and a Gulfstream G650. The planes were owned by Greensill Bank which leased them to Greensill Capital. All four were decked out in Greensill livery, and they were staffed by a full-time Greensill crew of pilots and flight attendants. Lex and senior executives used the planes to fly around the globe, meeting with shareholders and clients and politicians.

The Piaggios were used as runarounds to fly about the UK, visiting clients or investors. The biggest aircraft, the Gulfstream, costs about $60 million, and is one of the fastest civilian aircraft on the planet. Lex could use it to fly non-stop from London to SoftBank's headquarters in Tokyo. Sometimes, he would retire mid-flight to his own cabin at the back of the plane, where there was a bed and a separate area for him to work. It was always all business talk on the plane – work meetings and phone calls.

At home, Lex remained relatively understated, walking his dogs near his house in Saughall, Cheshire, and hanging out with his wife and children or visiting a local farmers' market. Sometimes he'd wear a flat checked tweed cap – like an English country squire – and a green fleece jacket, or a blue Patagonia one with General Atlantic's logo stitched onto it.

Lex didn't talk much about his home life. He rarely mentioned his wife or his children at work. Very few, if any, people seemed to feel they knew him well. But there were signs of how his new, vast wealth was changing his life.

He donated £2.5 million to Manchester University to support the appointment of a 'Greensill Chair in FinTech Investment'. The vice chancellor said the donation would help boost the university's fintech credentials. In a press release, Lex said, 'We are delighted to be able to give back to an institution that was so important to the foundation of our firm.'

The old vicarage where Lex and his family lived underwent a multimillion-pound makeover that included a hi-tech wine cellar, games room and pool. After Covid-19 hit, and everyone was working from home, Greensill's senior executives smirked at what they could see in the background on Zoom calls: through the window behind Lex, they watched a team of gardeners, dressed in Greensill farming outfits, working away on the estate.

Lex even tried to buy a tract of land in the local area for a 'rewilding' project. With the SoftBank money pouring into Lex's bank account, he made a proposal to the local parish council to buy hundreds of acres around Saughall. Lex personally met with local councillors and residents to pitch his idea. The minutes of the Saughall and Shotwick Park Parish Council meeting outline the scale of Lex's plans to erect a 'two-metre-wide hedge, plant thousands of trees to create forests, orchards and wildflower meadows and introduce some rare breeds of livestock, etc.'

Lex met again with councillors and residents several times to promote the project. He told them that 'our natural world has come to face many threats including climate change, wildlife decline and the loss of natural habitats . . . [The] project is my dream to make a small impact on these very important issues.'

A local newspaper speculated that Lex's 'green vision' might have been an attempt to offset the carbon footprint from his private jets. But when executives at Greensill Capital talked to Lex about it, he gave a different reason: 'It's the kind of thing that billionaires do with their money.'

Lex and his brothers were included in lists of Australia's richest people. He also bought property in Australia. Greensill director John Gorman had a huge Florida home. Sanjeev Gupta owned an Italianate mansion overlooking Sydney Harbour. Lex spent A$4 million on an ocean-front home in Bargara, near Bundaberg where he grew up. A real-estate listing for the property, known as The Glass House, calls it 'a multi-award winning architectural masterpiece of sophisticated style in an ideal location . . . Exclusively nestled amidst a tropical garden oasis, this sublime absolute beachfront property exudes privacy and tranquility.'

The house, which had a heated pool and glass lifts, was near another luxurious home owned by Peter and a few minutes' drive from his parents.

Greensill's farming business was also benefiting from the influx of money into the family. The farm expanded rapidly. Peter's seed money into Greensill Capital had harvested a fortune. 'It was a pretty good trade for me in hindsight,' he told an Australian paper. The family acquired more land and spent millions buying the best farming equipment. Lex bragged to finance types he met in London that they owned some of the most expensive agricultural machinery money could buy, including the largest water carrier in Australia.

A video, posted to the Greensill Farming Facebook page, opens with a shot of Lex, Peter, their brother Andrew and their parents, standing in front of a farm building under a sign for 'Greensill Sweet Potatoes'. Everyone is in the bright yellow and blue overalls that all Greensill farm workers wear – except for Lex, who is in smart black shoes, grey slacks and a blue banker's shirt with a white collar and white cuffs, like an Australian Gordon Gekko.

On its website, Greensill Farming said it had grown from the original 66 acres managed by Lex's grandfather to more than 8,000 acres. It grew more than 5 per cent of all the watermelons in Australia.

Not everyone was happy with their progress. Some local farmers were upset that Greensill Farming used money from the finance business to expand aggressively, paying over the odds for vast tracts of land, then driving down the price for sweet potatoes, piling pressure on other farms in the area. One of the critics was Rodney Wolfenden, chairman of Australian Sweet Potato Growers, who told *The Times* that 'The Greensill farming business is cutting prices to buy market share. Some local growers have gone broke. Others have been forced to cut production and lay off staff.'

The story quoted another farmer: 'There is no way this money was coming from sweet potatoes. If they are, then why am I not sitting in the f***ing Taj Mahal? . . . They have been cutting the cost of sweet potatoes to drive us out of the market.'

The flood of money was also making waves through Greensill Capital. Lex was a generous employer and placed a high value on loyalty to the cause. Staff were well paid, often salaries were two or three times the going rate, and many were given stock. Lex told me this was a sign of his generosity, giving away a stake in his company. Some senior executives who left on bad terms felt that Lex used their stock as leverage, to secure their silence about Greensill's riskier strategies and tactics – keep quiet and he might let you keep the shares. Another source told me that Lex took the idea for giving out so much stock from WeWork's Adam Neumann, whom Lex described as a friend. Even very junior staff flew business class and stayed in expensive hotels. He even once flew his tailor from the UK to New York to make bespoke suits for the Greensill team there. Staff were supposed to pay half the cost of the suits, with Greensill footing the rest, but no one ever got a bill. Perhaps it was just as well – the tailor mostly specialized in making shirts, and some of the suits fitted badly.

Corporate events were often staid – a reflection of Lex's own demeanour. But they were not cheap. A Christmas party for London staff in 2019 was held at the swanky Gothic revival St Pancras Renaissance Hotel. Chris Bates, who was the most senior figure at Greensill's Warrington campus, also held a second party for staff at a hotel in Cheshire. It was informal – Lex turned up in a pair of red chinos and a green waistcoat, with some staff remarking that he looked like a Christmas elf.

There was also an annual ski trip for staff. The 2020 version was held in Sweden, and a couple of hundred people took advantage of the heavily subsidized trip. This was the sort of thing that used to happen at big investment banks, though mostly it had ended after the financial crisis led to belt-tightening. At Greensill, Lex instead auctioned off use of the private jet to company insiders – the highest bidder could take the jet to the ski trip. The winner was Roland Hartley-Urquhart, who diverted the plane via Helsinki, where he first went to visit a yacht-maker, before continuing to the ski hills. Lex himself had not learned to ski until he was an adult. 'He skied fast and loose,' one former Greensill executive told me. 'The same way he did business.'

The hiring spree also really gathered pace at this time too. The SoftBank and General Atlantic investments made Greensill Capital a much more credible career move, as did the growing relationship with Credit Suisse. Several new senior hires came on board around this time, including Sean Hanafin, an experienced banker with a career at Citi and Standard Chartered under his belt, and a handful of top executives from technology start-ups and supply chain finance technology platforms such as Taulia. Neil Garrod, the former treasurer at the major Greensill client Vodafone, also jumped across to Greensill to become CFO. Greensill opened offices in Singapore, São Paulo and Johannesburg. New senior hires were told to recruit their teams without restraint.

Lex also spent millions to acquire other companies. He paid about $50 million to acquire Finacity, a US-based firm that specialized in securitizing receivables and had a big client base in the global shipping industry. Finacity, run by entrepreneur Adrian Katz, processed about $100 billion of transactions a year, multiples of what Greensill was dealing with up to that point. (After Greensill collapsed, there was a protracted sale process for Finacity, which was held up partly because of Katz's claims to payments he said he was still owed by Greensill. In the end, Finacity was bought by White Oak Global Advisors for $7 million, and Katz stayed on as CEO. Bloomberg reported that he dropped demands for $21 million in payments related to Greensill's earlier acquisition of Finacity.)

Lex also bought FreeUp, a UK-based start-up that was trying to find ways for workers to access their pay more effectively. Lex paid $5 million for FreeUp in October 2019, and effectively wrote its value down to zero the following summer. He also bought a similar Australian company called Earnd for another $12 million in February 2020 – $8 million of this was booked in the accounts to 'goodwill', effectively the excess purchase price over and above its fair market value. Flush with cash, Lex hardly seemed to be driving a hard bargain.

For new senior executives joining Greensill, there would be an invite from Lex to visit the farm in Australia for a few days. Beforehand, they'd typically get a message from Lex's personal assistant, asking them their clothing size and measurements. When they arrived, they'd be presented with a set of the yellow and blue Greensill farming overalls, boots and hat to wear on the tour of the extensive farmland, all in their size, with the Greensill logo embroidered into the jacket. Some thought this was a silly unnecessary expense. Some thought it bizarrely cultish. Others thought it was a nice gesture, which reflected Lex's focus on fine details and showed how much the family farm meant to him.

Greensill's accounts for 2019 showed a business transformed. Revenue had almost doubled, from $270 million in 2018 to $476 million in 2019, though Greensill's profits fell. The number of employees had almost tripled in twelve months, from 214 staff to 618.

IN JANUARY 2020, Lex was sitting beneath a vast sky, a small cup in his hand, basking in the warming glow of a well-kept campfire. He could have been back home on the farm with his brothers. But Lex had come a million miles by then.

Instead of farmers' overalls and heavy boots, Lex wore a dark blue suit, double-cuffed shirt and sober blue tie. His black R.M. Williams Chelsea boots – a nod to his Australian heritage – were partially tucked under as he sat on a thick, red carpet. Alongside him, the former prime minister of the UK, David Cameron, was dressed in almost the same way. They reclined against red and gold velvet cushions, a collection of shiny tea kettles at their feet. This was the desert retreat of the Saudi prince Mohammed Bin Salman, one of the richest – and most controversial – figures in global business and politics.

Lex had worked his way into the upper echelons of global power. Like Cosimo de' Medici, whose bank pulled the strings in

Renaissance Europe, Lex knew that money could make politicians dance to his tune.

Lex was enthralled by the Saudi trip, even if Mohammed Bin Salman, known as MBS, was just re-emerging from a brief period of international censure. The CIA had concluded in 2018 that MBS himself had ordered the assassination of the journalist Jamal Khashoggi earlier that year, according to a report in *The Washington Post*. The murder and ensuing investigations had caused many top business and political leaders to shun MBS for a while and avoid visiting the Gulf country. But the lure of the Saudi kingdom's vast oil riches, and MBS's ambitious and costly plans to reinvent his country, were enough of a draw for the bankers to overcome their concerns. By October 2019, the global business elite were flocking back in their thousands, attending the so-called 'Davos in the desert' finance summit in Riyadh and showing up with the aim of striking big deals.

Lex had good reason to join the parade of bankers to the Gulf. For starters, the Saudi sovereign wealth fund, known as the Public Investment Fund (PIF), was the single largest investor in SoftBank's Vision Fund. That stake also meant Saudi Arabia was effectively a major shareholder in Greensill too.

There were also potentially lucrative projects to work on. MBS's modernization plan for Saudi involves huge infrastructure spending – including a vast new, futuristic city that would feature high-speed trains and skyscrapers on a scale that dwarfs the tallest buildings in New York or London. All of this would need financing.

Lex and some of the executives at SoftBank also at one point discussed a plan to create investments that were tied to the hajj, the annual Muslim pilgrimage to Mecca. SoftBank and Greensill executives discussed how to ease the logistical pain, and enrich themselves, by making loans to hotels, infrastructure projects and transport operations that were needed to support the pilgrims. Their plan was to bundle up these loans into securities and sell them on to investors. It was outlandish, but potentially incredibly lucrative.

There was another, more down-to-earth deal to be done too. Saudi Aramco, the part state-owned oil and natural gas company, is one of the largest companies in the world. Aramco – which had listed some of its shares in December 2019 on the Saudi stock exchange, the Tadawul – processed as much as $2 billion in supplier payments each month. There was a huge supply chain finance programme in the pipeline. Such were the potential opportunities – and the vast pool of wealth to be tapped – that Lex flew into Saudi regularly in the early months of 2020 on his private aircraft. He was even planning to open an office in Saudi, with several staff permanently on the ground.

After the camping trip, Lex pinged back to Greensill executives a photo of himself and Cameron fireside, with a message that said, 'We have lots of work to do.' In the end, none of these deals came to fruition.

It didn't matter. To the outside world, Greensill's business appeared to be booming. In early 2020, Greensill held a meeting with a small core of the top management team, board members and a group of bankers from Credit Suisse. Top of the agenda was a planned IPO of Greensill's shares. SoftBank was targeting a sale of the company in 2024. General Atlantic had a similar timeline. Lex and some of the other insiders had already pocketed a fortune. But Lex, Peter, John Gorman and others still held a huge amount of stock that would pay out in bundles if the company could get to launch an IPO. The Credit Suisse bankers were bullish. Given Greensill's recent trajectory, if the company could hit $800 million in revenue in 2020, an IPO could follow quickly after, and the IPO could achieve a staggering valuation of up to $40 billion, the bankers estimated. Shane Galligan, Credit Suisse's Australian private banker, who counted Lex as a personal client, delivered a rousing speech to pump everyone up. 'Your firm is worth billions, and we're going to take it to the market!' he exhorted.

Greensill would become one of the most valuable financial firms in the UK, rivalling the likes of Lloyds or Barclays.

As the meeting ended, the collected executives left the room half stunned, like lottery winners who had just discovered they held the winning ticket. Lex was beaming. He could hardly contain his thoughts. 'If we pull this off,' he said, 'me and my brother will be the richest men in Australia.'

TWENTY

# Making Finance Less Fair

Lex's big promise was that he would bring supply chain finance to the little guy, like his parents' farm. He would democratize capital and make finance fairer. But that's not what happened.

There was a legitimate supply chain finance programme at Greensill, and it counted among its clients some major organizations like Boeing, Vodafone, General Mills and the UK National Health Service. This was all funded with money from Global Asset Management or Credit Suisse or Greensill Bank, or sometimes other Greensill funding partners like Italian bank UniCredit or the Japanese banks Mizuho or SMBC. Greensill's role was to connect the funding partner (usually the big bank or its clients) with the borrower (usually the big corporation). None of this was particularly unusual. It was the kind of traditional supply chain finance that the big banks had been doing for years. The only thing disruptive about it was that Lex was willing to do it at such a low cost that he hardly made any money. But that wasn't the point. These big names brought volume and credibility, even if serving them meant running at a loss.

These programmes also mostly ran on someone else's technology.

This was one of the biggest misdirections under Greensill. Despite claiming to be a fintech, Lex didn't really have much in the way of unique technology, and so relied on third parties like Taulia or Prime-Revenue. The fintech branding only really came to the forefront after Lex got a big round of funding from General Atlantic.

The other big misdirection was that Greensill was making finance fairer. Supply chain finance can help small businesses – it can give them some certainty around payment times and it can be an alternative to more expensive forms of financing. But it can also harm small businesses. The programmes that Lex ran had a mixed track record.

In Australia, where Lex had become the dominant provider of supply chain finance, the small business ombudsman launched an investigation in 2019 into a wave of SCF that was sweeping across the country. Several big Australian companies were using SCF programmes, including telecoms company Telstra and the construction giant CIMIC, both Greensill clients.

What followed was a confusing tug of war between the ombudsman, Kate Carnell, and Lex Greensill. Carnell's office had heard stories about bullying by big companies, who were using SCF to force unfair terms on to their smaller suppliers. They found suppliers were being told that either they signed up to a supply chain finance programme or they wouldn't be paid for months. In some cases, they might find they would be shut out of the supply chain altogether. In other words, get paid on time, but at a discount, or don't get paid for months, if at all.

In October 2019, Carnell announced a review into the impact of supply chain financing on small businesses. A position paper published then said that SCF was being used inappropriately by large businesses. Some of them were stretching out their payment terms, telling suppliers they wouldn't get paid for much longer than previously, and then offering SCF as an alternative. It was bullying.

'Small businesses have very little bargaining power compared to large entities who have a number of potential suppliers in any marketplace,' the report said. 'This impacts their ability to demand fair payment terms for goods supplied and services rendered.'

SCF on new technology platforms had 'brought an insidious new front to the war small businesses are waging to get paid within a reasonable time frame.'

A few months later, in March 2020, Carnell's office published their final report. It was critical of several big Australian companies, including Telstra and CIMIC, explicitly accusing them of unfairly forcing smaller suppliers into accepting longer payment terms or SCF discounts.

The report cited a detailed example. It involved a small Australian company that was a supplier to a construction sector business that had recently been bought by CIMIC. Under its new owners, the company stretched its payment terms from thirty days to sixty days. That, according to the report, would have forced the small supplier to take out a costly A$1 million overdraft to cover the delay in cash coming into its coffers. Alternatively, the CIMIC subsidiary offered the small supplier an SCF deal with Greensill to get paid more promptly.

The report bluntly says, 'The small business owner was left with a choice to use the Greensill SCF offering or go out of business.'

Carnell's office also said that some SCF providers were unfairly using artificial intelligence techniques to squeeze even more out of the suppliers.

The stinging criticism embarrassed CIMIC, which had become one of Lex's biggest clients in his home country. The firm responded by slashing its SCF programme. The construction company's SCF balance fell from $850 million at the end of 2019 to just $140 million a year later. Telstra too was scaling back its SCF exposure. Carnell later acknowledged that the GFG companies of Sanjeev Gupta were also a special focus. She told Australian media that GFG companies were especially slow payers. Greensill's SCF programmes meant GFG's suppliers were paid earlier but they got less than they'd invoiced for.

By the time of the report, Lex was on the record saying Carnell's review had caused him to rethink the business model, and that he wouldn't be providing SCF to clients that wanted to push out payment terms beyond thirty days.

Carnell's report cautiously said, 'We are looking forward to seeing the evidence of significant improvements made by Greensill and the other SCF providers in this regard.'

Despite this, the bad smell around SCF programmes lingered for months in Australia. In May, it blew up again as local media reported a CIMIC subsidiary had pushed out payment terms and offered a Greensill SCF programme as the alternative for suppliers willing to accept a discount. Greensill quickly dropped the client, and earned the praise of Carnell again, which was followed by the usual sort of Greensill press release, this one touting the ombudsman's praise.

The whole episode was like a naughty child scolded by their parents for misbehaving, then earning faint praise for doing the right thing. Greensill was claiming credit for no longer helping its clients bully suppliers.

IN AUGUST 2020, the Global Supply Chain Finance Forum, an industry lobby group, put out its own report on the industry bullies. The decision to speak out was a sure sign that the problem was significant, although the report predictably claimed that bullying was rare.

Authored by the likes of the International Chamber of Commerce and the European Banking Association, the report clearly sought to put some distance between best practices and the kind of approach taken by some of Greensill's clients. 'Reports of suppliers being forced into accepting unfavourable terms are extremely worrying,' it said. 'Yet our understanding is that these incidents remain isolated and uncommon. We believe that, while they have attracted significant media coverage, they are not representative of how [SCF] programmes are used by the majority of buyers and sellers in mutually supportive supply chains.'

At Greensill, Lex and Doran had considered putting out a position paper – a piece of 'thought leadership' – on SCF that would put their side of the controversy. When it was circulated among executives though, the plan hit a wall. The paper was misleading and full of errors. Roland, who had taken out a patent on a kind of SCF programme twenty years earlier, politely deconstructed it over email. Other executives who were concerned that publishing the document would have been embarrassing breathed a sigh of relief. The paper went nowhere.

IN AUSTRALIA, THE small business ombudsman Kate Carnell was not the only authority to have taken a critical eye to Greensill's business. In October 2019, the Australian Taxation Office decided that Lex would have to pay tax on about A$58 million in capital gains from the sale of shares in his company. A trust set up in Peter Greensill's name had sold the shares between 2015 and 2017. Lex wouldn't normally pay tax in Australia because he was resident in the UK. But the Australian tax authority determined that because the trust was based there, tax should be paid there too. The decision meant Lex was on the hook for an enormous, unexpected back tax bill. It was also personally embarrassing and a source of constant irritation that would bring his temper to the fore. The Greensill Trust appealed, and appealed again, but lost each time. Perhaps Lex wasn't so smart after all.

# TWENTY-ONE

# Wild Bill and the NHS

Bill Crothers was one of Greensill's top lieutenants. The Belfast-born accountant had spent most of his career at the management consultancy Accenture, where he had a reputation as an aggressive and skilled negotiator. He sat on the firm's UK board and had been a leading partner at Accenture during one of its most controversial UK projects, a £300 million-plus contract to implement a new billing system for British Gas in the early 2000s that was beset by a series of failures, leading to a deluge of customer complaints and an embarrassing and protracted legal battle. The affair had led to tens of millions of pounds' worth of legal wrangling, and was one of several bungled projects that had tarnished Accenture's name in the mainstream media.

After that, Crothers became a civil servant. He told *The Guardian* in a 2012 interview that he joined the public sector 'to travel less and because of a sense of wanting to give something back to society.' In the post-financial crisis world, when austerity was the keystone of government policy, Crothers became chief procurement officer with a mission to extract big savings from billions of pounds of government contracts. (Crothers later rebranded his role as the more all-encompassing and altogether more impressive-sounding chief commercial officer.) Sponsored by Francis Maude, the former Morgan Stanley banker who was minister for the Cabinet Office, Crothers shook up the government's procurement process, drove private sector-style reforms and claimed billions in budget savings. But he also created a whorl of animosity. Other civil servants queried his savings claims and referred to him as 'Wild Bill', after the famed Western gunslinger, for his tendency to shoot from the hip, firing off missives and making snap decisions and only asking questions later.

In 2014, Crothers had also appointed Lex to the Crown Representatives programme, which recruits private sector experts to help the government work with suppliers. Just one year after that, Crothers turned around and joined Greensill – initially part-time while he still worked in government before he took on a full-time role. By 2019, Crothers had a stake in Greensill that was worth well in excess of £5 million, had he been able to cash it all in.

At Greensill, one of Crothers' goals was to find ways to ingratiate the company with government agencies, particularly the NHS. Government organizations had vast swathes of suppliers, steady cash flows, and billions of pounds' worth of transactions – all of which could be bundled up into securities and sold off to investors. What's more, if Greensill became more deeply embedded in government, that could potentially save it from disaster. Greensill could become too important to fail.

NOT LONG AFTER Crothers officially landed at Greensill, one of the cornerstones of Greensill's relationship with the NHS was put in place.

The Pharmacy Earlier Payment Scheme, known as PEPS, had been launched by the Department of Health and Social Care a few years earlier, in 2013, to streamline payments to small pharmacies.

The idea had partly come out of Lex's own work for the government. Citi, the giant US bank where Lex had briefly worked, was awarded the first PEPS deal under an existing government contract without a structured procurement process. In 2018, the PEPS contract was up for renewal. Executives at Citi thought they'd won it again – they believed they had been told as much by government contacts – only for bidding to be reopened. Greensill swept in and offered to run the programme at a slightly lower cost, undercutting Citi at the last moment.

In effect, it meant Greensill had been awarded a contract to provide a supply chain finance programme to the public sector that Lex himself had proposed while working inside Whitehall. Regardless, it was a major coup. Lex frequently invoked the NHS pharmacies contract as a sign of Greensill's credibility and scale.

In truth, the PEPS business was doing little to help Greensill's bottom line – and little to help the small pharmacies that were supposed to benefit from it either. Although Greensill was processing more than £100 million of pharmacy-related payments monthly, PEPS was not a success. A government investigation in 2021 found that far fewer pharmacies than anticipated had taken part in the programme, and that those that did were more likely to be larger pharmacy chains rather than small, family-run pharmacies that most needed help. The same investigation also found there was no evidence that the much-vaunted savings to the NHS – which were calculated based on Lex's estimations and advice – ever resulted.

PEPS was not the only NHS business at Greensill.

Almost everything SoftBank had put into Greensill in October had gone out of the company, either to Greensill Bank or to the pockets of the founder shareholders. But not all of it. In late 2019 and early 2020, Lex was in acquisition mode.

FreeUp was a small start-up founded by a group of entrepreneurs who wanted to give employees access to their salary in real time. There were several similar businesses around. The idea is this: each of us who works for a wage and is getting paid fortnightly or monthly is effectively providing a kind of credit to our employers. We supply our work up front, and the employer pays later. A clutch of fintech believers say that the traditional payroll process is deeply unfair, woefully outdated and ripe for disruption. Instead, businesses like FreeUp aimed to let workers draw down their salary whenever they wanted – even daily.

Most of the companies that do this charge a fee – maybe £2.50 for each withdrawal. It's a bit like the fee you reluctantly pay at some ATMs for withdrawing cash from your bank account. The companies that provide this service often portray themselves as a better, fairer alternative to payday lenders, which have been heavily criticized by poverty action groups and government inquiries for charging exorbitant rates to desperate customers. But the fees that these alternative payroll companies charge can still be costly.

FreeUp's small group of founders came from big tech and consulting backgrounds and had also worked in quasi-governmental and non-profit organizations. They were backed by the venture capital investor Public, which is run by a former Number 10 policy adviser. As well as being a fintech, FreeUp was one of a new breed of so-called 'GovTech' firms that were pushing new technologies into the public sector around the world. The company's name, FreeUp, signalled that its founders wanted to find a business model that would allow workers to draw down their salary without incurring any fees at all. It was a socially conscious organization, not just another company out to make huge profits.

Although FreeUp was little more than an idea – it had no customers at this point – the company had been noticed by Bill Crothers.

Crothers met with the founders. He was clearly impressed. FreeUp had plenty of potential. Imagine if it could be integrated into the NHS. The UK's health service is one of the world's largest employers, with 1.4 million staff and an annual payroll of more than £50 billion. Between them, FreeUp and Greensill could turn that into a gold mine.

Crothers introduced the business to Lex. He was interested. He saw it as similar to supply chain finance but, instead of transactions between suppliers and buyers, FreeUp dealt with payments between employers and their staff. Those payments, the obligations to pay staff, could be bundled up into securities and sold in the market just like supply chain payments.

Lex quickly made an offer to buy out FreeUp. At first, the shareholders rejected him. They were interested in having Greensill provide some funding to turn the idea into reality, but they weren't looking to sell. If they lost control of the company, they would lose control of its mission-driven agenda too. Lex came back with another offer – £5 million. It was an extraordinary bid, given there really was no business at that point. FreeUp's founders said yes.

Characteristically, Lex lavished FreeUp with grandiose praise. Combining Greensill and FreeUp had 'the potential to revolutionize the way workers are paid around the world', he said at the time.

But it soon became clear that the new venture would need a lot more development to deliver any meaningful income. In March, Lex sought to hasten that along. Greensill went out and bought Earnd, an Australian start-up that was in the same field. The Sydney company had been started less than two years earlier by a couple of entrepreneurs with a similar socially conscious mission to the founders of FreeUp. The big difference was that Earnd already had about twenty business customers and it was used by about 10,000 people.

But things didn't go to plan. First, merging FreeUp and Earnd into one business was not straightforward. Second, the Greensill vision did not match the ethical purpose of the founders. Lex planned to give it away for free to employees of the NHS, sure. But there were good commercial reasons for that. It would give the service enormous credibility to be working with such a huge employer – in effect, the free NHS service was a massive marketing cost. Also, Greensill wanted to use the service as a kind of loss leader. It could be used to seal a relationship with a client – including the NHS or other government agencies – and then upsell them loans or supply chain finance programmes. And finally, the service worked via an app, which could be furnished with a range of pop-up ads and other offerings, like insurance or remittances services or shopping discounts. Employees who drew down their pay would immediately be bombarded with ads and tempting ways to spend their money. This didn't seem anything like the ethically driven service the founders had envisaged. Several of the key executives involved in the business more or less immediately lost interest.

Still, Crothers began approaching NHS Trusts directly, asking them to adopt the Earnd service. Because the service was offered free, he told the trusts, there was no requirement to go through a formal tender process. In a handful of cases, Crothers was successful.

He wasn't the only cheerleader for Earnd. David Cameron was an especially proactive supporter of the business. He personally wrote to hundreds of business chiefs, asking them to adopt Earnd for their employees. Greensill also hired a high-profile advisory board for the business that included David Blunkett, the UK's former Home Secretary under Prime Minister Tony Blair; Dame Louise Casey, a parliamentarian and prominent advocate for homeless people; and Stephen Greene, an American 'social entrepreneur' who had been one of the leading lights of David Cameron's 'Big Society' policy efforts, aimed at integrating free-market thinking with volunteerism and social awareness. Blunkett took his role to heart, even weighing in on a branding and logos discussion with Greensill's marketing team, suggesting his own ideas for how the designs should look.

But Earnd was going nowhere fast. At the handful of NHS Trusts who had taken the service on, only a tiny group of employees were using it – barely 2,000 in total across the entire NHS. They were hardly drawing down any funds either, and opened the app very rarely. There were other problems. The trusts had put measures in place to prevent employees from drawing down so much that they got into financial trouble, putting a cap on how much they could draw or limiting when they could get access to their money. Still, a handful of employees who had left the NHS were able to draw down more than they were owed before they left. This was an issue the NHS Trusts had brought to Greensill even before Earnd was implemented, but nothing had been done to address it. In at least one case, Greensill agreed to pay the trust to compensate.

By early in 2020, just weeks after buying the two businesses, Greensill planned to write down to zero the value of its investment. An internal Greensill memo said that the product was likely to generate 'negative revenue' in 2020 as it was offered to governments for free, and because there was commission payable to an NHS agency for helping to get it launched. Earnd had attracted only a tiny handful of users and a meaninglessly low volume of assets.

Greensill's official position was still characteristically optimistic. It was budgeting for 2.8 million users of the platform by 2024 and $126 billion of assets flowing through the programme. Yet by 2021, in the chaos following Greensill's collapse into insolvency, Earnd in the UK simply disintegrated. The entire staff and business of Earnd in Australia was picked up for a bargain price by Wagestream, a competitor.

Greensill had promised Earnd would revolutionize employer payments. Like most of what Lex and Bill Crothers did with the NHS, it turned out to be time-consuming, expensive and fruitless.

# TWENTY-TWO

# Fault Lines

By early 2020, Lex was living large. The company had four private jets. Lex, his brother Peter, and several other top executives had squirrelled hundreds of millions of dollars out of the company. He had remodelled his Cheshire home and acquired the Queensland beachfront property.

The business was hiring at a clip. Managers were faced with few restrictions or processes to go through. The company's workforce already numbered a few hundred and was headed towards a thousand employees. Lex signed a lease on an enormous new office in the northwest of England, near his home.

The roster of big businesses and individuals who'd staked their reputations on Greensill was large and growing.

But there were some serious fault lines – and they were starting to widen.

Outwardly, the biggest problems appeared to be a wave of ugly defaults at Greensill's clients, several of them financed through the Credit Suisse funds. Some of these were long-troubled businesses that finally ran aground. Brighthouse, a UK-based rent-to-own retail business, was a longstanding Greensill client. The Credit Suisse funds had loaned it tens of millions of dollars over several years. Its fortunes had been declining since 2017 after it was accused of charging excessive interest rates, leaving some of its relatively poor customers owing huge debts. The UK's Financial Conduct Authority (FCA) had slapped Brighthouse with a £15 million fine, from which it had struggled to recover. By late 2019, Brighthouse was barely surviving and it went into administration early in the new year.

Other businesses that Greensill had loaned money to were mired in fraud allegations.

Agritrade was a Singapore-based commodities trading company that Greensill financed out of the Credit Suisse funds. In early 2020, Agritrade ran into financial difficulties. A group of European banks that were owed money by the firm – ING, Natixis and Commerzbank – filed court documents accusing its management of a 'massive, premeditated and systematic' fraud. The allegations included that Agritrade had used forged documents to finance the same trades several times over – like getting several mortgages on your house at once. When the firm filed for insolvency, it owed Greensill about $30 million.

Gulf Petrochem, known as GP Global, was another troubled commodities trader, this time based in Dubai. Greensill had loaned GP Global more than $30 million from the Credit Suisse funds. But the company was caught up in a protracted restructuring through much of 2020, while its management, customers and legal advisers fought a very public battle over allegations that some of its senior executives were engaged in widespread fraud, including using fake documents and financing the same transactions more than once.

Greensill was also party to the high-profile default of NMC Health, a Dubai-based healthcare chain and distribution business whose shares are listed in London. In late 2019, NMC was in the crosshairs of Muddy Waters, a US-based investment firm run by an investor named Carson Block, which publishes investigative research on public companies. Block was infamous in investing circles after unearthing a series of frauds at Chinese companies. Typically, his research notes seek to reveal some big accounting fraud and are often characterized by flowery language. Muddy Waters profits from making investments that increase in value when his research goes public and shares in the target company sink.

Regarding NMC, Muddy Waters' allegations included that the company overpaid for investments, overstated cash balances, and reported profit margins that were too good to be true. Block's report also singled out NMC's use of reverse factoring, which, he said, made it hard to tell how much debt the company had taken out. It mentioned the Credit Suisse funds specifically and noted that NMC had been less than forthcoming about the nature of these loan facilities.

Block also told a colleague of mine at Dow Jones US-based investor magazine *Barron's* that, 'Accounting standards don't really address reverse factoring . . . There's not necessarily a standardized way to report. That's the whole point of financial engineering, to take something that's not flattering and to hide it.'

Greensill had loaned NMC $137 million from the Credit Suisse funds.

NMC was eventually placed into administration and revealed that debts of $2.7 billion had not previously been reported. (There was another oddity about NMC. Companies linked to its founder, Indian businessman B.R. Shetty, were audited by a tiny London accountancy firm called King & King. The same tiny firm, whose main office was based in a trading estate on the outskirts of London, also audited several companies owned by Sanjeev Gupta.)

Between these borrowers, the Credit Suisse supply chain finance funds had loaned well in excess of $250 million. When the Greensill board asked about them, Lex seemed open and direct. They weren't life-threatening. They were too small for that, and several were covered by trade credit insurance.

But the defaulting loans seemed like a series of toppling dominoes. Each one that fell was a blow to Greensill's reputation and its relationship with insurance providers and potential funders. After the GAM scandal, Greensill could hardly afford to be linked to another. And while the insurance cover provided a safety net, claiming on it didn't come without a cost. For starters, Greensill usually had to take a 'first loss' – like a deductible on your car insurance. That was painful enough, eating directly into Greensill's profits. And with each claim, the premiums that insurers would charge Greensill were likely to rise too, cutting into the already fine margins of Greensill's core business.

Inside Greensill, there were other concerns about several of the companies Greensill had loaned money to. Staff in risk management were worried that invoices from some of these companies all seemed to be very similar. You could see that they all followed the same template. It was troubling. It suggested that maybe the invoices that backed the loans weren't real.

There were also questions about the amount of exposure that the company was building up to Sanjeev Gupta. But when staff raised their concerns about any of these issues, there appeared to be little appetite for further investigation. At times, the credit risk team would joke that there was no point in their existence at all – if Lex wanted a loan to go through, then it would go through.

One of the loudest dissenting voices was that of Brett Downes, a dour Australian veteran risk manager who had joined Greensill in 2015. He had previously built out Citi's commodity trade finance business, a type of financing similar to supply chain finance but for traders of raw materials. Downes had been hired by Lex to be the chief risk officer (CRO), and had been given the task of building up a proper risk function, capable of weighing up the various loans Greensill had extended to its clients and assessing what could go wrong. In practice, he frequently clashed with Lex and was frequently overruled by Lex too.

For months, Downes had highlighted the Gupta Family Group (GFG) issue at management group and board meetings, presenting the problem in stark detail. GFG was dominating the assets placed at Greensill Bank – Gupta's companies accounted for 80 per cent or more of the bank's assets – and made up more than half the assets in at least one of the Credit Suisse funds. Not only that but 40 per cent or more of the GFG loans in total were backed by 'Future Receivables'. This referred to one of the most controversial aspects of Greensill's business, and Downes was highlighting it for everyone to see. Typically, supply chain finance programmes involve extending loans backed by actual transactions – actual amounts owed by one company for goods received from another. Lex and Sanjeev had entered new territory altogether. In order to extend even more financing to Gupta, they'd come up with a new category of loans – they would extend financing based on transactions that might happen at some time in the future. The guesswork to come up with these numbers might have made some sense if it had been based on a detailed analysis of past purchase orders, inventory levels, demand and market prices. None of that was involved. Instead, the future receivables balances were calculated by little more than plucking a number out of thin air.

Downes's team highlighted several other worries heading into 2020. Greensill was moving too far, too fast. Too many functions were still manual. The company was moving into risky new geographies and its systems were not ready to deal with the consequences. Half of Greensill's staff had been with the firm only a few months. Key processes were still not up to the level you would expect in a big company, including for data protection, whistle-blowing, and for policies to deal with financial crime, anti-bribery and corruption.

Downes's team also pointed out problems with key partners. A single insurer, The Bond and Credit Company (TBCC), provided $6.8 billion of cover and needed monitoring. Suddenly, there were lots of loans to other SoftBank Vision Fund companies, many of them start-up companies whose creditworthiness was questionable.

The risk reports also focused on sanctions and anti-money-laundering (known as AML) questions. The complexity and volume of cases were growing rapidly. The team noted that Huawei, the Chinese telecoms business that Greensill worked with through Deal

Partners, was under expanded US government sanctions. The reports made specific mention of GFG companies, noting that there were several Gupta-company transactions where one of the parties involved had filed 'Iran Notices' with US regulators – a type of required disclosure indicating that you have done business with the sanctioned country. There was no indication of any wrongdoing, but these were serious issues, and the worry was that Greensill's risk function was struggling to keep up.

The reports show that there was never a shortage of disclosure at Greensill. The board and senior management were furnished with plenty of warnings about the risks the company was facing, whether related to insurance or GFG or bad loans or poor processes. From time to time, someone at a senior level would ask about these issues in a high-level meeting. Lex would always have an answer. The issue – TBCC, GFG, AML – was under control. But the impression from reading these reports was of a business too reliant on a single client, GFG, and too dependent on a single insurer, TBCC. The impression was of a business growing too fast and rapidly running out of control.

Downes was becoming increasingly agitated. As Greensill expanded, the risk of a major issue was rising sharply. Downes appeared to be especially stressed out about GFG. Greensill was lending about $7 billion to Gupta's companies. And much of that was backed by future receivables. A lot of it was in the bank, but some of it was stuffed into the Credit Suisse funds, often packaged up in the so-called multi-obligor programmes named after streets and districts in Lex's hometown.

By early 2020, some of Gupta's businesses weren't even paying the interest or fees they owed on Greensill debts. Instead, Greensill just kept adding the outstanding amounts to the total owed by GFG, while booking the revenues as though nothing was wrong. Senior Greensill staff sometimes asked Lex about the rising risk of concentrating too much of the business with Gupta. Lex would calmly say that he expected to outgrow GFG. If Greensill became ten times the size it was currently, and GFG stayed the same, then the problem would be ten times smaller.

Lex's relationship with Downes was increasingly fraught, and the strain was starting to tell on the CRO. Lex and Downes were regularly going toe-to-toe. It sometimes seemed to others as though the two would come to blows.

Downes's behaviour on calls became erratic. He frequently yelled at junior staff and colleagues. In early 2020, Downes and Lex had another stand-up row. Lex told him he could either walk out, with his shares, or face legal action. In May 2020, the board asked Downes to take some leave. Effectively, they fired him but kept him on payroll indefinitely. At Greensill, he was replaced by his understudy, who had arrived at the firm only a few months earlier. The move did little to ease tension among staff. If an experienced hand like Downes could be sidelined, how could a relatively new joiner – with far less experience – stand up to Lex? What would happen to the overhaul of the entire risk function that Downes had been working on? Who was left who could apply the brakes to Greensill's reckless acceleration? There were no good answers.

Lex had never showed the risk team much respect. They were like a necessary evil, tolerated but not really listened to. The situation certainly didn't improve after Downes's departure. One Sunday, some members of the team called a meeting to discuss a loan that Lex was planning on pushing through. Greensill grumpily joined the call. Before anyone else could speak, Lex set the tone, telling them: staff are welcome to hold a call like this, but I'm the CEO and it will be my decision. Talk for as long as you want, but the decision's already been made. We're going to do this deal.

IN MARCH 2020, the global financial markets were swooning over the possibility that the pandemic would stifle the world's economy and trade. Investors pulled money out of all sorts of funds, including the Credit Suisse–Greensill funds. Billions of dollars left the funds in just a few days. It threatened disaster for Greensill. When investors demand their money back, fund managers are forced to liquidate assets to make the payments. If investors pulled too much money out of the Greensill funds, then eventually the fund managers would find there were not enough good assets left to liquidate quickly. Many of the loans couldn't be repaid in short order, in ninety or 180 days. Some of them likely would not be repaid in a year, or at all. If the market chaos continued and investors kept demanding their money back, Greensill – and Credit Suisse – would not be able to liquidate enough assets to pay them all back.

Lex increasingly turned to an inner circle, a kind of Star Chamber of favoured Greensill executives, including his chief legal counsel Jonathan Lane, chief operating officer Chris Bates, and vice president Sean Hanafin. It was a dysfunctional group. They were loyal to Lex but had varied knowledge of the business as a whole. Hanafin had only joined recently. The others had been there from the start. As the world moved to remote working, information – which had always been concentrated in and around Lex – dried up almost completely. For the most part, internal communication was reduced to weekly Zoom meetings. Lex would usually show up late, give a rosy view of the business, and end the meeting.

Even as the problems mounted, Lex was presenting a very optimistic picture of the future to senior management and investors alike. He projected revenue doubling every year for years ahead, and the potential for a lucrative initial public offering of the company's shares seemed just around the corner.

In reality, the business was souring fast. What Lex later described as 'a perfect storm' was already brewing.

# TWENTY-THREE

# The Vision Fund Family

In April 2020, I published a story in the Dow Jones publication *Financial News*. The focus was on a strange new twist in the way the Credit Suisse–Greensill funds were operating.

Credit Suisse published monthly summary reports about the funds on their website and distributed them to investors in the fund too. They were emphatically bullish about the funds and didn't say exactly how much they loaned to each borrower. But they did say what proportion of the fund was loaned to each of the top ten clients. It was a straightforward task to reverse-engineer a calculation that showed how much in dollars each of the top ten borrowers had received. I kept tabs on them regularly for any unexpected shifts.

That month, there was a surprising new development. Suddenly, companies that were backed by the SoftBank Vision Fund popped up in the list of top ten clients. I knew Greensill was effectively making all the decisions about who the funds loaned to. Coupled with that knowledge, this new revelation meant Greensill was directing those funds to companies that, like Greensill itself, counted the giant Japanese firm as a major investor.

There were four Vision Fund companies that stood out.

OYO Hospitality is an Indian hotel company that operates budget accommodation around the world. SoftBank had invested more than $1 billion into the company, but in early 2020 OYO was struggling. The global Covid-19 pandemic had already started to hurt the travel and tourism sector. Even before that, a rapid expansion plan, encouraged by SoftBank, had been accompanied by widening annual losses of several hundred million dollars. The company had begun laying off staff and scaling back its ambitions.

Fair Financial was in a similar position. Fair had started out offering subscriptions to customers who paid a fee to drive used cars. Along the way SoftBank had ploughed more than $300 million into the company, becoming a major shareholder with influence over the direction of the company. Fair had morphed into a broader car leasing business, including a major deal to lease cars to Uber drivers. According to Bloomberg News, the Vision Fund's Colin Fan had led the investment and told Fair's executives that the biggest risk to the company was if it did not grow fast enough. That ambition too had proved wrongheaded. Fair began rapidly cutting costs, reducing staff numbers and exiting unprofitable deals such as the one with Uber. Senior management ranks were shuffled and shuffled again as the company hurtled into financial difficulties. The CEO stepped down after a round of layoffs. The company allegedly broke the lease on its office, failed to pay its $500,000 security deposit, and was sued by its landlord. Even as Fair borrowed from the Credit Suisse–Greensill funds, it was facing a major financial headache. It wasn't quite there in early 2020, but by the end of the year, Fair was deep in trouble. By the middle of 2021, it was potentially heading for insolvency.

Smart window manufacturer View Inc. had received an investment of about $1.1 billion from the Vision Fund in 2018. The Californian company makes 'dynamic glass' that is meant to reduce heat, glare and eyestrain. View too had been hit by the pandemic, which had slowed the US construction industry. And it was burdened by huge debts. The company was laying off staff and generating hundreds of millions of dollars in losses. View had received more than $80 million in financing from the Credit Suisse funds, loans that it didn't have to pay back for a year. That was odd. Most of the financing in the funds was for around ninety days, and hardly any loans were for more than six months. (In March 2021, View went public through a so-called SPAC – special purpose acquisition company – raising about $800 million. The move allowed it to restructure its debts, although its share price fell by about 40 per cent over the next six months as questions about its long-term profitability hung over the company.)

The other Vision Fund company that got a Credit Suisse–Greensill loan was Chinese online auto sales firm Chehaoduo. The Vision Fund had invested $1.5 billion into the Beijing-based firm in 2019. It too was struggling with the fallout from the pandemic, which had put a dent in Chinese auto sales. My colleagues at *The Wall Street Journal* had also written previously that some investors in the Vision Fund objected to the decision to put their money into Chehaoduo, which had been accused of fraud by a rival Chinese firm. A spokeswoman for Chehaoduo had denied the accusations, while SoftBank's leaders said they had conducted their own due diligence and found the accusations groundless. The Credit Suisse documents referred to it under the name Guazi, which is the name of Chehaoduo's online car-trading platform. It wasn't uncommon for these documents, which were sent out to investors, to include information that was not quite right, out of date, or just flat out wrong.

In total, these four companies – OYO, Fair, View and Chehaoduo – had received as much as 15 per cent of the loans provided by the biggest of the Credit Suisse–Greensill funds. That worked out at about $750 million – all of it Credit Suisse's clients' money, and all of it loaned to Vision Fund companies that were, to a varying degree, facing financial difficulties of their own. None of the four companies had been among the big borrowers from the funds a few months earlier, indicating that financing to them picked up after SoftBank bought into Greensill. Some of the deals were hugely lucrative for Greensill too. By the fourth quarter of 2019, Greensill was counting on the four Vision Fund companies to deliver about $90 million in revenue, about a fifth of the total revenue for the year. The whole arrangement appeared to represent a huge conflict of interest. I called some investment and governance experts I knew and they were all in agreement: it was potentially very problematic, and possibly riddled with conflicts, especially so if investors in the funds were blind to what was going on.

I checked through all the documentation from the funds that I could get my hands on, to see whether Credit Suisse or Greensill disclosed to investors in the funds the ties between Greensill, the Vision Fund, and four of the biggest obligors. There was nothing.

When I called Credit Suisse, it was unclear to me that anyone there even knew about the Vision Fund loans. Instead, a spokesperson for the bank sent me a bland, on-the-record statement, by email, that said the funds are 'highly regulated and [have] a thorough investment and due diligence process in place' and that everything was 'in line with the prospectus, investment guidelines and marketing material.'

Greensill was equally unhelpful. I got another email, this time apparently highlighting the SoftBank connection as a positive: 'The investment from and relationship with SoftBank has provided Greensill access to numerous new relationships, from across the Vision Fund and externally, for us to evaluate.'

It seemed like a vague reference to something Masayoshi Son had said about the 'Cluster of No. 1' strategy. SoftBank's website explains that SoftBank-backed companies 'are encouraged to form synergies to evolve and grow together based on capital ties and a shared vision while making decisions independently.'

The story we published in *Financial News* had raised a serious red flag about the multifaceted role of SoftBank in the Greensill funds. It also made another point. The Credit Suisse–Greensill funds had ballooned in the past couple of years – from about $2 billion in aggregate at the end of 2018 to more than four times that much in early 2020. But that trend was now in a dramatic and swift reversal, with investors pulling billions of dollars out of the funds in a matter of days – part of a broad market upheaval caused by the pandemic.

The same Credit Suisse spokesperson emailed me: 'During this unseen market correction, the fixed income asset class has generally seen record outflows. Despite the adverse markets, the supply chain finance funds of Credit Suisse Asset Management have delivered a solid performance and are outperforming the [sic] peers. All redemptions have been met.'

In fact, the wave of redemptions was much more significant than that. Lex knew that not all the loans were short term, and that some of them might not be recoverable at all. If redemptions continued to grow, it was possible that Credit Suisse would not be able to pay back investors who demanded their cash. That would be catastrophic, revealing that the funds were not as liquid or safe as many investors had been led to expect. The whole house of cards would come crashing down, and fast.

I didn't know this till later, but Lex was as panicked as the markets. Weeks before my story about the potential conflicts of interest, he had called Masayoshi Son in Tokyo from his chauffeur-driven car on a rainy day in London. Lex pleaded for his mentor's help. He blamed the impact of Covid-19 and the markets. It was critical. If SoftBank could put $2.5 billion into the Credit Suisse funds, it would immediately stop the bleeding. From the outside, no one would know where the money had come from, and such a major inflow of investment money would send a signal that the funds continued to be stable and reliable. Lex also knew that getting the cash was potentially existential for Greensill.

It was a huge ask. Masa and SoftBank had a well-deserved reputation for making big, multibillion-dollar bets, and fast. But even for

Masa, $2.5 billion was a high-stakes gamble. On the other hand, if the Japanese investor didn't put the money in, the $1.4 billion that Soft-Bank's Vision Fund had already invested in Greensill could be at risk.

Masa offered $1.5 billion – less than Lex wanted but a staggering sum, nonetheless. It would have to do. The money came with terms attached: SoftBank got an extra stake in Greensill, of about 3 per cent of the company's shares. Greensill and Credit Suisse also agreed a side deal that the funds would only invest in loans brokered by Greensill. In practice this was the case anyway. It was a formalization of a built-in conflict in the way the funds were run.

I didn't uncover all these details until months later. But in June, Robert Smith and Arash Massoudi, journalists at the *Financial Times*, reported that SoftBank had poured more than $500 million into the funds. Though I believe they underestimated the true size of the investment, the story was the first to report the additional twist.

The pressure on the funds was becoming too intense for Credit Suisse to simply keep quiet. Something would have to give. In June, the bank's senior management launched an investigation into the funds.

By then, the bank was under new stewardship. Thiam, the charismatic French-Ivorian, had been pushed out in February after a nasty boardroom standoff. Inside the insular world of Swiss banking, he had never really been accepted. The previous year, Thiam walked out of a birthday party for the bank's chairman, Urs Rohner, after a black performer dressed as a janitor danced on stage and some bank executives donned Afro wigs.

Iqbal Khan, Credit Suisse's wealth management chief, had also fallen out with Thiam and decided to leave the bank for its crosstown rival UBS. Khan and Thiam had clashed frequently, with Thiam trying to curb the wealth management unit's long-held appetite for selling riskier investments to its clients. But Khan was popular inside the bank and his exit had damaged Thiam. Then it emerged that one of Thiam's top lieutenants had hired a corporate espionage company to follow and spy on Khan after his departure. In the worst incident, Khan and his wife were allegedly engaged in a car chase through the streets of Zurich before a physical altercation between the banker and the spooks. Thiam pleaded his ignorance of the spying debacle, and he was formally cleared of any involvement by an external law firm. But he was pushed out of the bank anyway.

His replacement, Thomas Gottstein, was a Swiss national who had represented his country at golf and had worked for Credit Suisse for twenty years. Over the next few months, it would be Gottstein who would have to deal with the crisis that emerged at Greensill.

The new CEO was quickly facing several crises all at once.

Among his biggest problems was how to untangle a mess at Luckin Coffee, a Chinese challenger to Starbucks. Credit Suisse had touted Luckin, and its founder Lu Zhengyao, as a poster child for its strategy of banking wealthy entrepreneurs. The Swiss bank had underwritten Luckin's New York IPO in 2019 and sold hundreds of millions of dollars in bonds for the Chinese company. But in April 2020, the coffee company imploded after revelations that its top management had made up $310 million in sales. It was an embarrassing – and costly – black eye for the bank.

There were other blows too. The bank's reputation had been called into question in 2019 after it had helped finance a controversial bond sale for Wirecard AG, a German payments company that collapsed amid fraud allegations. And, later in 2020, Credit Suisse announced it would take a hit of at least $450 million on a stake it had bought in hedge fund York Capital Management, which was winding down after being pummelled in the markets.

The Greensill–SoftBank issue might have seemed the least of Gottstein's worries at that point. It wasn't the first time the funds had come into the crosshairs of the bank's top management. In the wake of the crisis at GAM, there had been a discussion at Credit Suisse about whether their own Greensill funds needed a closer look. The discussions went as high as Lara Warner, the bank's head of compliance. Warner was seen by some colleagues as a stickler for the rules, although she was also known for trying to find ways to come up with commercially friendly solutions. Credit Suisse's fund managers in Zurich were very defensive about the GAM questions. The Greensill funds were growing and making tens of millions in management fees. The fund managers – the team that included Mathys and Haas – pushed back hard, belittling the concerns from compliance and pointing out that the insurance coverage meant the funds were fully protected against any downside.

In the end, the bank's managers, including Warner, decided they had not uncovered enough to make any changes to the ways the funds were run.

But the questions didn't go away. In 2019, some bankers in the credit-structuring team had come across the Greensill loans too. They sent messages to the bank's reputational risk committee, alerting it to the possibility of some wider problem, suggesting that Greensill was taking shortcuts in documentation and the way it was running its loan book. Again, the questions went nowhere. Some of the bank's staff who had spoken up felt that there was no point. The funds had grown rapidly. Everyone was making money. And there was still the potential Greensill IPO to think about. No one wanted to hear any negativity or scepticism.

My own regular questions about the funds – as well as those of other journalists – were also escalated from the bank's media relations team to people further up the hierarchy. Ultimately though, the inquiries always hit a senior executive, someone like Warner, and the questions would stop. Warner was part of Thiam's top ranks and had been expected to follow him out of the door. Instead, Gottstein promoted her to chief risk and compliance officer.

When the revelations about SoftBank's multiple roles in the Greensill funds broke, the bank's senior executives initially talked about a wide-ranging review of the funds. There were many questions. How were they run? What did they invest in? Should they do more due diligence on Greensill?

The bank's investigators reviewed phone records and emails from the key staff working on the funds, Mathys and Haas. There was nothing incriminating. Nothing like the free flights and tickets to Buckingham Palace that GAM's Haywood had taken.

Top bank executives were also concerned that the portfolio managers had struck the separate side agreement, not disclosed to investors in the funds, which said they would only invest in supply chain assets from Greensill. In theory, the funds could previously invest with assets sourced elsewhere, but this agreement had formalized Greensill's exclusivity, and would have ensured a steady stream of business for Greensill.

At Greensill, meanwhile, there was little to indicate that a serious investigation was underway. Lex told his board and top executives that it was a Credit Suisse issue – they were happy with the funds' performances and happy with Greensill's role. The questions were all about their own internal procedures. It was the same playbook he'd employed when the GAM crisis had blown up. Nothing to see here. Someone else's problem. Many of those close to him were inclined to believe Lex. He had got out of bigger scrapes, after all.

In late July, Credit Suisse sent a letter to investors in the funds. The bank said that it was committing to taking further steps to protect investors – though it never explained what those were. It also said the funds were performing well, and that no investors had incurred losses because of the matters under investigation. To me, this only showed they still didn't understand the way the funds worked. So long as investor money kept coming in, then Lex could continue rolling bad loans over, and writing up whatever performance he wanted.

Meanwhile, staff working for Eric Varvel, the bank's head of asset management who had once said he would help Lex fund a new capital for Indonesia, were assigned to investigate individual obligors beyond the SoftBank Vision Fund borrowers. That would have meant looking at the many Sanjeev Gupta GFG companies or a host of other odd loans. An investigation like that would have uncovered some of the billions of dollars of loans that might never be paid back. It might even have unearthed major problems at Greensill Bank and with Greensill's biggest insurance partner. But nothing substantial ever came of it. The wide-ranging review of the funds that the bank's senior management had talked about in June faded into the rear-view mirror as Greensill headed straight towards a cliff.

IT TURNED OUT that SoftBank wasn't the only Greensill shareholder that had got itself entangled in Greensill's Credit Suisse funds. In 2019, General Atlantic had been seeking financing for an investment it was making into a joint venture with German exchange operator Deutsche Börse. The private equity firm needed about $350 million, which would be secured against its stake in the deal, and the company put out a request to lenders to see who could come up with the best deal. There were four or five bidders. In the end it came down to Goldman Sachs and Greensill, which were offering similar terms. GA decided to give it to Greensill. An internal Greensill document said the deal 'provides Greensill with the opportunity to strengthen its relationship with a significant sponsor while achieving a strong return.'

Greensill parked part of the loan in Greensill Bank. There are limits on how much banks can lend to their own investors. So the rest, a little under $100 million, sat in the Credit Suisse funds.

ALTHOUGH CREDIT SUISSE'S investigation had fallen short, it was not without an impact. The probe had very publicly shone a light on Credit Suisse's relationship with both Greensill and its biggest investor, the SoftBank Vision Fund. It was another blemish on Greensill's reputation, at least among those who were paying attention –

potential corporate clients and insurance partners, for instance. Eventually, Credit Suisse's fund managers asked that Greensill cut the exposure to GFG. At the end of 2020, about 13 per cent of the funds were invested in GFG loans and, Lex told his senior staff, Credit Suisse wanted that down to about 9 per cent as soon as possible, with a further reduction to 5 per cent by the end of June 2021. The bank's demands meant Lex would have to find somewhere else to put another billion dollars of GFG loans at some point.

# TWENTY-FOUR

# Bluestone

In July 2020, negative publicity had forced Credit Suisse to launch its Greensill investigation – and it seemed like a good time to publish some findings of our own. My colleague Julie Steinberg and I wrote a story in *The Wall Street Journal*, uncovering details of some of the companies that were borrowing money from the funds – the 'obligors'. Collectively they had received billions of dollars of loans, all money that came from Credit Suisse's own clients.

We focused on companies whose businesses were inherently odd, or that had troubled financial histories or a poor track record when it came to repaying debts. There were quite a few to choose from.

But one of the biggest obligors was a company called Bluestone Resources Inc. It had received about $40 million in financing from one of the Credit Suisse funds, and we knew from some other sourcing that it was one of Greensill's biggest clients in terms of the amount of revenue it generated.

At first, it wasn't easy to track down Bluestone. There are several companies named Bluestone, or that have a similar name. Any Credit Suisse investor tracking the obligors could easily have looked at the wrong company. We figured out the one we wanted was a coal-mining business based in West Virginia.

Bluestone Resources made for an interesting, oddball case study for our article – later, we realized just how important it was to the entire Greensill story, as loans to Bluestone ballooned and Credit Suisse's ability to recover the debts foundered.

The coal-mining company is owned by one of the most colourful politicians and businessmen in the US. Jim Justice, the billionaire governor of West Virginia, is six feet seven inches tall, an avid basketball fan, and an imposing and controversial figure.

Justice grew up on coal. His father had made a small fortune in the coal industry, and Justice built an empire off it. Over several decades, he bought and sold hundreds of farming, timber and coal companies. In the 1970s, he ran Justice Family Farms, which grew soybeans, corn and wheat. He was US national corn-growing champion seven times, according to CNN. In 2008 and 2009, he negotiated to sell off the coal mines to various buyers, including a Russian-owned metals and mining company called Mechel. The Russians reportedly agreed to pay about $4 billion for the mines, which were collectively known as Bluestone. When the financial crisis hit, the deal was restructured and Mechel paid only about a tenth of that price. Even then, the acquisition didn't work out. The owners of Mechel had loaded up with too much debt, and they were under some political pressure, facing stinging criticism at one point from Vladimir Putin for exporting raw materials too cheaply.

In 2015, when coal prices were hitting rock bottom, the Justice family bought Bluestone back for $5 million. They had acquired a substantial operation, a small but genuine player in the metallurgical coal sector. The Justice family's coal interests mined more than a million tons of coal in 2018, most of it metallurgical coal used in steelmaking. It sounds like a lot, though the largest metallurgical coal miners in the US produced about ten times as much.

Back in 2009, Justice had also acquired the Greenbrier, a

sprawling hundred-year-old resort hotel in the Allegheny Mountains, renowned for its golf course and Cold War bunker, and because it has hosted dozens of illustrious guests including prime ministers and presidents. The Greenbrier was bankrupt, and the Justice family picked it up for just $20 million. It was a typically opportunistic deal. The resort is likely valued at many multiples of what Justice paid for it, although perhaps not the $1 billion that he has claimed.

In 2016, Justice ran for governor of West Virginia – one of the poorest states in the US. He was a controversial politician and a frequent pundit on cable news. Although Justice was a registered Republican, he ran as a Democrat in the blue-collar state.

After he won, Justice switched camps again, back to the Republicans, a move he announced at a rally with President Donald Trump. It was a strange turn of affairs – in a period of major electoral surprises, the political news publication *Politico* asked, 'Is West Virginia Holding America's Weirdest Election?'

Justice had also become known for something else: not paying his debts. In May 2020, the US investigative journalism outlet ProPublica published an investigation into the Justice family's businesses. The investigation found that Justice's companies had been involved in more than 600 lawsuits in the past thirty years, including suits filed by the company's workers, business partners – and suppliers. In most cases, the plaintiffs alleged that Justice's companies hadn't paid their debts. In a story accompanied by a photo of Justice in full camouflaged hunting gear, carrying a rifle, the magazine *Forbes* called Justice 'The Deadbeat Billionaire' and documented tens of millions of dollars in unpaid bills.

In other words, Justice made for a strange client for an investment fund that makes loans to supposedly super-safe, low-risk borrowers.

But here's how it happened. Bluestone wasn't the bargain its $5 million price tag suggested. The acquisition of his old business also saddled Justice with about $300 million in environmental and legal liabilities. Justice said Mechel had mismanaged the company, 'burdening it with substantial reclamation, union and trade obligations.' The Justice family – Jim and his son James 'Jay' Justice III – set about restructuring Bluestone's finances and operations. The long-term makeover would not come cheap. Step forward Greensill Capital.

Jim Justice had been introduced to Roland Hartley-Urquhart through a mutual acquaintance. This was Roland's world. The Greenbrier was his comfort zone. He became a confidant of Jim Justice, emailing regularly and talking frequently in person or on the phone. And he sold Justice a bunch of Greensill debt.

Initially, Bluestone signed up to a small supply chain finance and receivables programme – this is what we wrote about in *The Wall Street Journal* in the summer of 2020. We had noticed something odd about the loan. In that first round of financing, Bluestone repaid Greensill with a combination of cash and $25 million in equity warrants. This was strange. Typically, SCF loans are paid back with cash alone. Typically, *any kind* of loan is paid back with cash. A lender would only expect payment in any other way as a last resort. Bluestone was paying its loan back with a financial instrument that gave Greensill the right to own a few Bluestone shares. It certainly didn't help counter the view that lending money to a Justice business was risky.

It was even more eye-opening in the context of Greensill's business. The $25 million was equivalent to more than half of Greensill's entire profits for the whole of 2018. Depending on what you thought the shares were worth, their valuation could have a huge impact on Greensill's profitability.

Accepting payment of the loan in equity warrants rather than cash suggested Bluestone had Greensill over a barrel. You'd only accept this deal if there was no other option.

When we wrote the story, Bluestone's lawyers told us that the company had been working with Greensill to improve its working capital. The lawyer also said that the equity warrants were 'very soon after redeemed fully in cash' – though it wasn't exactly clear what that meant. (Later, after Greensill collapsed, the administrators Grant Thornton issued an update on their work in October 2021. The update said that Greensill held an equity warrant related to a US mining business that had been booked at a value of $50 million. The administrators said it was unclear how much of that could be recovered. It is also unclear whether this was a new warrant, different to the one we wrote about in 2020, but it almost certainly relates to Bluestone.)

The strange deal we wrote about had been just the opening act. Bluestone was quickly becoming a significant Greensill client. Though Roland was the key contact, Lex himself flew down to West Virginia to meet with Greensill's increasingly important business partners. The amounts Greensill loaned to the coal company grew rapidly too. And Greensill was becoming increasingly dependent on Bluestone revenue. Within a few months, Bluestone was responsible for a third of Greensill's revenue, more than any other Greensill client in 2018, including all of Sanjeev Gupta's companies put together.

Here's how the loans were structured. The Greensill and Bluestone executives discussed an 'enterprise financing' agreement that would fund the comprehensive rebuilding of Bluestone. That process would take several years to bear fruit, and the financing from Greensill would need to be preserved for all of it. The Justice family understood the loans were long term and didn't have to be paid back for several years. Within Greensill, the Bluestone loans were also counted as 'committed facilities' that were longer term too. An extra level of security for Greensill was that the Justice family personally guaranteed their side of the agreement – they would be personally on the hook if Bluestone did not pay up.

Greensill and Bluestone also agreed that all the loans would be backed by receivables – amounts owed to Bluestone for coal it sold. The agreement stretched the limits of conventional financing. Bluestone could also borrow from Greensill based on 'prospective receivables' – amounts attributed to potential buyers of Bluestone coal in the future. Greensill provided Bluestone with a list of potential buyers and put a number alongside their name for potential revenue. Greensill was no longer financing actual transactions, but possible transactions that might or might not take place sometime into the future. They were literally making up the numbers.

All of this was financed out of the Credit Suisse supply chain funds, which were supposed to be making short-term SCF loans. Bluestone and the Justice family later claimed they didn't know about Credit Suisse's role until Greensill collapsed. In any case, Greensill managed the short-term/long-term issue by making a series of shorter-term loans to Bluestone, which were continuously rolled over on maturity.

A lawsuit Bluestone filed against Greensill in early 2021 included an illustration to show how this worked:

'By way of example, on January 4th, 2019, $15 million of Prospective Receivables were scheduled to 'mature' or be rolled over. On that day, Greensill Capital was to 'purchase' new Prospective Receivables in the amount of $15 million from Bluestone by wiring to Bluestone a discounted amount of $14,543,186 (with the 'discount' corresponding to the interest to be paid from the date of the new purchase until the next roll date). Bluestone then wired to Greensill Capital the $14,543,186 just received from Greensill Capital plus the difference between such amount and the $15 million to be repaid ($456,814 in this instance) back to Greensill Capital. The net result of that exchange was Bluestone's payment to Greensill Capital of only the $456,814 in interest.'

The result of this was that Bluestone didn't have to repay its loan, or even pay the interest on the loan – those payments were coming directly out of the funds extended from Credit Suisse to Bluestone via Greensill.

In summer 2020, this remarkable process was streamlined even further. Greensill modified the system, so that Bluestone no longer rolled the loan over. Instead, the coal-mining company just paid Greensill the net amount of fees owed. This became known as a 'cashless roll'.

Around the same time, Greensill had also agreed to extend the life of its commitment to Bluestone. The initial four- to five-year lending arrangement was upped to six to eight years. In September, Justice met Roland at his home in Westhampton, a wealthy enclave of Long Island. Greensill wanted to do even more business with Bluestone, Roland said. We will continue rolling Bluestone's existing loan facilities, he assured him. You're a valued partner, and Greensill as a firm was a believer in Bluestone and its management.

By 2020, Lex had another plan. He had begun to connect the dots between his two biggest clients – Sanjeev Gupta and Jim Justice.

If Bluestone had a steady stream of sales for its metallurgical coal, then Greensill could provide even more financing. And if GFG had a reliable supplier of coal, then that could be financed too. By getting Bluestone and GFG to work together, Greensill would have plenty of cash flows against which he could make loans.

Roland made the case to Bluestone. A first delivery of coal from Bluestone to GFG followed in mid-2020. But when the payment for that shipment fell due in December 2020, GFG failed to pay. Another shipment of coal was due the same month. Justice put a block on it.

Between 2018 and 2021, Greensill loaned Bluestone $850 million, and Bluestone paid $108 million back to Greensill in the form of fees. Greensill also received warrants to purchase a stake in Bluestone that was worth another $100 million. But the relationship was increasingly strained.

# TWENTY-FIVE

# BaFin

Lex had built a business that avoided the toughest regulators. Greensill's parent company was registered in Australia, but mostly operated elsewhere. The Australian securities authorities left it alone. His auditor in Australia was a tiny firm called Nexia Sydney that had only a few million dollars in revenue.

Greensill's operations were run out of the UK, where the company was registered with the Financial Conduct Authority through a so-called registration agent – a kind of outsourcing shell that offers a light registration, typically for very small hedge funds and individuals who don't want to go through the costly and time-consuming red tape of a full registration. His UK auditor, Saffery Champness, was relatively small too, lacking the scale to typically work on a multinational client running billions of dollars of transactions.

The funds Lex operated with Credit Suisse were registered in Liechtenstein and Luxembourg, where the regulators didn't have oversight across the whole Greensill business. Swiss regulators kept an eye on GAM and Credit Suisse, but they weren't keeping tabs on Greensill.

The European regulator with a reputation for being among the most toothless, however, was in Germany. BaFin, Germany's banking regulator, was heavily criticized for its role in the downfall of Wirecard, the credit card payments company that, like Greensill, had once been backed by SoftBank. Journalists at the *Financial Times* had spent years writing critical stories about Wirecard, only to face a concerted effort by the company, German authorities and large swathes of the German establishment to undermine their work.

In 2019, I found out that Greensill had taken a huge new round of funding – from the SoftBank Vision Fund – and parked it in the bank. The press release announcing the funding round had talked about using the money to 'accelerate new technology' and expand into emerging markets. In fact, the money was mostly sent straight to the bank. 'I can't hide from the fact that's what I have done,' Lex told me. He said that putting the money there was more efficient than trying to build the business in China or India, and that it could provide a buffer for a potential economic downturn. 'My board and I are pretty bearish about the economy going forward,' he told me. Having a bank 'with oodles of cash' was a hedge against the uncertainty ahead.

In that interview, there was also a stunning admission, one that revealed the true purpose of Greensill Bank. It was, Lex told me, 'as much as anything a warehouse that provides us with the ability to manage the liquidity requirements of our business.'

In other words, Greensill Bank would buy the loans Lex was selling even when no one else would take them off his hands.

Greensill Bank, which was regulated by BaFin, grew rapidly after Lex bought it. He had used a good chunk of the SoftBank money to build its balance sheet, and then attracted more money from ordinary Germans, as well as German town councils. The bank pulled in huge amounts of deposits by offering interest rates that were better than you could get elsewhere. Then Lex used the bank to buy loans that couldn't be squeezed into the Credit Suisse funds, especially loans to Sanjeev Gupta's business.

The challenges arising from this period of supercharged growth were everywhere. A report on the bank by credit rating agency Scope in August 2019 said that 'the ambitious growth strategy requires the group to invest heavily in staff, systems and processes.'

The bank was heavily reliant on other people's technology. It depended on platforms such as Taulia's and others to originate, structure and service loans. Because it did not have a big network of branches, it had to rely on external platforms and brokers to attract deposits. Its assets were narrowly focused too. Scope reported that in August 2019, two-thirds of the loans it had made were to parties connected, one way or another, to Sanjeev Gupta. There were mitigating factors that reduced the risk of too much concentration. Almost all the loan book was covered by insurance. And the Gupta Family Group-related business was mostly receivables financing, meaning the money was owed to the bank by a diverse range of businesses. Still, the transactions that were financed by the bank were all related to GFG, meaning that Greensill Bank was little more than a funding source for GFG.

The injection of the SoftBank money had certainly seen Greensill Bank grow at a rapid clip. Its loan book was just about €200 million in 2016, but it had grown to about €2.8 billion by the end of 2019, according to Scope.

BaFin's leadership was suspicious about Greensill Bank. Having been caught out on Wirecard, they would hardly want to be in the same position again. They were particularly concerned about the exposure the bank had to Gupta's companies.

The German regulator initially started to make inquiries about Greensill as early as the start of 2019. At first, these were fairly benign questions about Greensill's ownership structure or the insurance coverage that Greensill had in place to protect bank depositors. Greensill was able to deter further probing by providing a self-certification that the insurance policies were adequate.

BaFin's inquiries ramped up a few months later. In January 2020,

BaFin contacted the Financial Conduct Authority in the UK. The German regulator was keen to know what to make of what had happened at GAM in relation to Greensill. Shortly afterwards, the German regulator received the first in a series of whistle-blower tips, alleging there was a fraud at Greensill Bank.

The allegations from an anonymous whistle-blower were serious. Someone inside the bank claimed to have knowledge of wrongdoing connected to loans the bank was making to its biggest – by some way– client, Sanjeev Gupta. The allegations included the suggestion that some of the loans were not backed by real invoices, as was supposed to be the case. In fact, they were backed either by fake invoices or by nothing at all. All of that would mean Greensill Bank's balance sheet was far weaker than it looked. Depositors' money was being handed out to a single, rather tenuous, steel and metals business in the form of effectively unsecured loans. It would put at serious risk money deposited at the bank by ordinary German citizens and municipal governments too.

Over the next few months, BaFin received several more tips from the whistle-blower. Some of these focused on Greensill Bank and the loans to Gupta. They pointed to more fake invoices and more unsecured loans. Other whistle-blower tips came in, making allegations focused more broadly on the financial health of the bank's 100 per cent owner, Greensill Capital.

By March, the regulator was considering asking Greensill to bulk up the amount of capital held at the bank, to further safeguard against the risk of a major blow-up. BaFin's supervisors had also told Lex Greensill and the bank's senior managers that they had to reduce the amount of exposure the bank had to Gupta.

Through May, June and July, the regulator had monthly calls with Greensill's board and management to get an update on efforts to reduce the GFG loans. The regulator also sent a series of letters to the management of Greensill Bank. BaFin repeatedly complained that some of the bank's senior executives were not properly qualified.

They warned of a series of governance violations. And they started demanding more and more information from Greensill Bank.

WITHIN GREENSILL, THE problem with the bank's exposure to GFG had been on the agenda for at least a year. It was in the reports that Downes's team submitted to management meetings, which had noted that most of the loans the bank made were to GFG, and that many of those were backed by so-called future receivables.

By the time BaFin was asking for regular updates and launching its task force, though, Downes had been put on leave. The subject still came up at management meetings. Some of it had leaked into the media – reporters from Bloomberg had first published a story about BaFin looking at Greensill Bank in the summer. When I and other journalists asked Lex about these leaked reports of an investigation, he would get tense. Either Lex or Doran would then insist that there was no special investigation, that the German regulator's questions were just part of its regular oversight of all the banks it supervised. This was patently false.

At that point, management meetings were still on Zoom. Whenever one of Greensill's managers asked about the German investigation, Lex would repeat the same mantra: 'We're all set with BaFin.'

Except that they were not. His risk management team – inexperienced, with their leader Downes gone – was left to pick up the pieces. While Lex would insist all was fine, the team would discover the reality on their own calls with BaFin. The regulator wanted more information, more action. They wanted the GFG loans to go away.

While Lex remained outwardly calm and in control, the BaFin probe was potentially life-threatening for Greensill. The Germans wanted him to reduce the proportion of assets tied to Gupta from about 90 per cent of the assets in the bank to around 30 per cent.

Lex had other sources of financing. Greensill sometimes placed supply chain finance programmes or other assets directly with a handful of big banks, including Lloyds, Mizuho, Sumitomo and BBVA. These banks would buy billions of dollars of assets between them. But they were only interested in the good stuff. They wouldn't take Gupta debt.

His other pool of available cash was the Credit Suisse funds. He could hardly hide the Gupta loans there. For starters, the Credit Suisse funds were already stuffed with vast amounts of lending to Gupta companies. The ongoing investigation into those funds – provoked by the piling up of loans to Vision Fund companies – meant they were definitely off-limits for more controversial assets. Lex couldn't place more GFG debts there without attracting further unwanted attention to the funds.

In June and July 2020, Lex told Neil Garrod, the CFO, and Wasif Raza, Greensill's head of distribution, to investigate alternative sources of funding. The two put together a report that went to the board and senior management. In theory, the report was supposed to be looking at ways to expand the available funding to cover the expected growth in Greensill's business. In reality, it was a scattergun review of the possible escape hatches that could deliver Lex from another looming crisis.

The Greensill team figured they had a little under $25 billion in available funding. This included all the Credit Suisse funds, all their banking relationships, the rump of the GAM Greensill Supply Chain Finance fund (GGSCF), which had somehow survived the Haywood debacle, and Greensill Bank. But $23.5 billion of that funding capacity was already invested in assets. There was very little spare capacity, and not enough funding even to hit Greensill's revenue target for the year. To meet that goal, they'd need to find about $6 billion in funding from somewhere, according to Garrod and Raza's calculations.

There were several short-term options under consideration. These included a new securitization programme with Mizuho and Lloyds, and a new facility potentially provided by a combination of Morgan Stanley, Barclays and BNP Paribas that would finance cash advances through a government Covid-19 loan scheme. They also hoped to boost Greensill Capital's own balance sheet by $500 million by issuing bonds in the company. It wasn't clear whether any of these could really be delivered or whether they were just pipe dreams.

A longer-term plan seemed even more ambitious. By the end of 2023, Garrod and Raza's report said, Greensill aimed to have access to $91 billion in funding. Some of this, they said, would come from Credit Suisse. They projected the bank's Greensill funds would grow to more than $15 billion, partly because Credit Suisse was planning to market the funds in the US. They planned for Greensill Bank to provide $7 billion in loans. There'd be more funding from bank partners too. Where would the rest come from? Even if the existing sources of funding grew at the aggressive rates that the Greensill team projected, they'd still need to find about $45 billion in new funding sources to hit their targets.

They came up with another ambitious list. They wanted to build $9 billion worth of new funds, like the Credit Suisse funds, and identified giant asset manager BlackRock and Spanish bank Santander as the likely partners. They planned to develop more investment-grade rated securities, by putting insurance wrappers around the underlying loans to non-investment-grade companies. They also planned to convince the rating agencies to attribute 'shadow investment-grade ratings' to assets that weren't investment grade and didn't have an insurance wrapper either – Raza and Garrod acknowledged this would be a challenge, but told Lex that 'the prize is sufficiently large that this is a route we must pursue.'

The biggest source of funding – the big prize – was to tap the US capital markets. Though Greensill loaned money to plenty of US clients, it had not been successful trying to tap US investors. US regulations stated that they would have to retain at least 5 per cent of the credit risk of any assets they securitized. Greensill didn't have the balance sheet to do that. Garrod and Raza's report said that the firm could not afford to ignore the US for much longer if it wanted to hit its growth targets.

They also proposed buying several commercial banks – a move that would bring 'unfettered access to central bank balance sheets, which has proved so illusive [sic].' At least in this case, Garrod and Raza acknowledged that it could take years to pull it off.

Given everything Greensill was facing at that time – the BaFin investigations, the investigation at Credit Suisse, the governance issues on top of growing pains – it was an astonishingly optimistic plan. Some of the board and senior management thought it was delusional. These weren't plausible ideas to address Greensill's many problems. Raza and Garrod were just delivering what Lex wanted to hear, regardless of the blunt reality. Greensill had become like a cult, where no one wanted to upset the leader.

At the same meeting in which Raza and Garrod mooted their ideas, another report was presented, looking into short-term funding mismatches. Greensill had what it considered 'committed facilities' of $3.3 billion to seventeen clients. These were longer-term lending commitments that the firm was legally obliged to fulfil. The average remaining length of the loan commitments was twenty-one months, though some were considered 'evergreen' – essentially loans that never matured. The report, from a member of Garrod's team, said that Greensill had 'reasonably permanent' funding sources of $7.7 billion – theoretically plenty to cover its commitments. But there was a potential pitfall: some of the 'reasonably permanent' funding could not be deployed quickly enough to cover 'the more uncustomary credits that are commensurate with the majority of the Committed Facilities'. This tangle of jargon meant that the long-term commitments were largely loans to the likes of Bluestone, GFG, the SoftBank Vision Fund companies and other potentially problematic Greensill clients. Some of these long-term loans were hard to fund out of the longer-term funds Greensill could access. There was no real solution to this problem, other than crossing your fingers and hoping for the best.

Meanwhile, BaFin's focus on Greensill Bank was not wavering. Far from it.

In July 2020, BaFin put together a special task force that would be entirely focused on getting to the bottom of the issues at Greensill Bank. In August, the regulator sent a list of detailed questions to Lex. They wanted to know more about the business model, about the ownership structure, and the loans he made. That month, BaFin also reported to Germany's Ministry of Finance on its ongoing investigation into Greensill and GFG.

In September, BaFin sent more questions, and hired the accountants KPMG to start a forensic audit, looking at Gupta loans and pretty much everything else.

While Lex continued to downplay the regulator's questions, it was clear that they weren't going to go away. The only solution would be to reduce the amount of exposure Greensill Bank had to GFG. Even that might not be enough.

On 15 December 2020, Lex, along with the management and directors of Greensill bank, was summoned to a video conference with BaFin's representatives. The regulator asked yet more questions – about the business model, about the loans to GFG, about the measures it had demanded in terms of restricting further loans to Gupta.

When the first draft of KPMG's special audit report landed at the regulator a few days before Christmas, it was damning. The auditors had found plenty of reasons to be concerned, uncovering evidence of what they considered 'serious violations by the management' of the bank. These included the way the bank was accounting for some of the Gupta-related loans, and how the loans themselves worked in practice. They were supposed to be backed by real transactions, but in fact they were supported by guesstimates of future deals.

These were serious issues. Alone, it could have been enough to kill off Greensill. But there were other terminal problems too.

# TWENTY-SIX

# The Bond and Credit Company

There was one further, important revelation from that April 2020 story I wrote about the Vision Fund companies that were getting loans from the Credit Suisse funds. A spokesperson from the bank pointed out that investors were protected by insurance provided by several trade credit insurance companies. But that comment only served to highlight another looming issue that I had been talking to the Swiss bank about for several months.

The marketing materials for the funds repeatedly claimed that a diverse group of insurers were providing coverage. That was not accurate. A couple of high-profile insurers already flat out refused to work with Greensill because of unsavoury run-ins with Lex in the past. AIG, one of the biggest trade credit insurers in the world, had steered clear of Lex for years. And other big insurers that worked with him seemed cautious – they didn't like to talk in public about Greensill and limited their exposure to the business.

As a result, instead of a diverse pool, the insurance coverage for the Credit Suisse funds was dominated by a single, relatively unknown Australian firm called Insurance Australia Group or IAG.

And within IAG, all the Greensill business was conducted through a single, small unit called The Bond and Credit Company (TBCC). This was a concern that Greensill's own internal risk managers had highlighted for months.

In June 2019, I'd asked Credit Suisse too about this arrangement.

In my meeting with senior Credit Suisse staff in Zurich in late 2019, I pointed out that about 40 per cent of the insurance was with IAG at that time. At the time, given the size of the funds, that meant IAG was providing coverage for about $800 million in underlying loans. That was a huge amount for an insurer of IAG's size. No other insurance company was providing anything like that level of coverage, and most of the others covered just a tiny proportion of the funds overall – typically less than 1 per cent or 2 per cent.

There was surely a risk that IAG had bitten off more than it could chew, and that it would not be able to cover more Greensill assets. That would limit the potential for Greensill and the Credit Suisse funds to grow.

I thought I had found a potential flaw. But the bankers took the wind out of my sails. They told me that there was a new rule in the works, which would limit the amount of cover provided by a single insurer of the funds to just 20 per cent of the underlying loans. The purpose of the rule was to avoid too much concentration in one insurer and spread the risk more broadly. It made a lot of sense.

The only problem was that – by April 2020 – the proportion of coverage IAG was providing had grown – to 51 per cent. That was even more startling, given the funds themselves had about doubled in size. It meant IAG was now responsible for insurance on about $3.5 to $4 billion of the loans.

There was a further complication. IAG had sold its stake in TBCC in 2019 to giant Japanese insurer Tokio Marine. So why on earth was the coverage it was providing to the Credit Suisse–Greensill funds growing? When I called the Australian company, a spokesperson there said that the business was all 'run off' – existing business from before the sale of TBCC. All the existing run-off arrangements would expire by June 2020, he said. That seemed to make sense at the time, especially if the coverage was matched to short-term supply chain finance loans. So it made a lot less sense that IAG's coverage was growing.

Again, I was struck by the ticking time-bomb in the Credit Suisse funds – if TBCC could no longer provide insurance coverage to the Credit Suisse funds on the scale it had done previously, then the funds would quickly lose a key layer of protection. That would make them off-limits for a whole bunch of investors, who would have to be paid back, fast.

I went back to Credit Suisse several times to ask about the new rule – the 20 per cent cap. How come the proportion of coverage provided by IAG had grown to 51 per cent when I had been told there was a new rule in the works specifically to curb that kind of outcome? What they told me was shocking. I found out that the Credit Suisse–Greensill portfolio manager, Lukas Haas, and one of his bosses, Luc Mathys, had simply decided not to implement their own 20 per cent cap rule. They had told their colleagues that it wouldn't be hard to find more trade credit insurance if it was needed. So a key control they had proposed just didn't happen. A few months later, the issue that the rule was supposed to address became critical to Greensill and to the Credit Suisse funds.

INSURANCE WAS CENTRAL to Greensill's business model. Insurance premiums ate into Lex's margins. But without it, many investors simply could not put money into the sort of assets Greensill was selling. With insurance in place, the investors cared less about the quality of the underlying credits or the complexity of the structures that Lex had set up. In a sense, their investment was a bet on trade credit insurance.

Lex had always known this. The withdrawal of insurance is what had destroyed Robert Cleland's Transaction Risk Mitigation (TRM) business in the early 2000s. The Dragon Technology debacle – when AIG had abruptly stopped providing cover to Greensill – should have provided a harsh lesson too.

The board also knew that insurance had a critical role to play in the future of the company. At just about every board meeting through 2019 and 2020, someone asked the question: how are we doing on our capacity to get insurance? And just about every time they asked, Lex calmly reported that everything was fine. The company worked with a broad and growing pool of insurers. More insurers were coming on board all the time. There was no problem.

This was deeply misleading. No one ever meaningfully challenged it.

INSURANCE AUSTRALIA GROUP was born in 2000, evolving out of the insurance arm of Australia's National Roads and Motorists' Association, an automobile services group based in New South Wales. The company, whose shares are listed on the Australian Securities Exchange, has tried for years to diversify beyond its roots in NSW. It moved into new geographical markets around Asia. It signed up to joint ventures. It mulled mergers with bigger competitors. In 2015, Warren Buffett's Berkshire Hathaway bought a small stake. But ever since it was first created, IAG struggled to shape a strong new identity and deliver consistently impressive results.

In 2016, IAG signed a partnership agreement with what was then a brand-new business, The Bond and Credit Company, to launch a new trade credit insurance product into the Australian market. TBCC was a tiny firm, with a dozen or so staff in a Sydney office. It made a couple of million dollars in revenue each year. And it was rapidly becoming critical to Lex Greensill's burgeoning multibillion-dollar financing empire.

A single executive, Greg Brereton, was the main Greensill

connection at TBCC, providing billions of dollars of trade credit insurance. Brereton was well liked, quiet, and lived a modest, suburban life focused on his family, cricket and rugby league. TBCC's own website said Brereton's strength was in relationship-building, though he also had a strong commercial sense too. He worked hard, but there was nothing out of the ordinary that would signal to colleagues he held a pivotal role in the future of Greensill. They didn't twig, even when former UK prime minister and Greensill employee David Cameron showed up in 2018 for a brief personal meeting with Brereton at TBCC's Sydney office. The meeting puzzled other staff. It's not every day a world leader pops by the TBCC office, next to a parking lot and a Subway sandwich shop. But though the 'getting-to-know-you' meeting – as Cameron later described it – was odd, no one saw it as a warning of what was to come. Neither did anyone switch on to the crucial role of TBCC when Brett Downes, Greensill's chief risk officer, showed up with little notice to sniff around the firm.

In late 2019, I asked Lex why Greensill did so much business with IAG, a relatively small firm compared to the big global providers of trade credit insurance. Why are you getting so much insurance coverage from this one Australian company? Lex was usually serious and smart. His response at the time was a rare, flippant moment: 'I am Australian, and proudly so!'

He also pointed out that IAG had recently exited their partnership with TBCC and that Tokio Marine, a giant Japanese insurer, had stepped into its place.

That shift in ownership was far from the positive development Lex was trying to portray it as. It wasn't the beginning of a much healthier insurance situation at Greensill at all. It was the beginning of the end.

Downes, the chief risk officer, had raised the problem of TBCC in late 2019. Brereton was certainly easy to deal with. He agreed to GFG deals that Greensill could not insure anywhere else within minutes of being asked by Lex's staff. But that speed was not necessarily seen as a sign of a healthy, robust process. A report from Downes's team, circulated among senior management, said 'there is an increasing reliance upon a single relationship for insurance which leads to the emergence of associated risks.' At that point, 72 per cent of Greensill's insurance was with TBCC. Its next biggest insurance provider was Euler Hermes, at 16 per cent, and they were cutting back.

Even as Lex was telling his board – and nosy journalists – that everything was rosy, TBCC's new owners were themselves becoming increasingly nervous about the policies Greg Brereton had signed them up to. And Lex knew it.

In July 2020, Mark Callahan, a veteran Tokio Marine executive based in Houston, Texas, launched a worrying missive. Callahan called his counterpart at Greensill's insurance broker, Marsh McLennan. When he hit voicemail, Callahan followed up with an alarming email: 'Note that all existing limits on Greensill buyers have been set to nil in our policy system. No extensions will be provided to any existing policy.'

Not only would Tokio Marine not be writing any new insurance for Greensill, nor extending any existing policies, but the company had also already curtailed Brereton's capacity to write insurance policies a month earlier.

Marsh had been a loyal supporter of Greensill's for years. Julian Macey-Dare, a Marsh managing director, was an experienced broker who had frequently supported Lex's quest for a big insurance backer. He had helped Lex to get IAG on board. He'd personally worked on Greensill's business with TBCC.

In an email to Toby Guy, who was effectively CEO of TBCC, Macey-Dare questioned whether Tokio Marine could really pull the plug. 'We welcome your strong commitment to support Greensill Capital as your largest customer, as well as valuing support for Marsh as your largest broker,' he wrote. 'We recommend you engage with us and our Insured [Greensill] as soon as you have a full understanding of your Insured portfolio.'

The following month, the unfolding disaster was laid out for

Lex in full in another email from Guy. The message also went to Greensill Bank, which technically paid the premiums on the Greensill policies.

Brereton had been fired.

TBCC had launched a full-blown investigation into 'dealings between Greensill Capital and Greg Brereton'. The investigation had already found he had exceeded his 'delegated authority' – he had written more than A$10 billion in insurance to cover Greensill's loans in the previous twelve months, well above his personal limits. The investigation had also found that Greensill failed to submit signed paperwork and other documents including monthly status reports concerning the insured transactions.

A high-stakes legalistic back-and-forth was now zipping between Greensill, Marsh, TBCC and Tokio Marine. Mostly, the insurer was insisting that Greensill and Marsh had failed to provide all the right documents they were supposed to send to TBCC, and that TBCC was not providing insurance cover beyond Brereton's limits. Lex and his broker claimed they had sent everything and that they expected the insurer to honour commitments Brereton had made on their behalf.

What's striking is that even if Greensill had successfully argued his points (that Brereton was TBCC's problem, and that the existing policies he'd written should be left in place), the relationship between Greensill and its biggest single insurer, by far, was burning to the ground. It was typical of Lex, a constant blind spot, that he didn't seem to realize that winning another short-term victory would have just stacked up a bigger problem further down the line.

On 1 September, TBCC's Guy sent another message. TBCC is still working on its investigation into Brereton's previous dealings with Greensill, he wrote. TBCC would tell Greensill the outcome of their investigation in due course. In the meantime, Guy wrote, Greensill should consider his message as notice that the insurer won't renew any policies when they end on 1 March 2021.

The clock was ticking down. And all the time, Lex was telling his board and anyone else who asked that there were no issues with Greensill's access to insurance coverage.

OF COURSE, THE problem was abundantly clear from a cursory glance through the monthly updates that Credit Suisse published on its own funds. I had brought up the risk of this concentration with Credit Suisse several times, months earlier. The bank had even come up with a rule that would mitigate against the danger of having all the insurance eggs in one basket. But then they decided not to implement it.

As the TBCC problem escalated, there were few alternative places for Greensill – and Marsh – to turn to. My *Wall Street Journal* colleague Julie Steinberg and I had heard that Greensill was struggling to get trade credit insurance from a broader pool, despite what Lex and Credit Suisse said in public.

We already knew giant US insurer AIG had stopped working with Greensill after 2017. The trade credit insurance industry was a relatively small community, with executives swapping firms regularly. That meant Greensill's reputation for aggressive risk-taking and lending to companies with weak credit ratings had got around.

Another major trade credit insurer had also now stopped doing business with Greensill. Euler Hermes is a giant of the trade credit insurance industry. Its name on Greensill investments had been a big marker of credibility. In negotiations over renewing Greensill policies, Euler had said it wanted to raise the excess – this would have the effect of reducing the amount Greensill would recover in the event of a claim. The move came after Greensill made a claim earlier in the year related to the failed company, NMC Health. It was like when a car insurer increases your deductible after an accident.

When we went to Greensill with this story, Lex and Doran tried to play it down. We wrote: 'Greensill . . . rejected the terms and opted to replace Euler with other insurers, a Greensill spokesperson said, declining to name them.'

In November, Greensill had arranged additional insurance coverage, of about $3 billion, through Chubb, a Swiss insurance company. Lex later acknowledged that the Chubb policies were never used because they required Greensill Bank to pay a first loss deductible. The policies would only work if Greensill could provide a significant cash collateral to cover the potential deductible. But Greensill didn't have that kind of cash. Lex was running out of insurers and running out of time.

# TWENTY-SEVEN

# Covid and Connections

On 11 January 2020, the Chinese government alerted officials at the World Health Organization that a sixty-one-year-old man in the city of Wuhan had died from a mysterious new type of viral pneumonia. Over the next few weeks, the coronavirus rippled across the globe. By mid-February, airlines had isolated China and other hotspots, Italy was in the grip of a national lockdown, and governments around the world had convened their own emergency taskforces.

The pandemic rattled financial markets. How would trade cope with unprecedented restrictions on movement? How would the global economy survive as countries locked down their people? How much would companies suffer if their suppliers could no longer send them raw materials and their customers and staff could not go to work?

Investors were scared. Uncertainty reigned. Equity and bond markets were taking a beating.

Lex Greensill sensed fear, and opportunity. The fears were that investors might look at the Credit Suisse funds and prefer to have their wealth in cash; that no one would need trade finance if trade dried up; that trade credit insurance companies would stop writing insurance policies if they were faced with a wave of defaults; that clients who had borrowed billions of dollars would not survive the meltdown. GFG's steel business, Bluestone's coal business and a host of others to whom Lex had loaned other people's money would surely suffer as the global economy ground to a halt.

But there was great opportunity bubbling up too. Politicians were faced with dire predictions about the impact of lockdowns – many businesses relied on complex, protracted supply chains, and many of them had not set aside enough cash to survive for more than a few months. By early March, governments everywhere were planning emergency measures to bail out businesses, keep cash moving through the system, and provide guarantees that would keep key sectors alive. Record stimulus packages were passed in record time. Government loans and state guarantees were everywhere.

For Greensill, the moment had turned from existential crisis – billions of dollars rapidly yanked from the Credit Suisse funds, potentially exposing that money had been loaned to borrowers who couldn't pay it back – to a not-to-be-missed opportunity of the decade. Lex was already desperate to diversify his sources of funding beyond Greensill Bank – which was being scrutinized by BaFin – and Credit Suisse. There was no better funding partner than the government.

There was a similar dynamic playing out in the market for trade credit insurance. In April, the German government agreed to guarantee up to €30 billion in trade credit insurance. Other governments announced similar measures.

Inside Greensill, senior managers knew that this shift, this opportunity was what Lex wanted them to focus on. He told staff, confidently, that the Bank of England and HM Treasury were ready to provide funding.

*

IN THE UK that hectic and fear-filled spring, Chancellor Rishi Sunak announced the government's Coronavirus Business Interruption Loan Scheme (CBILS). The loans were intended to support small and medium-sized businesses that were struggling to make ends meet as the economic effects of the pandemic hit home. He then announced a similar plan for large businesses (CLBILS). The loans would help see them through a few months. Accredited lenders that distributed the loans would get a government guarantee: if the client did not pay it back, the government would repay up to 80 per cent. The loans would be administered by the British Business Bank, a state-owned economic development bank.

The Bank of England also unveiled a Covid-19 Corporate Financing Facility (CCFF), which would buy short-term securities from companies that made 'a material contribution to economic activity in the UK' and were in sound financial health prior to the pandemic. It was an alternative way to achieve a similar outcome.

Up until now, David Cameron's role at Greensill had been limited. He had helped open some doors in the Middle East and Asia. He gave Greensill the veneer of credibility in front of big clients. And he entertained Greensill's board and senior management at company meetings with tales from inside the corridors of power. He even asked somewhat probing questions at board meetings – not a deep, sophisticated interrogation on financial issues, but he did push for answers about how the company worked. Given his lucrative pay packet, some senior executives privately discussed whether Cameron really added enough value to offset the considerable cost of having him on staff.

When Covid-19 struck, it was Cameron's time to prove his worth. From as early as March, and for months thereafter, Lex hit Cameron with a barrage of text messages, urging the former PM to pull strings in Whitehall and at the Bank of England to get Greensill access to the suite of government bailout schemes. This intense lobbying, directed by Lex, was happening as the UK hit the depths of the Covid-19 pandemic, much of it when Prime Minister Boris Johnson was himself hospitalized with the disease. While the rest of us were thinking about how we might get through the lockdown and the worst healthcare crisis in generations, Lex was thinking about how he could tap an unprecedented pool of government money.

At the time, the Bank of England governorship was in transition, from Canadian Mark Carney to Andrew Bailey, a City veteran. Bailey had spent a large part of his career at the Bank of England (BofE), although he'd mostly recently run the Financial Conduct Authority, including during the period when the FCA had leaned on GAM over its handling of Tim Haywood and his Greensill investments.

Even as Bailey was settling into his Threadneedle Street office, Cameron and Lex began lobbying Sir Jon Cunliffe, the BofE's deputy governor since 2013. What they wanted was for the BofE to include bonds backed by supply chain finance loans in the list of securities that could be acquired through the CCFF.

'The disruption to supply chains and the financing of them is real,' Lex wrote to Cunliffe in an email on Sunday 15 March 2020. 'In the last week we have seen a great many fixed income investors who support the asset class step back – meaning liquidity could well become a major issue in the coming days.'

That was true, and Lex was in a great position to know it. Investors had pulled billions out of Lex's Credit Suisse supply chain finance funds since the pandemic hit.

Lex went on: 'You will recall that the Bank established a supply chain finance facility back in 2010 (as a part of your asset purchase facility). We think there is an urgent need to re-establish the same – given the millions of businesses that now rely on supply chain finance.'

It was a reference to the BofE's move to support Lex's supply chain finance programme at Morgan Stanley a decade earlier. If you could do it then, Deputy Governor, you can do it again now, Lex seemed to be saying.

Greensill and Cameron were pushing for a meeting with Cunliffe.

A couple of days later, they were given a call with a couple of more junior officials. Lex's pitch was that the traditional banks were not interested in helping small and medium-sized businesses. Greensill was. Greensill already worked with government agencies. He pointed to the NHS deals. He pushed for the bank to set up a facility of up to £20 billion to buy securities backed by supply chain finance assets. Lex emphasized the need for urgent action and stressed that a large BofE facility would help bring confidence to investors in supply chain finance. It was an incredibly self-serving pitch, given the amount of financing bleeding out of the Credit Suisse funds at that time. And it didn't work. The BofE decided against admitting Greensill to the CCFF.

That decision left Lex furious. What was the value of Cameron's connections now?

The former PM sent another begging email to Cunliffe.

'Jon, Am writing to ask for your help,' he pleaded. 'Greensill – who I work with – have had numerous conversations with [Treasury] but have failed to get anywhere. The request is simple – please include in the CCFF the ability to purchase bonds issued in respect of supply chain finance. These allow us to pump billions into SMEs [small to medium-sized enterprises] (including every pharmacy that works with the NHS).' This was at best misleading. Greensill only worked with a small proportion of NHS pharmacies.

Cameron continued: 'At a time when we are – rightly – worried about how quickly banks can get loans out to small businesses, why are we potentially cutting off a market that already pumps cheap credit directly into SMEs? I think I must be missing something here. Am obviously talking to [Treasury], but would be grateful for any light you could shed on this . . . All good wishes. Dc.'

When Cunliffe replied saying it was out of his hands, Cameron turned his focus to the Treasury. He texted the top civil servant there, Sir Tom Scholar, saying he was 'genuinely baffled' that Greensill wasn't given access to CCFF, and that he would call Sunak, and 'everyone'. Minutes later, he went straight to Sunak, though the details of their conversation have never been made public. Pretty soon, Cameron was back at Cunliffe, asking for him to speak with Lex in person. Lex's belief in his own abilities as a salesman was unshaken, even by a global pandemic. Eventually, in late April, Cunliffe finally relented and agreed to hear him out. Greensill delivered his pitch, but Cunliffe was unmoved.

The lobbying effort went on, through April, May and into June. During that period, Cameron blitzed his former government colleagues with messages. In one early April dialogue, Sunak had told Cameron he was 'stuck back to back on calls' and promised to talk later. In another message, later in the month, he said he was pushing officials to look for alternative arrangements that might help Greensill out. In all, Cameron sent at least fourteen separate text messages to Tom Scholar, the top Treasury civil servant; eight WhatsApp messages and two phone calls to Sunak; two more WhatsApp messages to one of Sunak's top aides; four emails, a text and a call to Cunliffe; and dozens more messages to various senior civil servants and cabinet ministers.

In June, Charles Roxburgh, another top Treasury civil servant, personally spoke to Lex to explain the government's decision. In a letter to Lex and Bill Crothers, who'd also leaned on his government contacts, the treasury explained that CCFF would not include buying supply chain finance assets from Greensill. First, the letter said, the market disruption had subsided since March and April. Money was flooding back into bonds as the worst of the pandemic panic had passed. Second, the government was already getting money into SMEs and didn't need to go down the route Lex had proposed. Thirdly, the government didn't see much evidence that Lex's proposal would work anyway.

Greensill was shut out. He would try an alternative route.

The approach was scattergun.

Greensill tried to get a £500 million loan out of UK Export

Finance (UKEF), the government agency that helps UK exporters get business and win contracts overseas. The agency looked at Greensill's pitch, and kicked it out, having decided Greensill's proposal didn't support UKEF's brief, and because of the media reports that had raised red flags about Greensill itself.

Greensill tapped government-backed emergency loans in France, Italy and the Czech Republic. The loans totalled a little under €200 million, and in each case they were taken out by GFG companies. However, instead of using the loans to pay for operating costs at the GFG businesses, the money was deposited into Greensill Bank and then used as collateral to make even bigger loans to GFG.

Sanjeev Gupta's companies were in a critical condition. Liberty Steel, his flagship company, pleaded with the UK government for £160 million to £180 million. Without the funding, Gupta's company said, they might not be able to keep their operations running beyond May 2020. As many as 3,000 employees in the north of England, Scotland and Wales would potentially be put out of work.

Inside the government (the Department for Business, Energy and Industrial Strategy, along with the Treasury), the view was that a bailout for Liberty Steel was a last resort, and they weren't quite at that point yet.

Gupta's team suggested an alternative plan, which would involve a government guarantee designed specifically for Greensill's loans to Liberty. It was an astonishing request: a bespoke government bailout for a private steel company and a private finance business. The GFG requests did not gain traction.

Lex was also looking for access to the CBILS and CLBILS loan programmes. By mid-April, Greensill was seeking to become an accredited lender under both programmes. Lex directly emailed the chief commercial officer at the British Business Bank (BBB) three days before the scheme was even launched. Greensill's technology could 'help to quickly increase the reach of the CLBILS in the UK economy', he claimed.

He was politely told to go through formal channels. There was no back door.

Greensill prepared its pitch to the BBB – Lex applied to be allowed to lend £1 billion, based on a pipeline of up to fifty clients. He was granted permission to lend up to £400 million, 60 per cent less than he had asked for. Greensill was also told not to lend more than £50 million to a single group of companies.

The outcome was disappointing. The lending restrictions were more limiting than Greensill wanted them to be. But it would have to do. For the CLBILS programme, Greensill was one of only twenty-seven accredited lenders, and twenty-four of those were banks.

During the accreditation process, the government's business and industry department asked the BBB on eight separate occasions about Greensill's status – whether it had been approved to participate as a lender. The government department pushed for Greensill to be prioritized in the process and for it to be allowed to provide more than £50 million to a single borrower. At the BBB, executives thought the level of government interest in Greensill seemed extraordinary.

Inside Greensill, at the company's Warrington site, loan officers and risk management staff were told to prioritize the government loan scheme, and to figure out how much they could give to the GFG companies. Some of the Greensill staff were uncomfortable. They were concerned that the Gupta businesses weren't all compliant with the terms of the loans. Some of the steel businesses weren't in good financial health heading into the crisis – Greensill's own internal estimates suggested GFG's Hartlepool site was effectively insolvent by late 2019, for example. That would make them ineligible to take part in the government programme.

And there were concerns that Greensill was potentially ignoring the fact that GFG was a single borrower group and therefore could not take more than £50 million in loans in total. During the accreditation process, Greensill had been specifically warned by the BBB about the group lending limits. The bank had even cited as an example, 'British Steel', which would be 'one group with a £50 million limit, and it is not a £50 million facility limit per subsidiary.'

Those Greensill staff who raised questions, though, were swept aside. Executives who queried the work on GFG were reassigned to something else.

Despite the rumblings inside Greensill, the firm loaned £400 million under the CLBILS scheme – the maximum it was permitted to lend. This consisted of eight loans of £50 million each – again, the maximum. That compared with an average loan size across the whole CLBILS programme of just £3 million. It also made Greensill the fifth-largest lender in the whole programme, much bigger than even some major UK banks. The start-up accounted for 8 per cent of the value of all the loans under the scheme.

More alarming still, far and away most of the money Lex loaned out was going to companies within GFG. In total, seven loans worth £350 million pounds were dished out to Gupta's businesses. The other loan went to a company called Aar Tee Commodities, whose owner, Ravi Trehan, was a long-time Gupta associate and previously a member of GFG's strategic board. Aar Tee's core business relationship seemed to be with other GFG companies too.

Inside Greensill, the loans were questioned by staff working on the credit teams. They had been alarmed to see that Nicola Gupta, Sanjeev's wife, had bought a £42 million house in one of London's poshest neighbourhoods, just as one of the £50 million CLBILS loans from Greensill landed.

At the same time, sales staff who suggested using the CLBILS accreditation to lend to other clients simply found there was no capacity for anything beyond GFG.

By October, officials at the BBB understood Greensill's loans were all heading to Gupta's businesses. Although there were circumstances under which the bank would lift the £50 million limit for a single group, Greensill had not been given that approval. The bank started to dig in. Lex was told that the loans had breached the limit, but he pushed back, saying GFG was not a single borrower. It was an extraordinary claim. The bank messaged Treasury and the Department for Business, Energy and Industrial Strategy to register its concerns.

On 13 October, officials from the bank met with Lex's team. The meeting was tense. The bank's officials didn't know that Greensill was facing a war on several fronts. They didn't know that he was under pressure in Germany to shift GFG assets out of Greensill Bank. They were unaware that Lex's main insurance provider was shutting down his capacity to get trade credit insurance to cover the GFG loans too.

Lex was told he could not make any more loans until the bank's concerns about GFG were resolved. Greensill later said it had received 'political steers' that the loans to Gupta were welcome because they supported UK steel. Inside Greensill, the word was that Gupta had been told by vaccines minister Nadhim Zahawi to get several CLBILs loans to bail him out. Later, after Greensill collapsed, Zahawi was unable to provide records of his phone messages because they'd been deleted. (In January 2022, the *Financial Times* reported that Gupta wrote to Zahawi thanking him for his 'instrumental' role in getting the Greensill loans.) The bank hired accountants EY to investigate Greensill's lending. It was yet another investigation of a controversial aspect of Lex's business. It meant that in just a few months, several sets of external auditors had been sent to sniff around Greensill.

Around the same time, Gupta launched an audacious bid to buy the steel businesses of Germany's Thyssenkrupp. He never said how much he was willing to pay, although it was a substantial business, with around 27,000 employees and sales of €9 billion. Gupta said that his non-binding offer was 'fully financed' through a consortium of lenders led by Credit Suisse.

He also said a deal would be 'a perfect match' for his existing empire. The biggest benefit, however, would have been all that new financing, and – possibly – more leverage with European politicians down the line. In the end, no deal materialized. Gupta was struggling as usual for financing. He even asked SoftBank's Misra to help, connecting him to his former colleagues at Deutsche Bank – would they finance a deal to save German steel jobs? The answer was a resounding no.

TWENTY-EIGHT

# Impatient Capital

It's hard to overstate the credibility Lex got from having attracted a couple of billion dollars in capital from General Atlantic (GA) and SoftBank's Vision Fund.

GA was one of the most respected big investors around. The Vision Fund had a mixed reputation, especially after WeWork's initial public offering (IPO) debacle. But many of its bets were starting to pay off in 2020.

Behind the scenes, though, patience with Greensill was wearing thin at both firms, and Lex's relationship with his two giant backers was under strain.

At SoftBank, Lex's standing had taken a major hit, in large part because of the very public investigation into the Japanese company's multiple roles at the Credit Suisse funds. SoftBank didn't need the bad publicity this kind of investigation attracted. Lex, once the golden boy, was suddenly on the naughty step. His daily calls with Masayoshi Son, his mentor and biggest promoter, ended abruptly.

He also lost the support of his other big cheerleader at SoftBank. Colin Fan, the former Deutsche Bank executive, had been Greensill's main point of contact at the Vision Fund from the outset. He represented the Vision Fund at Greensill Board meetings and was well known to Greensill's senior management team. But his star was falling too. In addition to Greensill, he had overseen the Vision Fund's investments in Fair and Chehaoduo, both of which Greensill had loaned money to. He was also the main Vision Fund executive responsible for Zume, an automated food delivery business that had pitched Masayoshi Son on the idea of using robots to make pizzas. By early 2020, all these businesses were floundering. Fan stopped attending board meetings at Greensill; although it wasn't announced until months later, he was in the process of leaving the Vision Fund altogether for another part of SoftBank.

That left Rajeev Misra, who ran the Vision Fund. Misra had signed off on the Greensill investment, but he had never been a true believer. His scepticism had only grown in the months since SoftBank had poured billions in.

He had been against the idea of using the Credit Suisse funds to lend to other Vision Fund portfolio companies from the outset. Not because of the perceived conflict of interest. Misra was more concerned about the 'correlation risk' – the risk that the fortunes of several portfolio companies would become entangled such that the ups and downs of one of them would affect the lot. Part of the reason for buying stakes in a diverse portfolio of companies is to avoid exactly that problem.

In April, SoftBank used the predicament Lex found himself in – when he had come to SoftBank looking for emergency backing for the Credit Suisse funds – to leverage some concessions and do a kind of governance audit of Greensill. They hired PricewaterhouseCoopers, the giant audit firm, to look through the entire business that spring.

Greensill was still being run like a plucky start-up. Everything went through Lex. Processes were ad hoc. Key policies were non-existent. Many of the weaknesses they identified were like those highlighted by Downes and the risk group. The audit firm came up with a series of recommendations that they said were needed to improve the company's processes and bring its governance practices in line with what should be expected of a business of Greensill's size.

Off the back of this report, Misra and SoftBank demanded changes. They wanted a personal guarantee from Lex on some of the money SoftBank corporate had put into Greensill loans. They pushed Greensill to create a new reputational risk committee at board level to manage the company's growing public relations problems. They forced Greensill to add new board members and advisers – Patricia Russo, chair of the board at Hewlett Packard, joined as an adviser, and Tracy Clarke, the CEO for Europe and Americas at Standard Chartered bank, pledged to join as a non-executive director in 2021.

SoftBank also told Lex to get rid of the private aircraft. It looked flashy, and, more importantly, it was bad for the bottom line. Maintaining a fleet of aircraft was expensive. Lex had long argued that he needed the jet because of his constant travel. It was like a mobile CEO's office. Misra didn't buy it. He told Lex: hey, you're a billionaire, if you want a private jet, buy your own. Just don't use the company funds to do it.

It wasn't just Misra pushing Lex to get rid of the aircraft. The question had been lingering for years, and others on the board echoed the Vision Fund chief's message. The planes were an unnecessary extravagance that would raise questions from other potential investors in Greensill. They were also an obstacle to creating a sound environmental policy, which would be needed if Greensill was to be taken seriously as a major company.

By the autumn, Lex conceded defeat. He would sell the planes, if that's what the board wanted. If this sounded like a concession, though, it wasn't a big one. Lex told his inner circle that they would still fly private. He had not committed to any timeline to sell the planes, and he would find some way to keep them anyway, even if it meant shuffling ownership of them into some other Greensill subsidiary company where they would be less conspicuous.

SoftBank's demands didn't end with the aircraft. Misra was also pushing Lex to get a brand-name auditor. Greensill was still being audited by obscure firms in London and Sydney. If you are going to go public, he told Lex, that must change. Shareholders will demand that you have a recognizable auditor, probably one of the Big Four – Deloitte, EY, KPMG, PricewaterhouseCoopers. For all their own mishaps over the years, the Big Four were still the main firms to which credible, multinational corporations went for their audit sign-off. Misra even called around his own book of contacts to try to get one of the Big Four to work with Greensill, but none would bite. Some were concerned about Lex's exposure to Sanjeev Gupta, whose business was too opaque to properly account for it. Given how important Gupta's companies were to Greensill, that meant it would be difficult to give an opinion on Greensill's accounts too. Other auditors were concerned about Greensill itself, given the investigations at GAM and Credit Suisse. They were also unsure of supply chain finance, which still sat in an accounting grey area. Greensill even tried to persuade big audit firms including EY and BDO to do other work for him – non-audit work. The idea was that he would build a relationship through some tax or consultancy business. He would at least be able to say that he worked with a big accounting firm, even if they didn't sign off Greensill's accounts. That didn't work either. Lex's pursuit of a big-name auditor was ultimately unsuccessful.

Around that time, Misra had also sent his own senior credit risk expert to look through Greensill's book of loans. What he had found was distressing. First, Greensill's own risk team was dysfunctional. They were cooperative, smart, and answered questions. But they were often overruled by Lex. If their job was to be a key check on the business, then Lex completely undermined that function.

Second, the loan book itself was very problematic. There was some genuine supply chain finance business here. These were mostly safe loans backed by actual invoices between big companies and their suppliers. If the borrower defaulted, there was a real transaction that provided a kind of security to the investors. There was also insurance in place that provided protection against defaults. But far too much of the book of business just looked like unsecured loans, backed by nothing of any value if the borrower couldn't pay it back. In effect, the investments Greensill was pushing were highly dependent on the insurance they were sold with. Without that, there was nothing much to protect investors at all.

Finally, far too many of the loans were linked to Sanjeev Gupta. About $7 billion was tied to the steel magnate. That would have been too much even if the single client had been squeaky clean. The fact that Greensill's business was so concentrated in loans to Gupta was especially worrying.

Overall, the SoftBank credit review found that Greensill was, in several crucial ways, a very different business to the one that the Vision Fund thought they had invested in.

In August, the Vision Fund chief also told Lex that Greensill needed to stop spending so much money. Greensill was hiring too fast, and it was paying salaries that were too high. They were burning through cash far too quickly. If Greensill wanted to be taken seriously by investors, the company would have to show some discipline. It sounded a bit hypocritical, given that the Vision Fund had also been pushing Greensill to charge ahead, to build the business at lightning speed. Lex was not interested, telling Misra: 'You can't interfere in my business. I'm the CEO.'

Despite his bravado, Lex's position was not strong.

Lex's big backers at General Atlantic were also increasingly unhappy. The GA team had really felt uneasy since the SoftBank Vision Fund had become an investor.

In October 2019, weeks after SoftBank's second huge investment in Greensill, Gabe Caillaux gave an interview with *Private Equity News* – another Dow Jones publication – that almost read like a warning about the potential pitfalls. Too much money was 'polluting' the market for new investments, Caillaux said. 'I think that's disruptive for building great healthy companies. Some will work out but we feel really strongly that you should grow in a healthy way.'

The article, written by one of my colleagues, noted that the Vision Fund had followed GA's investment in several companies, including Greensill.

'If you look across the GA portfolio globally, SoftBank has invested in a number of our companies,' Caillaux said diplomatically.

Caillaux and the GA team knew that Lex had a strong appetite for big risks, and felt that the massive Vision Fund investment was like throwing oil on a fire. Some board members were terrified about what Greensill would do with it all. Their fears escalated at the first board meeting with a Vision Fund representative in the room – Colin Fan, the former Deutsche Bank executive, announced, 'We didn't invest in Greensill to be a $10 billion company. We invested for it to be a $100 billion company.'

Lex told executives at the firm and the board that his aim was to double the size of the business.

Caillaux worried that Greensill was addicted to growth when it should have been consolidating its operations. He wanted the company to clean up its act and end some of the riskier practices. These had made some sense when it was a small start-up, but not when it aspired to be a major global company. The business was growing too fast – costs were running high, and crucial systems were yet to catch up with the new scale of Greensill. Many of these issues were the same problems identified by PwC for the Vision Fund, and the same concerns raised by Brett Downes and the Greensill risk team. The real issue was whether Lex was listening.

Having helped turbo-boost Greensill in the first place, GA was rapidly losing its grip, and any ability to influence the company. GA had taken out half its stake when the SoftBank Vision Fund invested in Greensill, and there was a sense among Greensill executives that GA was 'playing with house money' – it no longer had real skin in the game. This was clear even as early as the summer of 2019. Lex had been looking to replace his long-time chief financial officer, Al Eadie, who had been with Greensill from early on. Eadie was smart and hard-working. But Lex and the board agreed that the company had outgrown him as a CFO. There was far less agreement, however, on the preferred replacement. Neil Garrod had been the treasury chief at Vodafone, sanctioning the telecoms company's various Greensill schemes. I caught wind of the plan to hire Garrod at that time and called James Doran to confirm the story. Doran urged me not to go to print, saying Garrod's appointment was uncertain because he was dealing with some personal issues. It turned out this was yet another misleading interaction with the Greensill PR man. Garrod's appointment had been held up because it had been questioned by some Greensill board members, including Caillaux. They felt that he was intellectually robust and competent, but that he was a risk-taker and a dealmaker. He was too similar to Lex. He wouldn't help them rein in Lex's worst instincts. Caillaux might have won the argument a few months earlier, when GA was Greensill's biggest shareholder outside of Lex and his brother. But after GA had sold down its stake, it was just another minority shareholder.

GA recommended that Greensill keep the hunt for a CFO open. Lex responded, 'Thanks for your input. I'm hiring Neil.'

Lex's behaviour was sending some bad signals. He was extremely smart but seemed to believe he was smarter than everyone around him and took risks that seemed reckless. There wasn't a loan that Lex didn't seem to want to make. He thought he could structure his way around any challenge. He was spending too much money. And he was attracting the wrong kind of attention.

In late 2019, Lex loaned about $170 million from the Credit Suisse funds to a company called Tradeshift Networks, a San Francisco-based platform for supply chain payments run by a Danish tech entrepreneur named Christian Lanng. Tradeshift had been something of a fast-rising fintech star that billed itself as a cloud-based platform for supply chain payments. It had attracted hundreds of millions of dollars in funding and counted investors like Goldman Sachs and HSBC among its backers. Like Greensill, Tradeshift was a so-called tech unicorn with a valuation of more than $1 billion. It had also run into some headwinds. Towards the end of 2019, the company was laying off staff, and it was incurring millions of pounds of losses. BDO, the auditor of its UK accounts for 2018, said it hadn't been given access to all the information it needed to give its opinion on the accuracy of the financial statements.

Greensill had funded the Tradeshift loan from the Credit Suisse funds. The deal was transacted in unusual circumstances. Lex and Lanng had settled on the terms over a glass of wine in a bar, with Lex sketching out key details on a napkin. The terms were unusual. Whereas supply chain finance deals are typically for just a few months, Tradeshift was given the loan for five years. What's more, if Tradeshift defaulted, Greensill got to take over the whole business – an odd clause given it would be Credit Suisse's clients, not Greensill, that would be out of pocket in those circumstances.

It was a huge surprise to GA. They had also looked at making an investment in Tradeshift but decided against it. Yet here was Lex pouring a huge loan into the same company.

By the summer of 2020, Caillaux was riding out the pandemic lockdown at a family home in Spain, where his wife is from. Work carried on remotely. GA was looking at an investment in an up-and-coming UK-based athletic fashion company called Gymshark. The private equity firm was thinking about putting about £200 million into the clothing company, which would value it at more than £1 billion. To close the deal, Caillaux and a few other members of his team had to visit Gymshark's headquarters in Birmingham, meet with the owners in person and complete their due diligence. You couldn't make an investment like that via Zoom.

Lex heard about Caillaux's planned trip. He had hardly seen some members of the board in person for months because of Covid-19. By then, he was also becoming desperate to secure more funding. Could he get another round of money out of GA?

More money would mean he could stave off the worst of the looming crises. It would buy some more time. The private equity firm was a highly credible investor – another injection of cash would offset some of the negative stories about Greensill too. And if he could get GA to put money in, maybe the Vision Fund would follow again.

Lex suggested he would fly Gabe back to Spain on his private plane. 'We can use the focused time to catch up,' he told Caillaux.

It takes a few hours to fly from the UK to the island of Ibiza, whose airport is closest to Caillaux's home. Still, Caillaux didn't have time for pleasantries. Lex might have been planning to try to secure more funding, but the conversation quickly took a dive. Instead of discussing another round of investment in Greensill, the GA executive brought up his long list of concerns about Greensill's risky behaviour.

'You're going too fast. You're making too many mistakes,' he warned Lex. He was particularly unhappy with the loans to the Soft-Bank Vision Fund companies, which seemed to have been based on a loose guarantee of SoftBank's support if things went wrong. But his frustration with Greensill was much more than that. Caillaux was losing his cool. The whole business was in jeopardy if Lex didn't rein himself in. He had to understand what was at stake.

There could have been no misunderstanding about the nature of the conversation, but it wasn't clear that the message ever really landed. Afterwards, back in the UK, Lex told his inner circle of senior managers that he expected GA would invest another $500 million into Greensill soon. That would have been a real vote of confidence, had it been true. Instead, it was deeply at odds with the tone of their airborne discussion.

A few weeks after the flight, Caillaux sent a long list of demands to Lex and the board, demanding improvements in the way the company was governed. He wanted a new audit chair and a new CFO.

GA's representative on the audit committee resigned. They wanted Greensill to make a renewed effort to get a bigger-name auditor.

Despite the role GA had played in accelerating Greensill, Caillaux and Lex were never especially close on a personal level. The two men, roughly the same age and each with young children, rarely socialized together. This was not the kind of master and apprentice relationship Lex had once had with Masa. By late 2020, though, Lex's connections to Masa and Caillaux were in a similar state – almost entirely broken.

# TWENTY-NINE

# Show Me the Money

As the crisis mounted, Lex shuffled cash from one pot to another. In May 2020, the Peter Greensill Family Trust provided a $100 million loan to the company. Julie Steinberg and I found out about it. Greensill had provided the trust with a charge over its assets as security for the loan, and that charge was registered on the Companies House website, in plain sight. It was an odd situation. Why would Greensill, which was running billions of dollars in supply chain finance facilities and working with some of the biggest companies in the world, a client of the biggest banks on Wall Street, need a loan from Lex's family? And why would the family insist that the company was used as collateral?

When we asked Greensill for a comment, James Doran and Lex were typically belligerent. Occasionally, Greensill needed some month-end cash flow to cover timing differences on payments. The documents we were looking at were just formalizing a long-standing agreement. And the family trust was cheaper than borrowing from a bank. If we wrote about it, we would look foolish.

We didn't know much about the loan at all, although they did let slip that it was a revolving credit facility to the tune of $100 million. That was huge, although the major questions remained unanswered.

Later, after Greensill collapsed, Lex wrote about the loan in a legal statement filed as part of the administration. It turned out that much of what he and Doran had told us had been false. The Peter Greensill Trust loan was entirely new. It was not some long-standing agreement at all. And it reflected the company's growing cash-flow issues, not a solution to short-term month-end timing differences. Greensill was burning through cash, and its biggest clients were not paying their bills.

The family loan was only paid off after Lex persuaded Credit Suisse to stump up an even bigger loan.

The $100 million Family Trust loan was the first of a series of Hail Marys – last-ditch, desperate attempts to stave off the converging crises that were landing at Lex's door.

THROUGHOUT 2020, GREENSILL'S future hung in the balance. On the one hand, investment bankers were still touting the firm's potential multibillion-dollar IPO. On the other hand, there were a whole series of issues, several of them existential.

BaFin was demanding Greensill shift billions of dollars' worth of loans to Sanjeev Gupta off the balance sheet of its German Bank. Its main insurer, Tokio Marine-owned TBCC, was threatening to pull the plug, leaving Greensill unable to sell the loans it generated to investors. There were also several third-party investigations into Greensill, with auditors and partners crawling over the business all year long. The UK government Covid-19 bailout schemes had proved of only limited use, and Greensill's role in them had attracted further scrutiny too.

Lex had some success in shifting the GFG loans elsewhere. He sold tens of millions of dollars' worth of GFG-related assets to an Italian bank, GBM Banca, a Milan-based firm that had also been the subject of a potential takeover by Sanjeev Gupta. In 2021, the bank, then renamed Aigis Banca, collapsed because of these loans.

Through spring and summer 2020, tens of millions of dollars of GFG loans also went to White Oak Global Advisors, a US debt investment firm. When White Oak's UK unit, based in Chester, had bought about $50 million of the GFG loans, the firm told Greensill it could not take any more. Lex wouldn't be foiled. He structured a new, complex deal – effectively promising to take the assets back from White Oak if they required him to. It had the effect of shifting GFG assets off Lex's hands, at least temporarily.

Despite all the strains on Greensill, Lex mostly appeared outwardly calm, rarely showing signs of stress. In late summer, Julie and I had approached Greensill as we had heard the business was struggling, clients were abandoning the company and its access to insurance was drying up. We had heard that Greensill was desperately trying to raise new capital to avoid going out of business.

As so often, Greensill pushed back. Doran and Lex said that it was raising the new funds from a position of strength. Lex and his new external public relations team, led by Craig Oliver – a former BBC journalist and Director of Communications for Cameron in Number 10 Downing Street – agreed to a call. Lex Zoomed in from his Cheshire home. Oliver, who had been knighted by Cameron in his resignation honours list following the Brexit referendum, was the latest in a long line of external Greensill PRs. He sat in his kitchen, hardly appearing to be paying any attention at all. Gabe Caillaux was also on the call, for moral support. They agreed that things were tougher than anticipated but insisted a planned fundraising – of up to $1 billion – was a sign their business was thriving. The hunt for new capital was a sign of demand from investors who wanted to back the business, they claimed. Caillaux said GA wouldn't be putting money in – they'd already maxed out on Greensill per the firm's internal investing rules.

The notion that Greensill was raising capital for further expansion or because things were going well didn't ring true, and certainly didn't stack up with what we were hearing from other sources in the market, who described Greensill retrenching. Hiring had stopped. Some previously loyal executives were asking around about jobs elsewhere. Greensill was no longer bidding on big supply chain programmes. More insurers and funding partners were becoming reluctant to work with Greensill or had stopped working with them altogether.

Greensill was indeed on a worldwide search for new investors for a round of pre-IPO funding. It is not uncommon for companies to sell a large block of shares this way to a big institutional investor ahead of listing its shares. The money is often used to help the company improve its governance and consolidate its business. The appeal to investors is that they get in at a discounted price, ahead of the IPO.

In September, Greensill's advisers from Credit Suisse investment bank launched 'Project Olive' – the code name for the funding round – and told Lex that they were confident of strong demand for an investment of up to $1 billion, at a valuation 'materially higher' than what had gone before, perhaps as high as $7 billion. They had sounded out nine big institutional investors from around the world, including massive global fund managers at BlackRock and Fidelity, and identified another twenty that might be interested. Some of the investors they had spoken with already had said they could potentially put money in. Almost all of them said they would need to know more about the risk of defaults, the credit due diligence process, and the relationship between Greensill and SoftBank.

A pitchbook circulated by Credit Suisse to all potential investors touted Greensill as a 'market-leading disruptor' with 'cloud-based integrated technology' and a 'best-in-class founder-led management team backed by an experienced Board and engaged advisers.' The document said Greensill had expertise in algorithms and artificial intelligence. It claimed Earnd had been adopted by the NHS – rather than just a handful of NHS Trusts – and was offered to all its 1.5

million employees. And it said Greensill's annual revenue was forecast to hit $1.4 billion by 2022.

All of this was wildly optimistic. Greensill was struggling to hit revenue targets. Its Earnd business was going nowhere. There was very little in the way of AI at Greensill. It was also the subject of several ongoing investigations by business partners and regulators. Some of this was already in stories in the media. The fundraising went very slowly.

In October 2020, Lex knew the firm was in dire need of cash. He turned to his bankers at Credit Suisse and asked for a bridging loan to see the company through the next few months until it could complete the funding round. He wanted $140 million.

In London, Credit Suisse's risk managers rejected the application. They had read the reports about the BaFin investigation, and they knew about Greensill's exposure to Gupta. Lex said he would put up additional collateral for the loan – there was $50 million in cash in a Greensill bank account and around $1 billion in trade receivables that he could pledge too, he said. He also had cheerleaders inside the bank, in Zurich and in Asia, who complained that not making the loan could see a potentially lucrative client turning to one of their competitors. If Credit Suisse didn't do it, Citigroup, which ran trust accounts for the Greensill businesses, could easily make a loan of that size, for instance.

The decision on the loan was pushed up the chain of command, to Lara Warner, the head of risk and compliance. She had previously brushed aside concerns about Greensill's business. This time too, she waved the loan through, partly on the advice of Greensill's supporters in the bank in asset management and in Asia.

In truth, it was little more than a stopgap measure – and one that Credit Suisse would regret a few months later when Lex's business collapsed, leaving the Swiss bank out of pocket.

In the meantime, Lex remained desperate for more funding from an inbound investor. With pots more – permanent – cash, Greensill could find a way to shift his problems around once more, buy a bit of time, and get back on track. Outwardly, he continued to express optimism that the firm's current investors would put more money in.

Lex had told colleagues in the autumn that General Atlantic was interested in investing $500 million more into Greensill. That was totally misleading.

Lex also told colleagues that SoftBank would put more money into the firm too. Misra would do it, so long as they could find another investor to stump up some cash first. This, again, was wishful thinking. There was no such commitment from the Vision Fund or from SoftBank, and Lex's relationships with both Misra and Masa were on the rocks.

The firm, meanwhile, remained under pressure to deliver a huge run-up in revenue, to meet targets that would determine whether investors saw Greensill as a fast-growing tech star in the making or queried whether its business model was foundering.

Greensill had originally budgeted that 2020 turnover would reach about $850 million – a staggering sum, considering that the company had made less than half that the previous year. It was proving way too ambitious. By July, Greensill had veered way off course, with just about $190 million in revenue. Halfway through the year, Greensill had delivered less than a quarter of the revenue it needed to stay on track for the year.

That was partly because of the pandemic, which had slowed some trade. But it was also just a factor of the Greensill business model – it was still over-reliant on just a handful of riskier clients to generate most of its revenue and profit. And now, outside scrutiny meant it was being forced to limit its loans to those same clients.

Given the struggle to hit its numbers, Lex and his senior lieutenants – Neil Garrod the CFO, and others – settled on a new budget for the year, slashing their target by about 30 per cent, or $255 million, to $600 million. Even that reduced benchmark was proving elusive. By December, Lex and his inner circle of top executives were hoping to hit just $500 million. The new number was a little more than half of the original budget target that Greensill had set for the year.

Lex knew that the numbers were going to fall short of what he had promised to deliver. For a hot tech company on the rise looking to show exponential growth, stalling like this was a disaster. Investors in tech companies buy into the idea that if they get in early, they can ride a wave of rapid growth to untold riches. If the pace of expansion slows, then the whole story looks suspect. Against the backdrop of all the other red flags at Greensill, the disappointing revenue numbers would put a massive dent in the company's reputation. The promise of a massive IPO payout was soon looking like less than a pipe dream. It looked utterly, completely hopeless.

# THIRTY

# The Nightmare After Christmas

By December 2020, the planned fundraising had come off the rails. Investment bankers from Credit Suisse had pitched the deal to some of their biggest clients, but no one was stumping up the cash.

Despite the crisis, Lex wasn't showing any stress. He rarely did. Instead, he had the firm send every Greensill employee six bottles of champagne or a hamper from Fortnum & Mason for Christmas. It was a lavish gesture after a difficult twelve months and it cost Greensill about £300,000. Some of the firm's top executives were incredulous. Given all the pressure they were under, the firm should have been conserving every penny. Jobs were at serious risk. Yet Lex was spending to impress, as though nothing was wrong.

A week before Christmas, Lex held his final board meeting for the year. Despite the pandemic, 2020 had been a stellar period for Greensill, he said. The firm had record revenues. Profits were up. The plan to go public one way or another next year was in train. Some of them wished Lex a happy birthday for the following week. 'We're crushing it,' Lex told the board.

In the next day or two, he peppered the board with optimistic emails outlining all the successes. They could head off for the holidays in happy, festive spirits. Next year, they'd all be rich.

That might have been the last time anyone in the team really believed in Lex.

Greensill executives were scrambling for revenue, and increasingly concerned about the failed capital raise and the tough position taken by the German regulator. Hardly any of them knew that the biggest threat was the looming end to Greensill's main insurance partnership.

Lex despatched Roland Hartley-Urquhart on a mission to West Virginia. He flew down with the aim of persuading Jim Justice, or one of his staff, to help Greensill out of its mess. There was plenty to talk about. Bluestone had refused to send more coal to GFG, and Justice was smarting over the previous shipment that hadn't been paid for. From Greensill's perspective, if Bluestone would pay off some of its debts, then Greensill could certainly use the cash right now. That would also help ease the pressure on Greensill's insurance policies, which were maxed out. But the Justice family were hardly in generous holiday spirits. Hartley-Urquhart's flight made no material difference to the state of Greensill's perilous affairs.

A few days after Lex's cheery holiday message to the board and senior management, his mood took a dark turn. Around Christmas Eve, Lex began delivering the grim truth. It wasn't clear what specifically had caused him to change his tune. But now Lex was saying that BaFin, the German financial regulator, wanted to kill Greensill. They wouldn't negotiate over the GFG problem. They might even seize the bank. As always, he seemed calm, despite the crisis. He'd figure a way out. SoftBank would put more money in, he told some of his board and senior executives.

Despite Lex's assurances, many of the senior figures were now deeply concerned. They'd bought into the delusion for too long already. They knew about BaFin. The warnings they'd been given for over a year about the GFG exposure now suddenly came into sharp focus. There was no way out. Several board members and executives started to talk about leaving the sinking firm. At SoftBank, Misra decided that the Vision Fund should write its investment in Greensill down to zero. A couple of billion dollars, all told, was completely worthless.

By New Year's Eve, it was clear that Greensill was in deep trouble. There was another emergency board meeting. Much of the world, including the UK, was back under tougher Covid-19 restrictions. The meeting was dial-in, and it was under the direction of administrators from Grant Thornton, appointed that very day by the board. Their role would be to help figure out a plan. Sell the business. Restructure it. Break it up. Declare it bankrupt. Nothing was off the table.

Lex was furious. Bringing in administrators was unnecessary, he thundered. Lex and the board could figure a way out of Greensill's problems, he urged. But the board was not listening. Their patience had run out. The consensus view was that Lex's battle with the German regulators had gone on long enough.

Some senior executives and board members were now worried, not just about the future of the company. They were also beginning to wonder if Greensill would be the source of a major financial scandal.

One loan caused particular concern. The Credit Suisse funds had loaned about $435 million to Katerra, a construction company part-owned by the SoftBank Vision Fund. The five-year-old company was based in Menlo Park, California, and claimed to be 'transforming construction through innovation of process and technology.' In fact, it was struggling to survive. Some projects were running well over budget, and its rapid expansion plans had stretched the company's balance sheet to breaking point.

The Vision Fund had invested $2 billion into Katerra over the previous couple of years. Yet by autumn 2020, Katerra was close to filing for bankruptcy. On 30 December, my colleagues at *The Wall Street Journal* reported that Katerra had received another $200 million SoftBank bailout to stave off insolvency. The company's CEO also told the *Journal* that as part of the bailout deal, Greensill had forgiven a loan to Katerra in exchange for a 5 per cent stake in the construction business. It was a strange arrangement. At Greensill, Lex made a cursory reference to the transaction on a regular all-staff Monday-morning video conference call.

The deal troubled Greensill's senior team. Some of them knew that SoftBank had transferred about $440 million to Greensill to cover the Katerra loan. The money was supposed to be paid to the Credit Suisse funds. The problem was that months after receiving the payment, Greensill was still sitting on the money. It hadn't been paid into the Credit Suisse funds. Some senior executives were deeply worried – the money wasn't Greensill's. It belonged to Credit Suisse's clients.

A little while later, a spokesperson at Greensill's external public relations agency told me that Greensill took something called 'flash title' on the 5 per cent stake in Katerra which was 'passed through' to an insurance provider. He said the amount involved was closer to $100 million rather than $435 million. And he also said that no investor had lost any money as a result of the transaction. Pretty much all of this turned out to be inaccurate. Later, a report from Greensill's administrators said Greensill had taken the money from SoftBank and put it in Greensill Bank. When everything blew up in March, Credit Suisse was still showing the Katerra loan outstanding. Soft-Bank and Katerra believed the loan had been paid off, while Greensill insisted the money was stuck in the German bank and it couldn't get to it. Months later, after Greensill fell apart, the same Katerra payment became the focus of a protracted public falling out between Credit Suisse and Softbank that played out in a US court.

LEX WAS FACED with a billion-dollar game of whack-a-mole. Deal with one existential threat and another popped up. Deal with that one, and the first came back again to threaten Greensill Capital with insolvency. It was hopeless. But Lex was not going to throw in the towel. Faced with terrible odds in the past, he had somehow managed to survive.

Early in the new year, BaFin was the biggest, most immediate crisis. If he could get the German regulator to cut him some slack or at least give him more time, then Greensill could use that space to potentially secure another financial lifeline, and Lex could turn his attention to another blazing fire.

Whatever else might be going wrong, Lex remained a firm believer in his own negotiating skills. So long as the regulator was still talking, then it was always a negotiation.

In early January 2021, the plan was for Lex, Sanjeev Gupta and Rajeev Misra to fly to Frankfurt, Germany's financial centre, on the Greensill jet. They would meet with the German regulators in person. And the three arch-dealmakers would score some kind of victory.

That was not what happened. Europe was still mired in the Covid-19 pandemic, and travel – even elite business travel on a private jet – was severely restricted. Germany was a no-go. The three executives couldn't fly, and the meeting had to be held online. If they were going to make a big impression, it would have to be on Zoom.

The day of the call came round. Misra showed up late, as he often did. The four BaFin regulators on the call were not in a generous mood. Lex had lost a lot of goodwill. He never seemed to have been fully transparent about Greensill Bank's overall exposure to Gupta. The regulators had been pushing for Greensill to unravel its own mess for well over a year and were unimpressed by his ongoing pleas for a compromise. They were not going to ease up.

Lex would either have to get the GFG loans out of the bank or put more capital into it. One of the regulators asked about an email Lex had sent them. It had said that SoftBank was ready to invest a billion dollars more into Greensill. When was that going to happen? Attention shifted to Misra, dialling in from Dubai. The Vision Fund chief was blunt and direct. I don't know what you're talking about, he told them. The size of this Gupta problem is news to me. And as for plans to invest more into Greensill: no way. Not a single dollar.

The call went quiet. Lex was ashen. He appeared to have been caught providing the regulator with misleading information.

Eventually, Gupta broke the silence. Look, if we can't resolve this, then you're going to be putting thousands of people out of work, he said. That's a terrible outcome and it will be because of your actions. Lex joined in. If BaFin continues on this course, then jobs and businesses will fail, Greensill added. Greensill loans were funding the NHS and some major global businesses. Some of them are in Europe. If BaFin doesn't give Greensill breathing space, the results will be very painful for all our clients.

The four German regulators were unmoved. None of this was their concern. It wasn't their job to protect steel industry jobs. Their role was to safeguard the German banking sector. Nothing more. And Greensill Bank was too big a risk. The regulators said Greensill Bank must reduce the exposure to Gupta loans to zero. And it should do it now.

After the call, the dire reality of Greensill's circumstances could not be hidden from most of the senior team any longer, but not because Lex wanted to be more transparent. The management team knew what the situation was because they had heard it for themselves. The call had included a conference line set up by Greensill's external law firm. Several of Greensill's top executives knew about it and had dialled in. They had been eavesdropping on the whole thing. Lex's humiliation in front of BaFin had been played out before an audience. The scale of the calamity unfolding at Greensill Bank was clear for all of them to see.

# THIRTY-ONE

# End Game

In those last few weeks and months, Lex discussed a series of increasingly far-fetched rescue plans.

In one scenario, he would engineer the acquisition of Wyelands Bank from Sanjeev Gupta. Wyelands had grown rapidly, in part by offering high interest rates on deposit accounts that lured in customers who were getting next to nothing if they put their money in a traditional bank account. By 2019, Wyelands had signed up around 15,000 savers and held more than £700 million in deposits. The bank had issued loans of about £400 million too. But something was not right. UK financial regulators were crawling all over Wyelands because of their concerns that it was lending too much to other entities related to Sanjeev Gupta's business empire.

Wyelands was under pressure to wind down the amount it was lending to other GFG businesses. But Lex had another idea: what if Gupta sold him Wyelands Bank for a nominal fee of £1? If Greensill owned Wyelands, then the GFG businesses would no longer be related to the bank. And if that was the case, then the loans to GFG would no longer be a problem for the regulator. What's more,

Greensill could shift some of his own GFG loans into Wyelands too, from the German bank or from the Credit Suisse funds.

Lex's senior executives weren't buying it. There was no way the regulator would approve such a scheme. Besides, with so much bad press swirling around Greensill and GFG, it made no sense to add yet one more entanglement. For once, strong opposition inside Lex's inner circle won out.

Another Hail Mary left senior executives equally incredulous. Greensill had security over lots of the GFG assets as a kind of protection for the loans to Gupta. If Greensill foreclosed on the loans, GFG would collapse, but Lex would own it. He would be top of the list of creditors. Lex could claim on the existing insurance policies to cover the defaults. And he would inherit a global steel empire with no debts. Greensill would be reinvented as a sort of financing and metals conglomerate. Lex could even offer Sanjeev a small stake in the new super-Greensill to sweeten the deal. It was a nuclear option. *Explode the whole thing, and hope we survive.* Lex's team were dumbfounded. There was so much that could go wrong. Again, the sceptics won another one.

EARLY IN 2021, Lex was still clinging to the hope that there would be a further capital injection into the business from an outside investor. He was on yet another Zoom call with the management team. First, he checked the phone lines to see who was listening in, and then stressed that the conversation was private and should not be discussed outside the meeting. He seemed paranoid and even more focused than usual. Among sections of the senior management regime, there was a feeling that Lex's briefings were becoming less and less accurate, and wilder in aspiration.

'I want to provide some context as to why our capital raise didn't close in December,' he said. Then he added: 'The message to team members who ask is that we expect it to close in January.'

There had been a potential investor: TDR Capital, a $14.5 billion private equity fund, based in Marylebone, London, which manages money for pension funds, sovereign wealth funds, and others, in North America, the UK and around the world. The twenty-year-old firm had stakes in Pizza Express and Asda. An investment from TDR would not only have introduced new equity into Greensill, it would also have added some much-needed credibility. Lex was hoping, too, that SoftBank would match the new investment.

However, TDR had drawn back. Lex explained that 'an inbound' from BaFin had landed in December, questioning the company's 'GFG reduction plans'.

'It's not actually a legal obligation on our company yet, although it will become one over the course of the next few weeks, we're going to need to reduce the net GFG position in our bank over the course of the next twelve months to zero.' The communication from the German regulator was particularly unhelpful, created uncertainty around Greensill's GFG plans, and, when it was disclosed to the potential new investor, caused them to pause, he said.

'Not surprisingly, they said, you know, why don't you get it all sorted out before we close,' Lex told the meeting. 'People who write out equity cheques don't want to do so with uncertainty around us.'

In fact, TDR had already told Lex that they would not back any Gupta loans. They only wanted the safest loans. They had also called other Greensill investors, who had openly told them of their own concerns about the direction the company was headed.

Lex continued by telling the team that he was working on a multibillion-dollar liquidity line 'into which we can deliver GFG assets.' The deal would close in a matter of weeks, and SoftBank and others would back it, he said.

This involved a more than $2 billion 'term finance facility', which Lex said was arranged by Cantor Fitzgerald, the seventy-five-year-old New York investment bank and brokerage. Lex told management he was personally arranging the funding with Cantor's CEO. That was

Howard Lutnick, the hard-edged finance veteran who had gained global notoriety and respect when he rebuilt Cantor after the 11 September 2001 terror attacks, which had claimed the lives of 658 of the company's employees.

There was another useful connection there. The president of Cantor was Anshu Jain, a veteran banker and former co-CEO of Deutsche Bank, the much-maligned German bank where he had once been the boss of SoftBank's Rajeev Misra and several other SoftBank Vision Fund executives.

This would be a completely private arrangement. There would be no press coverage, Lex insisted, 'unless you guys leak it.' The message was clear – keep this to yourselves. Lex had become deeply hostile to any outside scrutiny.

The idea was that Cantor would set up a new vehicle – a kind of 'bad bank'. Greensill and Cantor would find investors to put their money in, and the 'bad bank' would then buy loans related to Sanjeev Gupta's GFG group of companies out of Greensill Bank. Potentially Greensill could dump some of the other problem loans there too. Investors would be fine with it because they would know what they were buying, and price it accordingly at a discount, and because the loans would be protected by trade credit insurance, which would pay out if they defaulted. If everything went as planned, the investors would get a decent return.

Cantor was a credible name for Greensill to work with. It had expertise and experience in dealing with complex, difficult situations. If Lex could pull it off, Greensill could shift the bad loans off its books and restart as a business focused on the higher-quality corporate clients, like Boeing or Vodafone. He could leave all the problems behind. There was one major hurdle: the vehicle, Lex was told, would need three years of trade credit insurance before any investors would buy in. The whole thing would only work if he could get trade credit insurance. Lex didn't admit it, but that made the plan just about impossible.

On the call with Greensill's senior executives, he outlined the next stage of the plan. Both General Atlantic and SoftBank had advocated that Greensill should become a public company much more quickly than previously anticipated, he said. Instead of waiting for an initial public offering (IPO), the firm would tap one of the hottest trends in finance at that time. Greensill, Lex told the team, would go public through a special purpose acquisition company, or SPAC.

Special purpose acquisition companies had been around for a while, but their popularity soared in 2020 and reached fever pitch in early 2021. By some measures, SPACs had raised about $64 billion in the US in 2020, almost the same amount as companies that listed their shares in the traditional way. Typically, SPACs are shell companies that receive a bunch of cash from big investors. They're sometimes called 'blank cheque companies', because the investors essentially write a big cheque that the SPAC then uses to go out and buy another, undervalued business. Because the SPAC's shares are listed, the companies they acquire effectively become listed too. It's a much quicker path to public company status than the IPO process. It doesn't involve the usual hurdles, such as investor roadshows and months-long preparation of IPO documentation. That appeals to company owners, but it has caused a lot of consternation among some investors and regulators, who say the fast-track process is less rigorous and more prone to cutting corners than a traditional listing. The SPAC plan essentially meant switching from a two-year IPO process to a four-month timetable.

'The probability of that has gone up materially in the last week or so,' Lex said. 'Clearly with the GFG concentration dealt with, we have a very good equity story to tell to the market.'

Of course, the GFG concentration issue hadn't been dealt with at all. Still, Lex told the team that a specific SPAC had already expressed an interest. He outlined several positives. For starters, some private companies that had gone public through a SPAC had achieved valuations of more than $10 billion, he said. The implication was that

Greensill would get a higher valuation too, although there wasn't much to back that up. The deal would also result in $2–3 billion of additional equity capital, he said.

Greensill would also have 'public company currency' – meaning its shares, which would be listed on the US Nasdaq exchange, could be traded. Staff and board members who still held a lot of stock could sell it more easily.

Finally, Greensill would inherit the SPAC's auditors, meaning that Greensill's failed quest for an auditor of its own would be resolved too.

Some of the senior managers worried that Greensill was nowhere near ready for it. The company didn't have the right governance or systems in place to be a listed company. It was still running an aggressive plan to double revenue every year, even though that had proved impossible. As a public company, it would have to be on a much more disciplined, sustainable footing. It would need to be able to produce the quarterly accounts and dozens of reports that were required of companies whose shares were listed in the US.

The senior management group's belief in Lex's vision was stretched to breaking point. Many of them knew that it was incredibly unlikely SoftBank and GA were looking to invest more. They knew that Lex's relationship with his two main outside investors was strained. And they knew that both the Cantor 'bad bank' plan and the SPAC were wildly ambitious, given that Greensill Capital and Greensill Bank were under intense scrutiny from regulators.

Lex continued. He stressed a new focus on costs. Spending had to be much more measured. Hiring and bonuses – both of which had been running at a clip – were suddenly paused. A year earlier, the company had had 414 employees. That number had now risen to 1,001.

It was a major gear shift, and seemed like Lex was finally coming to understand the dire reality. Then he added the most chilling message of the meeting. There was the potential, Lex said, that Greensill could run into a 'liquidity crisis' as it dealt with BaFin. Everyone knew what this meant. They could run out of money. If that happened, Lex told the team, it would result in a threat to the company's solvency. It was a stark admission.

'I've just given you full transparency,' he told the team, before clarifying that none of the discussion should leave that meeting. If what he was saying got out, then investors and clients would run from Greensill with great haste, spelling the end of his company. 'Transparency in the marketplace is terminal,' he warned.

IN LATE JANUARY 2021, Storm Christoph swept across the Atlantic Ocean and Ireland and bucketed rain in north Wales and the northwest of England. Rivers rose and swathes of the country were under water. There was also snow now blanketing parts of the region. The country was deep into another Covid-19 lockdown. Events in the US were tense following riots at the Capitol Building ahead of the inauguration of incoming president, Joe Biden.

At this point, there were management or board meetings at Greensill every few days. At one Zoom meeting of Greensill Capital's top executives, discussion turned to whether the company's 1,000 or so employees – mostly based in the northwest of England – were caught up in the floods or the snow, or whether they should send a message of reassurance to staff in the US who might be concerned about the political situation there. It was mundane stuff for a company in crisis.

Lex had more urgent matters to deal with. He moved the meeting quickly on to two key issues. There had been huge progress, he insisted, on both. The company now looked like getting access to more critical trade credit insurance, and he had a major financing rescue plan in place.

'There's still some wood to chop to get everything wrapped up,' he told the core management team. 'But in the meantime, it's obviously important that [you] keep the troops pointed dead ahead, focused on closing the deals.'

The bailout plan Lex said he was working on sounded thorough. First there was the emergency liquidity plan – the Cantor plan – to bring in much-needed cash to the business. The transaction was planned to close in March, Lex said. That was two months later than Greensill had previously hoped. Timing on all of this was becoming critical. Lex said the legal team at Greensill had worked for days and through the weekend with Tokio Marine and IAG to make this a reality. He said that initial feedback from investors was that they would be interested so long as the insurance was in place. SoftBank would put $1 billion into the facility, Lex had told the management team. He didn't elaborate on who else would put money in. But he said he was also talking to SoftBank and others about potentially selling some of the GFG assets earlier.

If Greensill could pull it off, the move would get the GFG exposure out of the German bank. And that would get the German financial regulator BaFin off Lex's back. It was only one of several major problems Lex was dealing with. But if he could put out one fire, even for a short time, he could move on to deal with the next one.

THROUGHOUT JANUARY AND February, there were board meetings every two or three days. Lex gave serious updates on BaFin, though he said it was all under control. He talked about his search for new sources of funding. He said that he was hopeful that Misra would put more Vision Fund money in. He said that if SoftBank stumped up some cash, others would follow. But SoftBank's representatives weren't always showing up to board meetings to answer those questions for themselves. It hardly gave the impression of an investor ready to ride to the rescue.

Greensill began talks with a giant US private equity fund, Apollo Global Management. The thirty-year-old company has almost $500 billion in assets under management. It is a New York-based giant of the industry, one of the biggest so-called 'vulture funds' – a reference to the way these firms pick through the bones of distressed companies, stripping them of their useful assets. Apollo was only interested in the non-GFG business, the good loans, and was looking to pay less than $100 million for the lot.

Lex was also working on a plan to deal with the onrushing insurance calamity. Greensill Capital had several insurance policies representing about $10 billion of cover with TBCC, owned by Tokio Marine. The most important was the Standalone Policy, which had a limit of $4 billion. Tokio Marine had told Lex it wouldn't renew the policy when it expired at midday on 1 March. Without this, the Credit Suisse funds could not function and Greensill would be finished.

Lex's position was always that everything can be negotiated. For months, he had been acting as though TBCC, Tokio Marine and IAG would buckle and agree to an extension. The insurers were not showing much indication that they were willing to help. Lex believed that if he could come up with $1.25 billion in cash collateral, then there would be a way to get the insurance extended. But where would he get that kind of money?

As the end date closed in, he tried another approach. In February, Greensill filed a lawsuit in Australia to try to force the insurers to continue coverage. Greensill disputed that Tokio Marine had provided the required 180 days' notice of non-renewal. Greensill appealed to the court on the grounds that the outcome of non-renewal would be 'catastrophic'.

'If the policies are not renewed, Greensill Bank will be unable to provide further funding for working capital of Greensill's clients . . . In the absence of that funding, some of Greensill's clients are likely to become insolvent . . . That in turn may trigger further adverse consequences on third parties, including the employees of Greensill's clients. Greensill estimates that over 50,000 jobs including over 7,000 in Australia may be at risk.'

It was the same argument Lex had used with BaFin. And it had the same level of success.

The Australian court rejected Greensill's argument. There were no grounds to force the insurers to renew the policies, which could have serious implications for their businesses too. The court also made a further compelling point. Despite the fact Lex knew about the insurers' position eight months earlier, Greensill only sought legal advice in late February, days before the policies were due to expire. Lex's lawsuit looked like a last-ditch attempt. It looked like another Hail Mary. And it failed.

Although Greensill teetered on the brink throughout January and February, Lex had continued to cheer the company's long-term prospects. In interviews with Australian media and with Bloomberg News in early 2021, he reiterated the public aim of an IPO, even speculating that he might list the company's shares in his home country. To many of the Greensill executives, as well as to me and to others paying close attention to the company, these stories appeared to be astonishing hubris or wilful blindness to the company's predicament.

Most of the employees of the company had no idea of the utterly dire straits that Greensill now found itself in. But some senior executives had begun to see the writing on the wall and were already leaving the company, while others were actively looking to desert what they saw as a sinking ship.

In the first two weeks of February, Hanafin, Garrod, Crothers and several others were all taken off the board of Greensill Capital, the main UK operating company within the Greensill group. As other senior figures departed, Lex remained stoic. But each departure deepened the sense of crisis.

At the Daresbury offices in northwest England, staff continued to toil away, with little knowledge of Greensill's predicament. For many of them, Greensill continued to be a good employer with strong growth prospects. That myth was about to be blown out of the water.

*

IN LATE FEBRUARY 2021, Julie and I heard that Greensill was likely finished. We heard that Credit Suisse was considering pulling the plug on its Greensill funds or replacing Greensill as the source of supply chain finance assets the funds bought. Credit Suisse was also trying to figure out what to do with all the GFG loans sitting in the funds.

It was an explosive story. If we published, it would open the doors on Greensill's predicament. The company would not be able to contain the fallout. All weekend, we called our sources, carefully trying to confirm what we had heard without becoming the source of a self-fulfilling rumour. We called Doran for comment, though he wasn't in the mood to chat.

Finally, late on the evening of Sunday 28 February, after consulting with editors and our lawyers at the *Journal*, we pulled the trigger on the story.

The next day, Greensill began to unravel quickly. The insurance policies were not renewed. Credit Suisse suspended the funds to prevent a run – it was like GAM all over again, but this time on steroids. The bank sent a note to investors, saying that assets in the fund are 'currently subject to considerable uncertainties with respect to their valuation.'

In the following days, chaos ensued. More board members left the firm. Apollo pulled out of the deal to buy Greensill's better loans. The Swiss financial regulator called in Credit Suisse to ask what on earth was going on. In Germany, BaFin seized control of Greensill Bank and referred matters related to Greensill Bank to criminal prosecutors.

On Monday 8 March 2021, Greensill filed for insolvency protection. Lex began calling round his board and investors. He spoke to Gabe Caillaux at General Atlantic. Lex, typically so cool under extreme pressure, sounded broken. His voice was cracking. 'Gabriel, it's over. I'm very embarrassed about what I've done. I'm ashamed for what I've done to my family name.'

# THIRTY-TWO

# The Aftermath

By the time Lex held a group call with the senior management team to tell them that the company was finished, he had gathered himself again. He was his usual assured, confident self. It was over. He knew exactly who to blame. The insurance companies had let Greensill down and there was nothing anyone could do.

Next, there were two company-wide calls. One was with the people leaving – hundreds, mostly in the northwest, who had lost their jobs. Many of them had loved working at Greensill. It was an exciting place to be. They had bought into the idea that they were changing finance for ever. They were stunned. For months afterwards, many of them still felt loyal to Greensill and could not believe what had happened.

The second call was with people who were staying behind. These were mostly risk managers and people who worked on the worst of the Greensill loans, about a hundred people in all. They were needed by the administrators from Grant Thornton, who were trying to unwind the complex, convoluted tangle of loans and special purpose vehicles left behind by Greensill's collapse. Doran also hung on to his position.

In Germany, prosecutors began a deeper investigation into Greensill Bank, even as they delved into a deposit protection scheme to bail out individuals and municipalities that feared they had lost their money with Greensill's collapse.

At Credit Suisse, it quickly became clear that it would be tough, maybe impossible, to collect several billion dollars. Some of the loans to big corporations were paid back as intended and Credit Suisse doled out the cash to its investors. But then there was all the GFG debt, and the Bluestone loans too. Neither Gupta nor Justice were in a position to pay the money back quickly. Justice launched a lawsuit claiming he was the victim of an elaborate fraud perpetrated by Greensill. The Swiss bank began issuing regular updates on how much was still missing, listing some of the details of the obligors who hadn't paid up. To me, the list was incredibly familiar. There was Catfoss (and a host of related Catfoss companies), which had been a long-term Lex client. Tradeshift, the oddball loan Lex had written on a bar napkin, was also there. So too were loans to Tower Trade, Kerry Leeds, Special Needs . . . in fact, pretty much every obligor I had asked the bank about and queried with Lex and Doran was on the list of non-payers.

I had no sense of smug self-righteousness, though one or two Greensill staffers I tried to talk to accused me of exactly that. Lex and some of his lieutenants had helped perpetuate the idea that this was partly the media's fault. Instead, I felt genuinely sorry that I had not been able to stop it getting so out of control. The only satisfaction came when one of my best sources called, full of emotion. Greensill had been a festering problem for years, and the company had so many powerful fans. For those on the other side of that equation, who had called Greensill out and suffered for it, it had been an agonizing time. Greensill's demise felt like some vindication for people like Sheard, the GAM whistle-blower, and others who had suffered because they had stood against the tide of Greensill supporters.

The collapse of Greensill fomented a feeding frenzy among financial journalists. Suddenly sources who had been impossible to pin down were readily available. Some Greensill insiders had quit even before the end and were now sharing their insight. Others looked to distance themselves. In political circles, information about Greensill's access to government and David Cameron's entanglement with the firm was everywhere.

The fallout from Greensill's demise was widespread. Aigis Banca, the Italian bank to which Greensill had sold some GFG loans, had gone bust. Deal Partners, the firm to which Lex had loaned Credit Suisse money, filed for administration. Kerry Leeds was struck off the Companies House register, while a related company, Kerry Ireland Investments, filed for administration with a loan of almost £14 million to Greensill unpaid and assets of £2.6 million.

Many Credit Suisse investors began talking to lawyers who were readying lawsuits. The bank suspended Michel Degen, the head of asset management in Europe, the Middle East and Africa, as well as Luc Mathys and Lukas Haas, who had been much closer to the running of the funds. Lara Warner, the head of risk, left the bank too. Over the following months, the bank stumbled from one big scandal to the next. After Greensill, there was a multibillion-dollar loss on a relationship with a failed hedge fund named Archegos; the bank's new chairman was forced to resign for allegedly breaching Covid regulations; and there were revelations from a consortium of international journalists about the bank's work financing dozens of sanctioned or otherwise ethically problematic clients.

The Greensill story had gone mainstream. From his home in Dubai, Sanjeev Gupta was scrambling to keep his steel empire intact. As Lex had warned, thousands of jobs really were at risk. Gupta began hardball negotiations with Credit Suisse. There's an adage in finance that if you owe the bank £1,000, it's your problem, but if you owe the bank £1 billion, it's the bank's problem.

Gupta had other issues to worry about. In May, the UK's Serious Fraud Office said it was investigating his businesses over suspected fraudulent trading and money laundering, including its financing with Greensill.

Details emerged also of the lobbying by Cameron and Crothers and Lex himself. Their efforts to get access to government Covid-19 loans and the Covid-19 Corporate Financing Facility (CCFF) became a front-page sensation, and Lex's face was plastered across newspapers around the world. Several government inquiries were launched. Cameron, Lex and others were hauled in to explain themselves to parliamentarians.

In spring, Lex spoke to the Business, Energy and Industrial Strategy committee by video call from home. His hair was cropped shorter than usual. He wore a black tie, white shirt and navy suit. His collar sat uncomfortably high, as it always did. The wood-panelled wall in the background was covered with family photos.

In an opening statement, Lex initially sounded contrite.

'Please understand that I bear complete responsibility for the collapse of Greensill Capital.'

Lex said how sad he was for his staff, Greensill's clients and the investors in Greensill's funds. And then he blamed someone else.

'It's deeply regrettable that we were let down by our leading insurer, whose actions assured Greensill's collapse.'

Though Lex was typically verbose, the panel interview went downhill from there. MPs said he was running a Ponzi scheme. They asked if he was a fraud. Lex read out an email exchange with the former Treasury minister, Paul Myners, including personal details of Myners' health issues, in a crude attempt to undermine earlier testimony from Myners that had been critical of Greensill. He launched into a strange dispute with one MP over the use of the phrase 'prospective receivables' instead of 'future receivables'.

It struck me that one of Lex's biggest failings was that he could never admit he was wrong, he could never lose an argument. It meant he could not turn away a loan. It meant he would not back down to his risk committee. He wouldn't write off a bad debt if he could tuck it away somewhere else.

He was a persuasive salesman and a clever lawyer. But he didn't know how to manage risks. He didn't know when to stop. Fuelled by floods of cheap money (investment into both Greensill itself and into the funds he built up), this personality flaw had become an enormous, multibillion-dollar accident waiting to happen.

BY THE SUMMER of 2021, the inquiries into Cameron and Greensill were still rolling on. Credit Suisse was still trying to recover its clients' money. Lawsuits were swirling. Regulators in the UK were looking at changing the rules related to several critical aspects of the Greensill story. Sanjeev Gupta was still under investigation by the Serious Fraud Office, as was Greensill itself. Greensill Bank was still under criminal investigation in Germany too. Lex's own future was deeply uncertain.

For once, Lex was in a self-reflective mood, unsure of himself. At last, there was a crack in his armour. He told an acquaintance that his mental health was suffering. Of course it was. Without his family, Lex said, he might not have survived the last few months, when the Greensill name had been dragged through the mud.

For those of us who had been following this extraordinary corporate saga from the start, it was time to ask: how had we got here? Could it happen again? Are there other Greensills out there?

Part of the answer is that the 'system' played a critical role. Banks like Morgan Stanley and Citigroup had seen Lex's tactics up close, but had continued to work with him, earning millions of dollars in fees. Regulators, including the UK's Financial Conduct Authority, were warned of his behaviour, and red flags were waved in their face, but they ignored them because Lex's business didn't fall squarely within their purview. Asset managers like GAM Holding and Credit Suisse put billions of dollars' worth of their clients' money into Greensill's assets but failed to safeguard them properly. Investors in his business – like General Atlantic and SoftBank – saw that things were going wrong but failed to stop Greensill veering completely off the rails. Armies of lawyers, media relations people and bankers took huge fees to cover over Lex's tracks too. Certain journalists were also happy to boost Greensill's profile in the name of a scoop, without asking any tough questions. Greensill's board was far too ready to accept Lex at his word when a little digging would have unearthed many problems long before they became a crisis.

The role of some of these actors was to help Greensill grow, even when it was clear the business was rotten. Most of them had no incentive to kill the golden goose, or to tell the world the assets they had invested in were worthless.

Greensill Capital was also the product of circumstances of the post-financial crisis business world. The company was one of many shadow banks that exploded when the traditional giants of finance retreated from businesses that were no longer profitable because of new regulations that followed the financial crisis. Greensill also benefited from the global trend of persistently low interest rates, which were meant to boost flaccid economic growth but which left big institutional investors scratching around for a decent return on their investments. This 'hunt for yield' helped turn a mundane, low-octane business that didn't generate much profit at all – supply chain finance – into something relatively super-charged. The flood of money from tech investors like SoftBank into anything that looked new and disruptive also strapped a rocket to Greensill's growth.

All these trends have been around for years and still exist to some degree. They mean there are likely more companies running around with similar flaws to the Greensill model.

But the system only explains so much of what went wrong.

Lex blamed the Covid-19 pandemic and unreliable business partners for the company's downfall. In truth, though Covid-19 might have hastened Greensill's demise, the writing was on the wall long before the pandemic struck.

Large parts of Greensill's business made very little money, or no money at all. It was a lending business heavily dependent on loans to a series of interconnected, often directly related parties, as well as other loans to borrowers of questionable repute, many of whom had little or no ability to pay back the sums they had borrowed. Some of the loans were supported only by guesswork. Other loans were backed by invoices that appear to have been made up.

The company also relied too much on a tiny Australian insurance company for a crucial piece of the machinery. There was very little innovative technology to speak of. And lots of the financing Greensill provided had nothing to do with the sort of safe, steady business Lex purported to be promoting. Instead, it looked a lot more like dodgy loans to speculative businesses.

The Greensill business model was also a reflection of Lex's own deep flaws. Undeniably, Lex Greensill was smart, passionate, an arch-salesman. He persuaded a long list of influential people to lend him their support and take a bet on his supposed genius, including Maurice Thompson, the former Citigroup chief in the UK, David Solo, the banking and trading maestro, Jeremy Heywood, the most powerful civil servant in the UK, David Cameron, the former UK prime minister, and Masayoshi Son, possibly the most influential investor in the world. There were many other lesser lights who also got behind Lex along the way, fuelling his rapid rise and self-belief.

There were others, though, who told me Lex was 'psychotic' and 'a pathological liar'. Whether you're a believer or a sceptic, it's clear the rise and fall of Greensill is a deeply personal story. Lex was ambitious and wildly self-confident. There was no one he couldn't outsmart. There was no problem he couldn't solve. I don't think Lex planned to run a bad business from the outset. But, like a rogue trader, Lex kept on betting he could dig himself out of a hole by digging a deeper one. He cut too many corners, relied too much on shifty financial engineering, and showed more bravado than brilliance. And, in the end, it brought Greensill crashing down.

# Epilogue

The Greensill saga was white-hot for months. Cameron's work with Greensill has led to widespread demands for changes to UK lobbying rules, and it is a cornerstone of an ongoing debate about the revolving door between Parliament and business.

Several different parliamentary inquiries and reviews have been launched off the back of Greensill's collapse. There are those looking into the use of supply chain finance by the government, reviewing private sector positions held by civil servants, and considering the need for an overhaul of standards in public life. The names and reputations of several top politicians have been trashed, not least that of David Cameron. The affair also ignited a firestorm of criticism of the UK's Conservative government that spread through the summer and over the following months, reaching the door of Number 10 Downing Street. By late 2021, the accusations of sleaze that had started with Cameron and Greensill had become a defining characteristic of UK politics and was a major issue as the Tories faced headwinds in local elections and parliamentary by-elections alike.

In December, the UK's Financial Conduct Authority finally

settled its investigation into Haywood and GAM, citing 'conflicts of interest and gifts & entertainment matters.' The regulator hit the asset management firm with a £13 million penalty (reduced to £9 million because GAM accepted their findings) and landed Haywood with a £230,000 fine (£319,000 before discount). It was a relatively tame outcome, which had been achieved without much of an investigation, according to my sources. They had not even talked to some of the people directly involved in the Greensill investments, or the way GAM managed the affair. The settlement felt less like a definitive conclusion and more like a plea bargain designed to make the whole issue go away.

Other regulatory actions are still ongoing at the time of writing. The UK's Financial Reporting Council has also launched an investigation into Greensill's auditor. And the Serious Fraud Office is still investigating both Sanjeev Gupta and Greensill too.

The strain on Gupta's GFG Alliance steel empire is testing whether governments are willing to bail him out or face massive job losses. A pick-up in steel prices will help the value of GFG's assets. But there is little doubt that Gupta's business looks fragile. The findings of the SFO investigation will be critical to its future.

Greensill's access to the government Covid-19 bailout loans has come under particular scrutiny. In March, as Greensill was collapsing in on itself, the British Business Bank wrote a 'letter of concern' to the company and suspended the government guarantee on the loans it had made. The BBB said it couldn't verify some of Greensill's information. By some calculations, the UK government could yet be on the hook for several hundred million pounds for loans that Greensill administered.

In Scotland, there is a lingering issue too. Amounts guaranteed by the devolved government there in relation to loans and schemes involving Greensill and Gupta have left Scotland with a potential liability of hundreds of millions of pounds.

The ripples of Greensill's collapse are felt around the world.

Regulators in Australia are trying to figure out how an Australian insurance company played a pivotal role in a multibillion-dollar global scam. In the US, the divisive governor of West Virginia, Jim Justice, is facing damaging financial implications. His family personally guaranteed the loans they got from Greensill. In Japan, Tokio Marine now looks to be entangled in years of litigation, as investors try to recover funds they thought were insured. The Japanese firm said its own investigation into Greensill's activities found that for several years Greensill had fraudulently misrepresented and fraudulently failed to disclose material information related to the insurance policies it had taken out with TBCC. Those policies, which were meant to protect investors, were never valid, according to Tokio Marine. The burgeoning supply chain finance industry is almost certain to be heavily regulated – perhaps into oblivion. Global and US regulators are already moving to impose tighter restrictions on how it is used. The implications for hundreds of big companies that fund billions of dollars this way are not yet fully understood. Moving hidden debts suddenly onto company balance sheets could leave some businesses looking a lot less healthy.

Credit Suisse has quickly run up a bill of more than $150 million just trying to recover the billions of dollars of client money that is still missing. In early 2022, the bank said it expected litigation was needed to try to recover funds from some of the companies Greensill loaned money to. The legal cases could take up to five years, the bank said. The bank agreed to restructure a small portion of the GFG loans, backed by facilities in Australia – instead of paying them back in a few weeks, they will now be paid back over several years. It's likely that billions of dollars more will never be recovered, and it is unclear who will foot the bill for that.

The bank finds itself in a similar position to that which GAM faced a few years earlier. They have been sold a bunch of dud assets, but if they are too open about that, if they acknowledge the investments they're holding are riddled with problems, they'll never shift them on to someone else.

Meanwhile, clients are angry. But if the bank gives them all their money back, then Switzerland's financial regulator could plausibly tell Credit Suisse it must stand behind every fund it sells in the same way – that would cripple the bank, as it would have to set aside billions of dollars in additional capital to cover future payouts. Instead, Credit Suisse must first go through a painful process of trying to recover as much as it can, through insurance or by negotiating with the obligors. After that, it may resort to legal action to recover a bit more. Every step must be carefully managed so as not to prejudice any later lawsuits involving the Greensill funds or Gupta or the insurance companies or any number of interested parties.

The bank commissioned a report into what happened and hired Deloitte and a Swiss law firm to investigate. Initially, the bank's senior leaders indicated at least some of their findings would be made public, though later they decided none of it would ever be released. One can only imagine how embarrassing it might be. In late September, the bank's Zurich headquarters were raided by Swiss police as part of a criminal investigation related to the Greensill debacle. Its lawyers then set about trying to seal all the documents the police had seized, so that they would never become public.

Administrator Grant Thornton appears to be one of the big winners of Greensill's collapse. The accountants are charging a commission for every loan they recover, as well as fees for running the shell business during the loan recovery process. They're expecting to make tens of millions of pounds out of Greensill's collapse. Critics say the audit firm is conflicted. Grant Thornton advised Sanjeev Gupta for years on many of his more esoteric deals. They helped Gupta come up with a valuation for his metals businesses, against which he borrowed so much money. Each time, Grant Thornton and its partners billed millions of pounds for their work. A spokesman for the firm told me in an email that, 'Prior to accepting the appointment as administrators . . . Grant Thornton UK LLP gave careful consideration to the Code of Ethics relating to such matters and satisfied ourselves that there is no threat to our independence as a result of any prior relationships.'

The big investors General Atlantic and SoftBank each come away with a nasty black eye. GA got its money out before things turned sour. SoftBank may have sunk about $2 billion into Greensill all told. The Vision Fund can easily afford it. Stakes that don't pay off are inevitable when you are investing in hundreds of rapidly growing start-ups. Several other backers with smaller stakes were also left holding worthless shares.

And what of Lex?

It seems highly likely that Lex and his brother Peter took hundreds of millions out of the company, before sinking some of it back in. In the end, Lex may need what is left to deal with potential lawsuits from investors and others.

In Greensill Capital's final months, Lex took a series of steps that had the effect of distancing his personal fortunes from those of the rest of the family. He sold his stake in Greensill Farms to another company controlled by a Bundaberg accountant. His name was removed from documents related to the family business. The Greensill family say that if you want Lex's money, you better look elsewhere.

# Postscript

The aftershocks of the Greensill scandal are still being felt.

Several of Greensill's former clients – the obligors – have declared themselves insolvent. In some cases, that means the owners of those firms, including owners with long ties to Lex, walk away without having to repay the loans that they received from the Credit Suisse funds. Special Needs Group, the firm run by Lex's neighbour which received £23 million in loans, including a £5 million UK government Covid loan, was declared insolvent and its assets sold to another company also owned by the same Greensill neighbour.

GFG is still under investigation by the SFO, and its business is still reeling from the collapse of Sanjeev Gupta's favourite finance firm. Steel plants owned by the sector lurch from one crisis to the next, with no sign of a long-term solution to the woes of GFG any time soon. The depth of Gupta's problems are most clearly reflected in a lawsuit filed by the landlord of GFG's London headquarters in early 2023, which claimed the company owed £4 million in unpaid rent.

Several investigations are still ongoing. In Germany and Switzerland, criminal investigations into Greensill businesses are yet to be concluded. In the UK, the Insolvency Service is also investigating Greensill and the actions – or perhaps inactions – of its directors. The agency could ban any of them from holding similar positions in the future.

Perhaps the biggest impact was at Credit Suisse.

In February 2023 FINMA, the Swiss regulator, released the damning findings of its report into the bank's behaviour in the Greensill affair. The regulator fined Credit Suisse and said there are four 'enforcement proceedings' against former Credit Suisse employees resulting from its enquiries.

The report also said that Credit Suisse's senior executives had repeatedly ignored critical questions about Greensill from the media and elsewhere, and that it had relied on Lex Greensill and conflicted parties at the bank to assess the risks inherent in the relationship. Because bankers took Lex at his word, the report said, statements they made were 'partly false and overly positive.'

This phrase seems to me like an incredibly accurate assessment of Lex Greensill.

Meanwhile at the Swiss bank, a revolving door of senior executives struggled to right the ship. The bank's stock price sank to record lows, clients withdrew more than $100 billion, and, amid a broader banking crisis, management was forced to negotiate a $54 billion backstop loan from the Swiss central bank. Even that was not enough. Only a couple of days after this extraordinary measure, on Sunday 19 March, Swiss authorities ordered the country's other giant bank, UBS, to take over Credit Suisse. It was a shocking decision. After 167 years, Credit Suisse was to be no more. UBS paid just a few billion dollars to buy its rival. Some of the bank's bondholders were wiped out. Shareholders received a fraction of the value of their stock from even a few days earlier. One thing UBS's management were certain to agree before closing the deal was that several billion dollars were set aside to cover any pending legal costs from the series of scandals that had rocked the bank, including the collapse of the Greensill funds.

The reason for Credit Suisse's demise was clear. Customers no longer trusted the bank.

Where was Lex during all of this? He had spent the past few months flying between Australia and his home in the north-west of England.

The village of Saughall hardly seems like a centre of intrigue. But, like the quaint village setting of an Agatha Christie mystery, Saughall is now the bizarre backdrop for Lex's latest brush with infamy.

Back before Greensill collapsed, Lex had told Cheshire West and Chester Council that his proposed rewilding project in Saughall was for the benefit of all the local people. The council agreed to his plan on the basis that the local parish council supported the deal. But after Greensill's reputation was dragged through the mud following the company's bankruptcy filing, several of Lex's neighbours objected to the deal. Strangely, given everything going on in Lex's life – the lawsuits, criminal investigations, regulatory and political enquiries – he has been fixated on this deal. Sporting a beard and looking far less dapper than in the past, Lex has been knocking door to door and accosting Saughall residents in the street to persuade them to support his plans. The parish council has called several emergency meetings, which have become heated as neighbours argue with neighbours. At one point, a former parish councillor even called the police claiming that Lex was harassing him. One key piece of information that emerged during this local scandal was that the original proposal to purchase the land – which didn't go through any kind of competitive tender process – didn't include a firm obligation on Lex to actually rewild the plot once he bought it.

This seems like a massive oversight. Another problem was that Lex had promised to pay half a million pounds to the parish council if the deal went through.

All of this seems relatively small time considering the mess Lex is faced with. It's hard to fathom why he would want to pursue this course of action with so much going on. One explanation is that he really is passionate about the land. Another might be that a few million pounds for a piece of prime real estate seems like an absolute bargain. To a former billionaire, down on his luck, faced still with mounting legal and financial difficulties, a deal like that would be too good to be true.

# Glossary

**BaFin** – Germany's top financial regulator, the Federal Financial Supervisory Authority, or BaFin, earned a less than impressive reputation for its handling of a series of corporate scandals. BaFin's officials were the primary authority responsible for regulating Germany-based Greensill Bank.

**CBILS, CLBILS and CCFF** – The Coronavirus Business Interruption Loan Scheme, Coronavirus Large Business Interruption Loan Scheme and Covid Corporate Finance Facility were all set up by the UK government in response to the devastating impact of the Covid-19 pandemic and resulting lockdowns on the country's economy. Greensill Capital sought access to all of these facilities as the struggling company scrambled to find new sources of funding to support loans it had made.

**FCA** – The Financial Conduct Authority is the UK's main financial watchdog. Like BaFin, the UK regulator has been criticized for the effectiveness of its oversight.

**GA** – General Atlantic was founded in 1980 to manage investments for a charity set up by Charles Feeney, the co-founder of Duty Free Shoppers. Today, GA invests tens of billions of dollars across a portfolio of almost 200 companies. The firm's investors typically target young, fast-growing companies that require an injection of cash and management advice to accelerate their development. The firm invested $250 million into Greensill Capital.

**GAM** – Global Asset Management, or GAM, was founded in 1983 by the investor Gilbert de Botton. The company manages investments for wealthy individuals, pension funds and other institutions. The Zurich and London-based company has been owned by Swiss banks Julius Baer and UBS. It has been independent since 2009. The firm was one of the first major financial institutions to invest significantly in assets sold by Greensill Capital.

**Global financial crisis** – The global financial crisis of 2007 to 2009 was sparked by a crisis in the US mortgage market whose ripple effects shook stock markets around the world and threatened to topple the international financial system. Several major banks collapsed altogether while others survived only with billions of dollars in government bailout money. It was followed by a period of renewed regulation that rendered many traditional financial activities unprofitable for the banks and encouraged the growth of a so-called shadow banking sector where new firms filled the gaps left behind.

**IPO** – An Initial Public Offering is the Holy Grail of the modern business founder. Once a company achieves a desired scale, its founders and other owners will typically look to list the company's shares on a public stock market through an IPO. They must first go through a tightly regulated and arduous process, but the rewards can be enormous for existing shareholders, including employees, who can sell their shares and convert wealth on paper into real money. Greensill

Capital was targeting a multibillion-dollar IPO before its collapse in early 2021.

**SCF** – Supply Chain Finance, also known as Reverse Factoring, is a kind of banking service that promises to smooth payments between suppliers and buyers of goods. SCF has grown rapidly in recent years, grafting new technology onto centuries-old banking traditions. Typically, SCF sees suppliers of goods and services get paid very promptly, while allowing buyers to pay their bills later. The process is funded by a third party, such as a bank or other financial institution, which profits by taking a fee for their role. Greensill Capital became one of the biggest providers of SCF in just a few years.

**SPV** – A Special Purpose Vehicle is a type of company set up to undertake a very specific business activity. Their use is a legitimate and necessary part of the modern business world, but they can also add complexity and obfuscation to business transactions. Greensill Capital used several SPVs to process the assets it sold to investors.

**SoftBank Vision Fund** – The $100 billion Vision Fund, founded in 2017, was set up by SoftBank, a Japanese technology firm led by charismatic businessman Masayoshi Son. The fund, which is also backed by investors from the Middle East and Silicon Valley, is the biggest technology-focused investment fund in the world. It is based in the UK, and provided billions of dollars of backing to Greensill Capital.

**TBCC** – The Bond and Credit Company is a small Australian insurance firm specializing in trade credit insurance. TBCC was founded in 2013. In 2019, Insurance Australia Group sold its 50% stake in TBCC to Japan's Tokio Marine. TBCC was by far the biggest provider of trade credit insurance to Greensill.

**Trade credit insurance** – Businesses take out trade credit insurance (TCI) to protect themselves against the possibility that their customers will default on payments that come due. Several major global companies provide trade credit insurance, charging premiums based on the likelihood of non-payment. Many of Greensill Capital's supply chain finance loans were sold to investors on the basis that they were protected by trade credit insurance.

# Acknowledgements

The Greensill saga unfolded across continents and through business, politics, finance and markets. The number, location and expertise of excellent journalists that uncovered the story reflected the breadth of its impact. I have leaned on all their work to produce this book. To those of us who followed Greensill closely, two reporters stood out: John Collingridge's coverage in *The Times* and Robert Smith's in the *Financial Times* was exemplary and inspirational.

I was fortunate many years ago to get a job at *The Wall Street Journal*. My work here builds on more than a decade of trying to keep up with the best journalists in the business. To the extent that this book illustrates my abilities as a journalist, it is because of the skills, approach to reporting, and dedication to the craft that I witnessed working with reporters and editors at the *Journal* in Hong Kong and, especially, in London. I hope that some of it rubbed off on me.

In pursuing this story in particular, my former *Journal* colleague and editor Alex Frangos deserves much gratitude. His perseverance with a challenging storyline is deeply appreciated. My partner-in-reporting, Julie Steinberg, is one of the best journalists anyone could wish to work alongside. Thorough, diligent, always fair – and great fun too. I was fortunate to share bylines with Julie on the Greensill story.

I also wish to thank my former colleagues at *Financial News* who first ran with this story. There are many great journalists there, toiling away and displaying dedication to their work every day.

Almar Latour shares some credit for this book. A mentor and friend, Almar gave me the space and encouragement to pursue the story, even when I had other, more immediate work to do for him. Thank you.

I was incredibly fortunate during the period of reporting on Greensill to work with one of the finest, most supportive journalists anywhere in the world. Francesco Guerrera is not only a brilliant, immaculately sourced, thoughtful editor, arch-storyteller, and consummate media strategist. He is also a great, great friend.

Books like this don't exist without incredibly brave sources. They risk their friendships and their finances. They put their careers on the line. They often do this when others around them decide to keep quiet or cover up. I was lucky enough to talk to many brilliant, courageous sources for this book. The story in it is dedicated to them and to their determination to tell the truth, no matter what. Two sources require specific thanks. One of them brought my attention to Greensill in the first place. Their input, generosity and trust lit a fire and they refused to let it go out, even when it seemed another version of events might take hold. The other key source was incredibly trusting, patient, and as thorough as any great reporter I've worked with. I believe you will know who you are.

Other sources too deserve plenty of plaudits. 'Bobx' – thank you for your time and guidance. To the others: this book is an attempt to tell a fair, accurate and meaningful version of events, and I hope it does justice to your efforts and the risks you've taken in talking to me.

I also owe enormous gratitude to my agent, Martin Redfern at Northbank, who understood the scope, scale and exceptional circumstances surrounding the Greensill story from the start. My publishers at Macmillan saw that the Greensill saga needed to be told too. Robin Harvie and Matthew Cole, the editors of this book, worked wonders with raw material. Lucy Woods provided irreplaceable fact-checking and Immie Kaldor's reading was insightful.

Above all, I must thank my family. To Mum and Dad and Andrew: thanks for encouraging me to write. To my wife, Bambi: your tolerance of this labour has been heroic. Your patience, exceptional. Your support, inspirational. To Duke, Cooper and Robson: thanks for not interrupting too many confidential phone calls, and never stop asking questions.

# Index